THE FORMATION
OF THE STATE OF
OKLAHOMA

The FORMATION OF THE STATE OF OKLAHOMA

1803-1906

BY

ROY GITTINGER

· MCMXXXIX ·
UNIVERSITY OF OKLAHOMA PRESS
NORMAN

NEW EDITION COPYRIGHT 1939 BY THE UNIVERSITY OF OKLAHOMA PRESS. SET UP
AND PRINTED AT NORMAN, OKLAHOMA, U. S. A., BY THE UNIVERSITY OF OKLAHOMA
PRESS, PUBLISHING DIVISION OF THE UNIVERSITY.

TO MY WIFE
FRANCES PRICE GITTINGER

PREFACE

OKLAHOMA was the last state formed and admitted from the area included in the Louisiana Purchase. The territory within the limits of the present Oklahoma was long kept free from the jurisdiction of a state government as the outcome of a series of events that are of peculiar interest because of their intimate connection with the national Indian policy. The promise in the treaty of purchase to admit the inhabitants of Louisiana "to all the rights, advantages, and immunities of American citizens" was fulfilled by the organization of the settled districts near the Mississippi River. The country farther west was left to the Indians. Oklahoma was the last state formed from this Indian country.

The law of May 28, 1830, together with a series of agreements, set apart for the Indians the country lying west of Missouri and Arkansas and provided for the removal thither of numerous tribes. The separation of Kansas and Nebraska from the Indian country confined the Indians to what is now Oklahoma. In the years following the Civil War, the removal of remnants of Indian tribes to the diminished Indian Territory continued. In spite of this concentration of the tribes in a small part of their former domain, vast open spaces were left. The desires of land-hungry white settlers were aroused by glowing reports of the rolling prairies that lay unoccupied in the Indian Territory. These reports were circulated by eager officials of the land-grant railroads who hoped to secure a share of the Indian

PREFACE

country if it were opened to white settlers. As adjacent states became more thickly populated, the pressure on the Indian country became greater. Home seekers threatened and then crossed the border. The opening of the western half of the territory and the relaxation of the intercourse laws in the eastern half destroyed finally the barriers that had for a long time dammed up the stream of settlers. The rush was overwhelming. In a decade and a half the population rose from a few thousands to a million and a half and the creation of a new state became imperative.

The formation of the State of Oklahoma as it is now constituted is the subject of this study. The story was first presented as Volume VI of the University of California Publications in History, at Berkeley in 1917. The original edition has been out of print for some time and this new edition is presented, appropriately enough, in the year which marks the fiftieth anniversary of the first white settlement in the Indian Territory, the settlement of the so-called Oklahoma district, an event which set the stage for statehood in 1907.

The sources of the present work are chiefly the official reports published by the Government of the United States. Citations are made uniformly to the volumes of Congressional documents and not to the reports published separately. The bibliography lists not only works that were used in the preparation of the study, but also includes a supplementary list of important publications issued in the last twenty years. The more recent works have not affected essentially the conclusions here presented.

PREFACE

The year 1906 marks the end of a definite period in the history of Oklahoma. The story of the constitutional convention and a discussion of the constitution as adopted are not a part of this study. The adoption of the constitution and the organization and development of the state under the constitution belong in another work.

Acknowledgments for aid in the preparation of this book are due to many persons. The late Professor Henry Morse Stephens of the University of California gave friendly counsel and encouragement in the preparation of the first edition. Professor Herbert E. Bolton, also of the University of California, followed the work through its earlier stages and made many valuable suggestions and criticisms. Members of the faculty of the University of Oklahoma also gave valuable assistance, especially the late Professors James S. Buchanan and Joseph F. Paxton, and Professor John B. Cheadle. Mr. Joseph B. Thoburn, formerly connected with the University of Oklahoma and more recently with the State Historical Society, also made useful suggestions. Thanks are due to Professor Morris L. Wardell for aid in the preparation of the supplementary bibliography. Acknowledgment is also made to the University of California Press, publishers of the first edition, for permission to present the second edition. The cooperation of my wife from the inception of the work is here gratefully recognized.

Roy Gittinger.

University of Oklahoma,
September 1, 1939.

CONTENTS

CHAPTER	PAGE
I. BEGINNINGS OF THE INDIAN TERRITORY WEST OF THE MISSISSIPPI	3
II. THE ESTABLISHMENT OF THE LARGER INDIAN TERRITORY	13
III. THE SEPARATION OF NEBRASKA AND KANSAS FROM THE INDIAN TERRITORY	30
IV. THE PROPOSED STATE OF NEOSHO	57
V. THE INDIAN TERRITORY DURING THE CIVIL WAR	68
VI. THE RECONSTRUCTION OF THE INDIAN TERRITORY	96
VII. THE BOOMERS	118
VIII. HOW THE BOOMERS WON	138
IX. FOUR YEARS OF WAITING	158
X. THE SETTLEMENT OF OKLAHOMA TERRITORY	184
XI. THE SETTLEMENT OF THE INDIAN TERRITORY	211
XII. THE ADMISSION OF OKLAHOMA	236

APPENDICES

A. THE EASTERN BOUNDARY OF OKLAHOMA	261
B. THE GREAT AMERICAN DESERT	262
C. AREA OF RESERVATIONS IN THE INDIAN TERRITORY	263
D. INDIAN POPULATION AT DIFFERENT PERIODS OF THE AREA NOW INCLUDED IN OKLAHOMA	264

CONTENTS

	PAGE
E. PRINCIPAL BILLS RELATING TO THE INDIAN TERRITORY INTRODUCED BETWEEN 1865 AND 1879	267
F. TWO SAMPLE PETITIONS FOR THE OPENING OF OKLAHOMA	270
G. PRECEDENTS FOR THE BOOMER INVASION	274
H. CREEK AND SEMINOLE AGREEMENTS OF 1889	275
I. THE WORK OF THE DAWES COMMISSION	277
BIBLIOGRAPHY	281
INDEX	291

LIST OF MAPS

	FACING PAGE
1. States Formed From the Louisiana Purchase	4
2. Position of the Indian Territory Between 1830 and 1848	24
3. Territory of the Southern Indians Before 1855	60
4. The Indian Territory, 1855-1866	84
5. The Indian Territory in 1889	186

THE FORMATION
OF THE STATE OF
OKLAHOMA

CHAPTER I

BEGINNINGS OF THE INDIAN TERRITORY WEST OF THE MISSISSIPPI

THE jurisdiction of the United States was first extended over Oklahoma in 1803, by the purchase of Louisiana from France. It is true that the southwestern limits of Louisiana were very indefinite, as the boundary between it and New Spain had never been established, and the question was not taken up in the treaty of cession.[1] The description of the new acquisition which was sent to Congress by President Jefferson included the statement, "the precise boundaries of Louisiana, westward of the Mississippi, though very extensive, are at present involved in some obscurity."[2] Nevertheless, the agreement made with Spain some years later left all of the present state of Oklahoma in the possession of the United States except the narrow rectangle projecting west of the hundredth meridian, now known as the Oklahoma Panhandle.

The division of Louisiana into commonwealths of proper size began on March 26, 1804, when all of the new cession south of the thirty-third parallel was set off as the Territory of Orleans. All north of that parallel, that is, all north of the present state of Louisiana, became the District of Louisiana and was attached,

---

1 For a discussion of this subject, see Marshall, *A History of the Western Boundary of the Louisiana Purchase, 1819-1841.*
2 November 14, 1803, *American State Papers, Miscellaneous,* I, 344.

{ 3 }

THE FORMATION OF OKLAHOMA

for administrative purposes, to Indiana Territory.[3] One year later, by an act of March 3, 1805, the District of Louisiana was organized as the Territory of Louisiana.[4] The Territory of Orleans, however, took the name of Louisiana on its admission into the Union in April, 1812;[5] and two months later Louisiana Territory became Missouri Territory.[6]

The map was left unchanged after this for a little over six years, but in 1818 the inhabitants of a part of Missouri Territory began to ask for statehood.[7] While the controversy growing out of this request was still unsettled, Congress organized the Territory of Arkansas, including, in addition to the present state of Arkansas, all of Oklahoma south of the parallel of 36° 30'. This was done by an act of March 2, 1819,[8] and for the next five years Oklahoma south of a line drawn from the southwest corner of Missouri to the northeast corner of the Texas Panhandle was a part of Arkansas Territory. The boundaries of this territory, where it touched the Spanish possessions, were established by a treaty signed on February 22, 1819, and ratified finally on February 19, 1821. By the terms of this treaty the line between the United States and New Spain was drawn along the Red River to the hundredth meridian

---

[3] *Statutes at Large of the United States of America* (hereafter cited *Statutes*) II, 283, 287.

[4] *Statutes*, II, 331. The act became effective on July 4.

[5] *Statutes*, II, 641, 701. The act was approved on April 8, and became effective on April 30.

[6] Act of June 4, 1812, *Statutes*, II, 743.

[7] A petition was presented in the House of Representatives on January 8 (*Annals*, 15 Cong. 1 sess., 591).

[8] *Statutes*, III, 493. The act became effective on July 4.

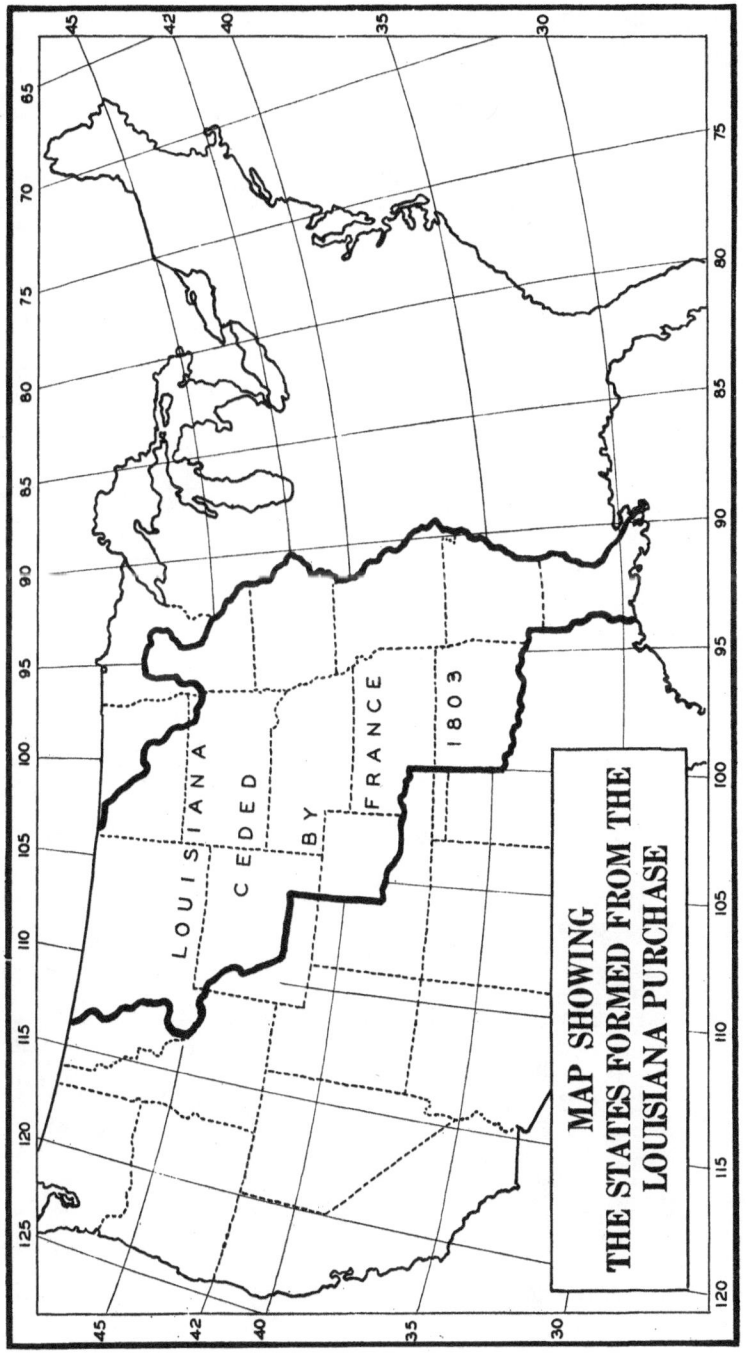

BEGINNINGS OF INDIAN TERRITORY

and thence extended north on that meridian into the present state of Kansas.[9]

While the limits of the future state of Oklahoma on the south and west were being determined by treaty, the eastern border was beginning to take form. By an act of March 6, 1820, the western boundary of Missouri was established on a "meridian line passing through the middle of the mouth of the Kansas River."[10] This line, especially the point of its intersection with the parallel of 36° 30', that is, the southwest corner of Missouri, later played an important part in the determination of the eastern boundary of Oklahoma.

Meanwhile, the movement had begun that supplied the dominant characteristic in the formation of Oklahoma. This was the removal of the Indians from their lands east of the Mississippi to the country set apart for them on the western frontier. The story of the events that brought about this great migration forms no essential part of the history of Oklahoma, and it has been told elsewhere.[11] Even before the purchase of Louisiana, Indians had drifted across the Mississippi— Cherokees, Choctaws, and Chickasaws in particular.[12] As early as 1803, Jefferson seems to have had in mind

---

9 For a discussion of the dispute arising much later over the location of this boundary, see below, Chapter X, footnote 62. The treaty is in *Treaties, Conventions*. . . (Malloy, compiler), II, 1651.

10 *Statutes*, III, 545.

11 See especially Abel, "Indian Consolidation," in American Historical Association, *Annual Report, 1906*, I, 233-450.

12 Jefferson's message, November 14, 1803, *American State Papers, Miscellaneous*, I, 350.

THE FORMATION OF OKLAHOMA

the removal of the Indians to Louisiana,[13] and a section in the act of March 26, 1804, which established two governmental divisions in the new cession, authorized the President to propose this to the tribal authorities.[14] In the latter part of 1808 delegates representing a large part of the Cherokees expressed a desire to remove beyond the Mississippi, and permission was secured easily for the migration of all who wished to go.[15] The lands lying on the White River and the Arkansas, in what is now the state of Arkansas, were chosen by them as their new home; and on July 8, 1817, a treaty was entered into between the United States and the "chiefs, head men, and warriors" of the Cherokee nation by which the United States ceded the Cherokees as much land on these rivers as they had given up east of the Mississippi.[16] It must be borne in mind that this cession was in northwestern Arkansas, but it seems that the Indians were given rights to an outlet indefinitely west, by an executive agreement made in March, 1818, and renewed in October, 1821.[17] The Cherokees who migrated at this time were known at first as the Western Cherokees, and afterwards as the Old Settlers.[18]

13 Draft of proposed amendment to the Constitution, July, 1803, Jefferson, *Writings* (Ford, ed.), VIII, 243.
14 *Statutes*, II, 289.
15 Preamble of the treaty of 1817, *Statutes*, VII, 156 (reprinted in Kappler, *Indian Affairs*, II, 140).
16 *Ibid.*
17 Preamble of the treaty of May 6, 1828, *Statutes*, VII, 311 (reprinted in Kappler, II, 288).
18 Treaty of August 6, 1846, *Statutes*, IX, 871 (reprinted in Kappler, II, 561). In 1822 they numbered six thousand, according to Jedediah Morse, *Report of the Secretary of War*, Appendix, 367.

BEGINNINGS OF INDIAN TERRITORY

The first treaty actually ceding land in Oklahoma to Indians from the country east of the Mississippi was made on October 18, 1820. By this treaty the Choctaws were given a tract that had just been relinquished to the United States by the Quapaw tribe. This tract included all of the land between the Red River and the Canadian. It extended east into what is now Arkansas, and indefinitely west beyond the present borders of Oklahoma.[19] The United States held, however, that the treaty with Spain, ratified finally a few months later, set bounds on the west, both to the territory of the United States and to this cession, and in the agreement with the Choctaws made in 1830 the description was amended to conform to this view.[20]

White settlers were already in the eastern part of the Choctaw country,[21] and they were naturally displeased with the government's plan. On May 26, 1824, Congress moved the western boundary of Arkansas Territory and provided that it should "begin at a point forty miles west of the southwest corner of the State of Missouri, and run south, to the right bank of the Red River."[22] It was planned at the time to secure the removal of the Choctaws to the country west of this

---

19 Treaty with the Quapaws, August 24, 1818, *Statutes*, VII, 176 (reprinted in Kappler, II, 160); with the Choctaws, *Statutes*, VII, 210 (reprinted in Kappler, II, 191).

20 Treaty of September 27, 1830, *Statutes*, VII, 333 (reprinted in Kappler, II, 310).

21 Nuttall, *Journal of Travel into the Arkansa Territory during the year 1819*, 152 (reprinted in Thwaites, *Early Western Travels*, XIII, 213).

22 *Statutes*, IV, 40. A law of March 3, 1823 (*Statutes*, III, 750), had proposed a line due south from the southwest corner of Missouri. The western boundary of Arkansas as established in 1824 ran just east of the present site of Muskogee. Until the admission of Oklahoma, it served as the boundary between the Creeks and the Cherokees for a few miles of its length.

THE FORMATION OF OKLAHOMA

line,[23] but it was possible to secure only a compromise, by which, on January 20, 1825, the eastern boundary of the Choctaw country was established on a "line beginning on the Arkansas, one hundred paces east of Fort Smith, and running thence, due south, to Red River."[24] The United States promised to compel the removal of all whites settled west of this line, a promise that caused a vigorous but ineffectual protest from the persons concerned.[25]

The Quapaw Indians in 1818 had ceded to the United States the entire tract that had been transferred to the Choctaws in 1820; but Indian claims often overlapped, and on June 2, 1825, the Osage tribe relinquished to the United States all the land now included in Oklahoma except the Panhandle.[26] The western boundary of the cession, it is true, was very indefinite, but the United States assumed that it extended to the Mexican frontier.[27] At the same time the Osages gave up all their lands east and north of Oklahoma except a rectangular plot, fifty miles wide from north to south, extending from a line parallel to and twenty-five miles west of the western boundary of Missouri to their

---

23 John C. Calhoun, secretary of war, to the Choctaw Delegation, November 15, 1824, *American State Papers, Indian Affairs*, II, 550.

24 *Statutes*, VII, 234 (reprinted in Kappler, II, 211).

25 Henry W. Conway, delegate from the Territory of Arkansas, to Calhoun, December 22, 1824, inclosures, *American State Papers, Indian Affairs*, II, 555-558.

26 *Statutes*, VII, 240 (reprinted in Kappler, II, 217). The cession in this treaty included all the land in Oklahoma, although a part of it had already been ceded to the United States by the Osages on September 25, 1818 (*Statutes*, VII, 183, reprinted in Kappler, II, 167).

27 Royce, *Indian Land Cessions*, 709 (cf. Abel, "Indian Reservations in Kansas," Kansas State Historical Society, *Collections*, VIII, 77).

BEGINNINGS OF INDIAN TERRITORY

previous western limits.[28] A strip twenty-five miles wide was left in this way to serve as a buffer between them and the white settlements. It soon received the name of the neutral land.[29] The southern boundary of the Osage reservation was fixed on a line forty miles south of "White Hair's village," but this proved to be so nearly the thirty-seventh parallel that it was soon given thus on maps. The southern boundary of Kansas was later established on this parallel as the supposed southern limit of the Osage country.[30] The immediate effect of this treaty was to free a large area between the Canadian River and the thirty-seventh parallel, and this was assigned at once to Indians from the country east of the Mississippi.

As early as February 12, 1825, the United States had proposed to give the Creeks lands in Oklahoma. At that time a treaty was made which provided for a delegation to select a home for the great body of Creeks. This treaty pointed out as the proper location the tract "running westward between said rivers Arkansas and Canadian." Here land was to be given "acre for acre" for the land that the Creeks were to surrender in Georgia and Alabama.[31] The treaty of January 24, 1826, annulled the treaty of 1825 and provided only for a delegation to select a suitable home for such Creeks as wished to migrate.[32] The lands selected, as

---

28 Treaty of 1825, *loc. cit.*
29 Abel, *loc. cit.*
30 This will be considered in Chapter III.
31 *Statutes*, VII, 237 (reprinted in Kappler, II, 214).
32 *Statutes*, VII, 286 (reprinted in Kappler, II, 264).

{ 9 }

THE FORMATION OF OKLAHOMA

will appear later, were those indicated by the first treaty.

By 1828 the Cherokees of Arkansas were so annoyed by white settlers that they agreed, as their neighbors the Choctaws had agreed in 1825, to move farther west. By the terms of a treaty concluded in Washington in May, 1828,[33] the western boundary of Arkansas, south of the Arkansas River, was made to conform to the eastern line of the Choctaw country as established in 1825—"a line beginning on the Arkansas, one hundred paces east of Fort Smith, and running thence, due south, to Red River." North of the Arkansas River, the new boundary of Arkansas was fixed on a direct line from the northeast corner of the Choctaw country to the southwest corner of Missouri;[34] and the Cherokees agreed to move west of this line. As a means of assuring them that this would be their last forced migration, the treaty guaranteed that henceforth their lands should never be included within the limits of a state or organized territory. The advantages of such a plan had already been discussed with the Choctaws,[35] and similar pledges were soon made to other tribes.

By the treaty of 1828, the Cherokees were given a tract of land amounting to seven million acres. Its limits on the south were fixed by the Choctaws' lands, and on the east by the new western boundary of Ar-

---

[33] *Statutes*, VII, 311 (reprinted in Kappler, II, 288). The treaty was signed May 6, and proclaimed May 28.

[34] For a brief history of the boundary between Arkansas and Oklahoma, see below, Appendix A.

[35] Calhoun to the Choctaw Delegation, November 9, 1824, *American State Papers, Indian Affairs*, II, 549.

BEGINNINGS OF INDIAN TERRITORY

kansas. The northern limits extended beyond the parallel of 36° 30' nearly to the Osage country; but, strictly speaking, the northern boundary was an impossible one, as it depended on a point determined by the intersection of the Missouri state line and the Neosho River, and these do not intersect. The western limits of the tract north of the Arkansas River were fixed at the old western boundary of Arkansas, but between the Arkansas and the Canadian the cession extended to "a line running north and south from river to river" that would "give the aforesaid seven millions of acres." As the northern boundary was indeterminate, this part of the western boundary was equally so.

The exact location of the western boundary could not have been considered important during the negotiations, as the Cherokees were guaranteed in the treaty "a perpetual outlet, west, and a free and unmolested use of all the country lying west of the western boundary of the above-described limits." The matter was not so simple as it seemed, however, for the Creeks had already selected land along the Choctaw border between the Arkansas and Canadian rivers in accordance with the agreement of 1826. The Senate accordingly amended the treaty with the Cherokees so that the prior rights of the Creeks to some of this land were recognized.[36]

Although the line between the Creeks and the Cherokees was not yet determined, certain facts stand out in 1828 as settled. The boundaries of the future state

---
36 Treaty of 1828, *loc. cit.*, postscript. At the same time the Senate inserted a provision that the northern limit of the outlet should not extend beyond the thirty-sixth parallel.

THE FORMATION OF OKLAHOMA

were fairly well defined. The southern and western boundaries, except of course those of the Oklahoma Panhandle, had been fixed by treaty with Spain. The eastern boundary had been established by the treaty of 1828 with the Cherokees. The thirty-seventh parallel, which became the northern boundary of the state, already marked a very real division. North of it lived the Osages, a western tribe that subsisted by hunting and fishing and was entirely without laws. South of it the land had been assigned to Indians who lived by commerce and agriculture and had laws and institutions to which they were attached.[37]

In spite of the conflicting claims of Creeks and Cherokees, the part of the Louisiana Purchase that lay west of Arkansas had been ceded to the Cherokees, the Creeks, and the Choctaws. The country had been definitely set apart for the southern Indians. The United States for this purpose had curtailed the limits of the Territory of Arkansas and had moved white settlers eastward. In addition to this, the Cherokees had been promised that no government save their own and that of the United States should exercise authority within their borders. An Indian territory west of the Mississippi had been established in 1828.

[37] McKenney to Barbour, December 13, 1825, *American State Papers, Indian Affairs*, II, 651; Clark to Barbour, March 1, 1826, *ibid.*, 654.

CHAPTER II

THE ESTABLISHMENT OF THE LARGER INDIAN TERRITORY

THE assignment of the western part of the Louisiana Purchase to the Indians, already well begun, was adopted as the formal policy of the United States by the act of May 28, 1830. This act authorized the President to set aside "so much of any territory belonging to the United States west of the river Mississippi, not included in any state or organized territory," as he thought necessary for the use of the Indians from the states east of the Mississippi. The President was further authorized to arrange for the government of the transported Indians and to assure them that the United States would "forever secure and guaranty to them, and their heirs or successors," the possession of their new homes.[1]

The act of 1819 creating the Territory of Arkansas, together with the treaty with Spain negotiated in that year, had divided what is now Oklahoma into three parts, which cornered at the point of intersection of the hundredth meridian and the parallel of 36° 30′. The part west of the hundredth meridian remained outside of the jurisdiction of the United States for over a quarter of a century. The part south of the parallel of 36°

---

[1] *Statutes*, IV, 411. On January 27, 1825, President Monroe had communicated to the Senate a plan for removing the several Indian tribes west of the Mississippi (*American State Papers, Indian Affairs*, II, 541). This plan, which was in part the work of John C. Calhoun, the secretary of war, was an important step in the development of the policy of removal.

THE FORMATION OF OKLAHOMA

30', including more than three-fourths of the present state, was soon separated from Arkansas, as has been said, and was assigned to the Indians. The section lying east of the hundredth meridian and north of the parallel of 36° 30' remained nominally in Missouri Territory, as after 1821 there were both a Territory of Missouri and a State of Missouri.[2] The territory, however, was left unorganized, as the last appropriation for the maintenance of its government was made in 1820.[3] In fact, all of the unorganized part of the Louisiana Purchase, whether cut off from Missouri or from Arkansas, was considered a unit; and the Cherokee territory, it will be remembered, lay on both sides of the line of thirty-six thirty after 1828.

All of the Louisiana Purchase was unorganized and open to Indian colonization in 1830 except the states of Louisiana and Missouri and the Territory of Arkansas. On June 28, 1834, the area now included in Iowa, Minnesota, and the eastern half of the Dakotas was attached to the Territory of Michigan.[4] Gradually, as Indians from eastern states were settled in the southern half of the vast unorganized area that remained, it came to be known distinctively as the "Indian Territory." This name at first had been used as an alterna-

[2] Since no positive action was taken at the time regarding the part of Missouri Territory not included in the State of Missouri, the name was still applied to the unorganized country north of the parallel of 36° 30', as will appear below.

[3] Act of April 11, 1820, *Statutes*, III, 559. The act of March 3, 1821 (*Statutes*, III, 631) made appropriations for the other territories, but not for Missouri.

[4] *Statutes*, IV, 701.

LARGER INDIAN TERRITORY

tive designation for the entire Indian country,[5] but in time it was applied especially to the section of the Indian country that had been set aside for the eastern Indians. In the treaty of 1838 with the New York Indians, their lands in the west were said to be in the Indian Territory.[6] Shortly afterwards it appears that this designation was applied specifically to the part of the Louisiana Purchase south of the forty-third parallel and west of the Missouri River and of the states of Missouri and Arkansas.[7] This use of the name was connected with the unsuccessful attempts to establish an organized Indian Territory within these limits.[8]

According to Josiah Gregg, the Indian Territory in 1844 included only the unorganized part of the Loui-

[5] Intercourse act of March 30, 1802, *Statutes*, II, 139. In 1833 the name "free Indian territory" was applied to all of the Louisiana Purchase north and west of Missouri (Maximilian, *Travels*, I, 120, reprinted in Thwaites, *Early Western Travels*, XXII, 252).

[6] Treaty of January 15, 1838, *Statutes*, VII, 550 (reprinted in Kappler, II, 502).

[7] Farnham, *Travels*, 1839, I, 114 (reprinted in Thwaites, *Early Western Travels*, XXVIII, 117), *Niles' Register*, November 30, 1844 (LXVII, 194).

[8] The Senate passed a bill on May 3, 1838, to establish an Indian Territory extending from the Red River to the Ponca, a small tributary of the Missouri just north of the Niobrara (*Congressional Globe*, 25 Cong. 2 sess., 348, 352). A bill introduced in the House in that session made the Platte the northern boundary of the proposed territory (*ibid.*, 348). An unsuccessful attempt was made in the Senate to extend the boundaries to British America. The North was unwilling to declare so large an area closed to settlement, as two-thirds of the Indian Territory proposed in the original bill lay north of the line of thirty-six thirty and could accommodate all the northern Indians east of the Rocky Mountains (*ibid.*, 347, 348). Moreover, the proposed territory included all the reservations that had been assigned to the eastern tribes. It seems that it was not possible to remove Indians to the country north of the Platte owing to the number and hostility of the native Indians (see below, this chapter, footnote 36). For other attempts to organize the larger Indian Territory, see below, pages 25 and 33.

{ 15 }

siana Purchase south of the Platte.[9] A tabular statement published by the government in December, 1848, gave it these limits and an area of nearly two hundred and fifty thousand square miles.[10] The larger Indian Territory was therefore more than three times as large as the present state of Oklahoma.

Other names were applied to the unorganized part of the Louisiana Purchase. The act of June 30, 1834, providing for a better system for the management of Indian affairs, referred to the country south of the Platte as the "Western Territory."[11] The country north of the Platte was called the "Northwest Territory" in 1848,[12] but on a map published in 1825 it was included in Oregon Territory.[13] The name Missouri Territory continued to be used for the unorganized part of the Louisiana Purchase north of the line of "thirty-six thirty" down to the organization of Nebraska and Kansas in 1854.[14] It could have been applied after that date to the strip between the parallels of 37° and 36° 30′, as it was not superseded there by any other statutory designation until after the Civil War. It is clear, however, from the debates over the Kansas-Nebraska bill that the usual name at the time

---

9 *Commerce of the Prairies*, 1844 ed., I, map facing p. 17.

10 *House Executive Documents*, 30 Cong. 2 sess., I (537), table on map 2 facing p. 48. (The number between the parentheses is the serial number of the volume of the Congressional Documents. The number of the document is given only when the volume cited contains more than one document.)

11 *Statutes*, IV, 736. See also below, p. 25.

12 Map and table cited above in footnote 10.

13 Turner, *Rise of the New West*, opp. p. 226, map based on H. S. Tanner's map of 1825.

14 Gannett, *Boundaries of the United States*, 3d ed., 124, 126, 127. Wyeth used the name in 1833 (*Oregon*, 29, reprinted in Thwaites, *Early Western Travels*, XXI, 50). Cf. Ray, *Repeal of the Missouri Compromise*, 250.

LARGER INDIAN TERRITORY

for the country from the Red River as far north as the Platte, at least, was the Indian Territory.[15]

The act adopting Indian consolidation as the policy of the United States gave new impetus to the westward movement of the Indians. In 1830, the very year of the passage of the act, the Choctaws of Mississippi agreed to join their brethren in the west. They acquired no additional land by the agreement, but a promise was made to them similar to the one made to the Cherokees in 1828; namely, that their lands should never be included within the limits of a state or organized territory.[16] The resulting migration of the Choctaws extended over several years, but in the end the tribe was practically united.[17]

In 1831 a movement began that added new elements to the Indian population south of the thirty-seventh parallel. In that year the Seneca band, living on the Sandusky, ceded their lands in Ohio to the United States and received in exchange a tract of sixty-seven thousand acres, which was described as lying just west of the state of Missouri and north of the land belonging to the Cherokees.[18] As has been said,

15 See in particular the speech of John Bell, senator from Tennessee, March 3, 1854, *Congressional Globe*, 33 Cong., 1 sess., Appendix 410 (cf. report of George W. Manypenny, commissioner of Indian Affairs, for 1854, *H. Ex. Docs.*, 33 Cong. 2 sess., I, i (777), 217). The forms, "the Indian territory," "the Indian Territory," and "Indian Territory," occur. The formal application of this name to the country south of the thirty-seventh parallel seems to date from the Revised Statutes passed at the first session of the Forty-third Congress (sec. 533).

16 Treaty with the Choctaws, September 27, 1830, *Statutes*, VII, 333 (reprinted in Kappler, II, 310).

17 Medill to Rutherford, October 9, 1847, *H. Ex. Docs.*, 30 Cong. 2 sess., I (537), 412.

18 Treaty of February 28, 1831, *Statutes*, VII, 348 (reprinted in Kappler, II, 325).

THE FORMATION OF OKLAHOMA

the northern boundary of the Cherokee cession of 1828 was an impossible one, but the Seneca tract was laid off near the southwest corner of Missouri at the bend of the Neosho River where it most nearly approached the state line. In the same year a mixed band of Seneca and Shawnee Indians exchanged their lands near Lewiston, Ohio, for a tract of sixty thousand acres adjacent to the Seneca tract. This band was promised that their land should never be included within the bounds of a state or territory.[19] In 1833 one hundred and fifty sections near these tracts were given to the Quapaws,[20] who in 1818 had ceded to the United States the country south of the Canadian. They had lived since that time on the Red River. The result of these cessions was the formation of a district less than twenty miles square that was never in the hands of the "Five Civilized Tribes."[21]

Meanwhile, the union of the Creeks and the Seminoles in the western country was brought about by the treaties of 1832 and 1833.[22] The Seminole or Florida

[19] Treaty of July 20, 1831, *Statutes*, VII, 351 (reprinted in Kappler, II, 327). By a treaty made with these bands on December 29, 1832 (*Statutes*, VII, 411, reprinted in Kappler, II, 383), it was agreed that these tracts should extend from the north line of the Cherokees, between the Missouri state line and the Neosho, as far north as was necessary to give room for the area called for by the two previous treaties. The reservations corresponded only approximately to this description, probably because of inaccurate surveys. The writer is unable to ascertain when the boundaries were surveyed.

[20] Treaty of May 13, 1833, *Statutes*, VII, 424 (reprinted in Kappler, II, 395).

[21] For the location of this district as finally delimited, see below, p.106. The five important southern tribes were not commonly referred to as the civilized tribes until after the Civil War (cf. report of the Board of Indian Commissioners for 1869, *H. Ex. Docs.*, 41 Cong. 2 sess., III (1414), 492). In the *Report* of the board for 1876, p. 8, they were spoken of distinctively as the "five 'civilized tribes.' "

[22] Treaty with the Creeks, March 24, 1832, *Statutes* VII, 366 (reprinted

LARGER INDIAN TERRITORY

Indians were considered a branch of the Creeks, as they spoke a common language.[23] The removal of these Indians was a gradual matter. The migration of the Seminoles was little more than half completed in 1844.[24] The treaty made in March 1832, guaranteed to the Creeks that no state or territory should ever have the right to pass laws for their government.[25]

The increase in the number of the Creeks in the West made it necessary to fix definite boundaries for their reservation. In February, 1833, commissioners from the United States met delegates from the Creeks and from the Western Cherokees at Fort Gibson to settle all conflicting claims. The northern limit of the Cherokee country was established definitely at the southern line of the Osage territory, practically at the thirty-seventh parallel. All the country between the Osages and the Choctaws from the Mexican border to Arkansas and Missouri was divided between the Creeks and the Cherokees, except the small district east of the Neosho and north of the south line of the Seneca tract. Roughly speaking, the line between the Creeks and the Cherokees, beginning at the Canadian River, ran north along the old western boundary of Arkansas to a point twenty-five miles north of the Arkansas River, and thence due west to the hundredth meridian. All

in Kappler, II, 341); with the Seminoles, May 9, 1832, *Statutes*, VII, 368 (reprinted in Kappler, II, 344); with the Creeks, February 14, 1833, *Statutes*, VII, 417 (reprinted in Kappler, II, 388); with the Seminoles, March 28, 1833, *Statutes*, VII, 423 (reprinted in Kappler, II, 394).

23 Report of William Armstrong, acting superintendent, for 1840, *H. Ex. Docs.*, 26 Cong. 2 sess., I (382), no. 2, p. 314.

24 Table in the report of the Commissioner of Indian Affairs for 1844, *H. Ex. Docs.*, 28 Cong. 2 sess., I (463), no. 2, p. 315.

25 *Loc. cit.*

THE FORMATION OF OKLAHOMA

north and east of this line was assigned to the Cherokees; all south and west of it, to the Creeks.[26]

The Cherokee country was divided nominally into two parts. The eastern part was ceded separately, and its western boundary was a north and south line that left just seven million acres of Cherokee land east of it. The western part was styled a "perpetual outlet west," but the Cherokees were promised the free and unmolested use of it. This method of ceding seems to have been only an echo of the cession of 1828. It in turn was based on the executive agreements of 1818 and 1821, which were supplementary to the treaty of cession of 1817. The supposed worthlessness of the far Western country made those concerned careless about forms of cession, but only one other tribe, the Delawares, acquired a similar outlet west.[27] The Cherokees agreed to share with other red men the use of the salt plain if that should fall within the limits of the outlet, but the same concession was exacted of the Creeks if this plain should lie within their boundaries. The

[26] Treaty with the Western Cherokees, February 14, 1833, *Statutes*, VII, 414 (reprinted in Kappler, II, 385); with the Creeks, February 14, 1833, *Statutes*, VII, 417 (reprinted in Kappler, II, 388). The boundary between the Creeks and the Cherokees was defined as follows in the Creek treaty: "Beginning at the mouth of the north fork of the Canadian River, and run [ning] northerly four miles—then running a straight line so as to meet a line drawn from the south bank of the Arkansas River opposite to the east or lower bank of Grand River, at its junction with the Arkansas, and which runs a course south, 44 deg. west, one mile, to a post placed in the ground—thence along said line to the Arkansas, and up the same and the Verdigris River, to where the old territorial line crosses it—thence along said line north to a point twenty-five miles from [the point on] the Arkansas River where the old territorial line crosses the same—thence running a line at right angle with the territorial line aforesaid, or west to the Mexico line."

[27] Treaty of September 24, 1829, *Statutes*, VII, 327 (reprinted in Kappler, II, 304).

LARGER INDIAN TERRITORY

difference in the method of cession of the two parts of the Cherokee country afterwards became a source of much confusion.

During the year 1835 delegates claiming to represent the eastern Cherokees agreed to sell their lands east of the Mississippi and to unite with the Western Cherokees in their country "without the territorial limits of the state sovereignties." As the Cherokees were afraid that there would not be sufficient land for all, the United States sold them the rectangle lying between Missouri and the Osage country. This tract, which had been known as the neutral land, now became the Cherokee neutral land. It lay north of the thirty-seventh parallel, but the Cherokees never occupied it. The United States agreed to include this land, the seven million acres, and the outlet, in one patent to be executed to the Cherokee nation by the president of the United States. The guaranty of freedom from the jurisdiction of a state or territory was renewed and extended to all the land included in the patent.[28]

Provisions for settling the Choctaws, the Creeks, the Seminoles, and the Cherokees, were thus made by the close of 1835. Four of the Five Civilized Tribes had rights in what is now Oklahoma. Only the Chickasaws were not yet settled. The Chickasaw people were "closely related to the Choctaw in language and customs."[29] Their home had been in Mississippi, but in 1834 they were forced to give up their tribal organiza-

---

28 Treaty of December 29, 1835, *Statutes*, VII, 478 (reprinted in Kappler II, 439).

29 Article on Chickasaws, by Albert S. Gatchet and Cyrus Thomas, in Hodge, *Handbook of American Indians*, I, 260.

THE FORMATION OF OKLAHOMA

tion. At that time they expressed a desire to remove beyond the Mississippi; but it was not until January, 1837, that a settlement was made. By an agreement between the Choctaws and the Chickasaws made at Doaksville, the Choctaw capital, the Chickasaws were received as a part of the Choctaw nation. The agreement provided for a separate Chickasaw district and for a certain separation of the Choctaw and Chickasaw finances, but the political organization of the two tribes was merged.[30] Thus by 1837 the Five Civilized Tribes were established in what is now Oklahoma.

Although the United States had received all of the present state of Oklahoma from the Quapaws and Osages and had distributed it among tribes from the states east of the Mississippi, yet the Kiowa, Comanche, and Wichita Indians and their allies, together known as the Plains Tribes, considered its western half a part of their hunting-grounds. To forestall serious trouble, United States commissioners called a great council of the tribes concerned. It met in August, 1835, at "Camp Holmes on the eastern border of the Grand Prairie, near the Canadian River, in the Muscogee nation." To this place came representatives of the Cherokees, Muskogees or Creeks, Choctaws, Osages, Senecas, and Quapaws, to meet representatives of the Comanches and Wichitas. These tribes agreed to remain on friendly terms with one another and with the United States. The "Great Prairie west of the Cross Timbers" was made a common hunting-ground, and licensed Indian

[30] *Treaty of May 24, 1834, Statutes,* VII, 450 (reprinted in Kappler, II, 418); treaty of January 17, 1837, *Statutes,* XI, 573 (reprinted in Kappler, II, 486).

LARGER INDIAN TERRITORY

traders were promised protection therein.[31] In May, 1837, the provisions of this agreement were extended to the Kiowa and Kiowa Apache tribes.[32] In this way, what is now Oklahoma was divided by a line drawn north and south almost through its center—a prophecy of the time when the civilized tribes were to have its eastern half, and "blanket" Indians its western half.

Meanwhile, the land north of the thirty-seventh parallel had also been assigned to the Indians. The Osage reservation set apart in 1825 has already been mentioned. In the same year the Kansas or Kaw Indians, who, like the Osages, were an indigenous tribe, were confined to a reservation on the Kansas River.[33] The process of moving tribes from the east side of the Mississippi to this region began in 1829, when the Delawares were located just north of the Kansas reservation.[34] Before 1840, the Shawnee, Kickapoo, Ottawa, Pottawatomie, Munsee, Chippewa, Wea, Piankesha, Peoria, and Kaskaskia tribes were transported wholly or in part and settled between the Osage country and the valley of the Platte, while the Otoe, Missouri, and Omaha tribes accepted reserva-

---

31 Treaty with the Comanches, etc., August 24, 1835, *Statutes*, VII, 474 (reprinted in Kappler, II, 435). According to Gregg (*Commerce of the Prairies*, II, 18, reprinted in Thwaites, *Early Western Travels*, XX, 107), Camp Holmes was located near a spring in latitude 35° 5', a mile north of the Canadian. He did not give the longitude, but on his map (*ibid.*, I, opp. p. 17, 1844 ed.), he placed it just across the river from the present site of Purcell.

32 Treaty with the Kiowas, May 26, 1837, *Statutes*, VII, 533 (reprinted in Kappler, II, 489).

33 Treaty with the Kansas, June 3, 1825, *Statutes*, VII, 244 (reprinted in Kappler, II, 222).

34 Treaty with the Delawares, September 24, 1829, *Statutes*, VII, 327 (reprinted in Kappler, II, 304).

THE FORMATION OF OKLAHOMA

tions not far from their previous homes.[35] The Pawnees were prevailed upon in 1833 to cede their lands south of the Platte, but they were not affected otherwise by this movement.[36] The tribes farther north were not disturbed.

Between 1840 and 1844 some additions were made to the population north of the thirty-seventh parallel. The Miamis were transferred in 1840;[37] the Wyandottes and the Sacs and Foxes, in 1842.[38] The map of the Indian Territory in 1844 shows that all the land along the borders of the states from the Red River north of the Platte, or even beyond, had been assigned to Indian tribes. The tract given in 1838 to the Indians of New York was never occupied by them.[39] The reading of the list of names or the study of the map alone gives an erroneous impression of the distribution of the Indians in the larger Indian Territory, as the bands settled between the Osages and the Pawnees were small remnants of once powerful tribes or, in some instances, represented only parts of tribes.[40]

35 Report of Richard W. Cummins, agent, Fort Leavenworth, September 30, 1840, *H. Ex. Docs.*, 26 Cong. 2 sess., I (382), no. 2, p. 317; of Joseph V. Hamilton, agent, Council Bluffs, September 30, 1840, *ibid.*, 318; of Anthony L. Davis, sub-agent, Osage River, October 15, 1840, *ibid.*, 320.

36 Treaty with the Pawnees, October 9, 1833, *Statutes*, VII, 448 (reprinted in Kappler, II, 416). The Pawnees did not move north of the Platte because of the hostility of the Sioux (report of the Commissioner of Indian Affairs for 1848, *H. Ex. Docs.*, 30 Cong. 2 sess., I (537), 389).

37 Treaty of November 28, 1840, *Statutes*, VII, 582 (reprinted in Kappler, II, 531).

38 Treaty with the Wyandottes, March 17, 1842, *Statutes*, XI, 581 (reprinted in Kappler, II, 534); with the Sacs and Foxes, October 11, 1842, *Statutes*, VII, 596 (reprinted in Kappler, II, 546).

39 Abel, "Indian Reservations in Kansas," Kansas State Historical Society, *Collections*, VIII, 83, 84.

40 This is apparent from the numbers given below.

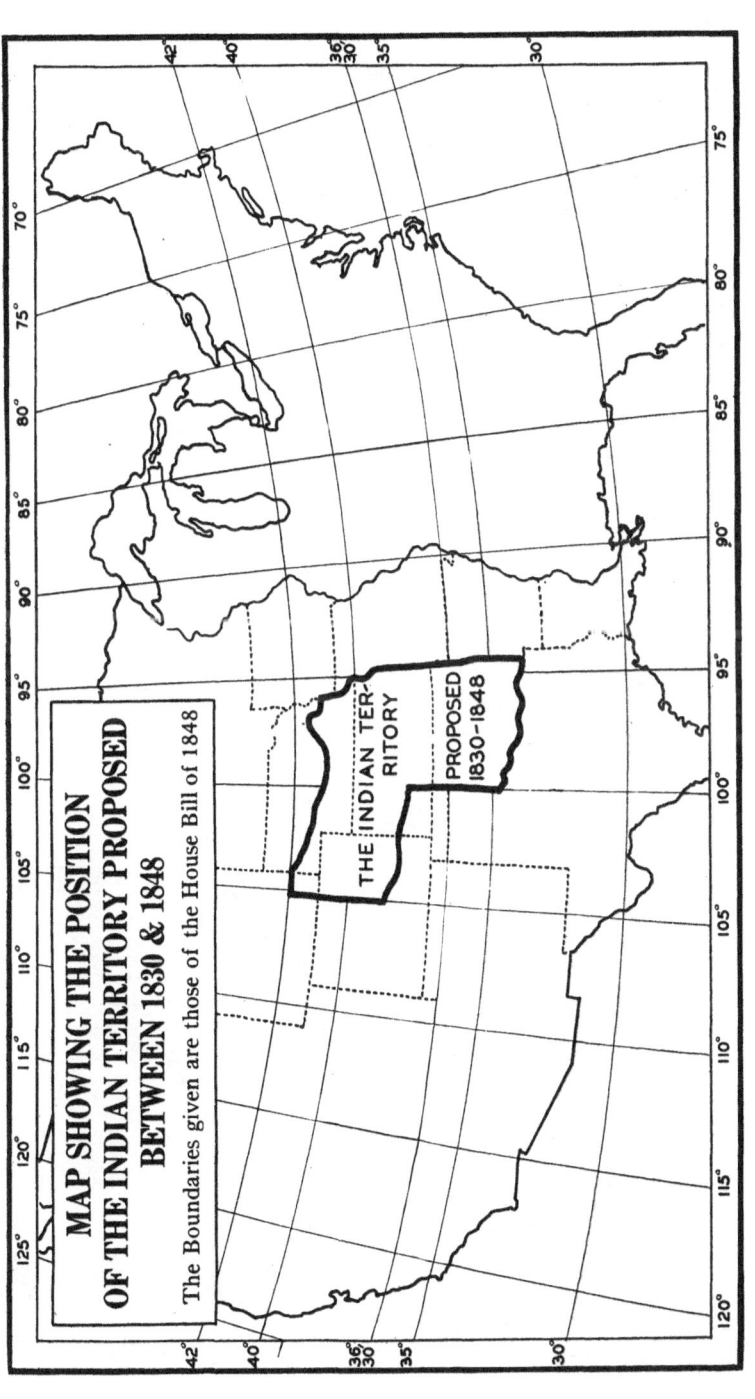

LARGER INDIAN TERRITORY

The progress of Indian consolidation had soon called for a better organization of the territory set apart for the Indians. Early in the year 1834, the House Committee on Indian Affairs prepared three bills designed to accomplish this purpose. The first provided for the establishment of the "Western Territory" for the Indians, bounded on the south and west by Mexico, on the east by Arkansas and Missouri, and on the north by the Platte. Only slight changes in the government of the territory were proposed. The Indians were to continue their tribal organization for the time, under the supervision of the United States. Apparently the development of an Indian state was expected finally within these boundaries.[41] This bill failed to pass, but its companion measures became laws.

The second measure provided for a reorganization of the department of Indian affairs. Assuming that the first bill would pass, the framers of this measure used the name Western Territory for the country between the Red River and the Platte,[42] and for several years thereafter this name appeared in the official records.[43] The third measure, known as the intercourse act, regulated trade and intercourse with the Indians. It forbade settlement in the Indian country

---

[41] The bills were introduced by Horace Everett of Vermont on May 20 (*Congressional Debates*, 23 Cong. 1 sess., X, Pt. IV, 4200, 4764-4779). For other attempts about this time to organize the Indian Territory, see Abel, "Proposals for an Indian State," in American Historical Association, *Annual Report, 1907*, I, 95-99.

[42] Act of June 30, 1834, *Statutes*, IV, 736.

[43] Its last use seems to have been in the Indian appropriation act of February 27, 1851, *Statutes*, IX, 575. Before this time its application had come to be limited to the country west of Arkansas (report of the Commissioner of Indian Affairs for 1848, *H. Ex. Docs.*, 30 Cong. 2 sess., I (537), 391).

THE FORMATION OF OKLAHOMA

and sought to keep white persons out as far as possible. It was a revision and re-enactment of earlier laws controlling commerce with the Indian tribes, in particular of the intercourse act of March 30, 1802.[44]

The most interesting part of this act was incidental to its main purpose. The Indian country west of the Mississippi was divided into two judicial districts, and the courts were given power to enforce the sections that regulated trade and intercourse with the Indians. The boundary between the two districts was the north line of the Osage reservation, a line parallel to and fifty miles north of the present northern boundary of Oklahoma. The Indian country south of this line was attached to Arkansas,[45] and the remaining Indian country west of the Mississippi was attached to Missouri. All of the territory of the United States west of the Mississippi that was not included within the limits of a state or organized territory was declared to be Indian country. Because of this partial judicial organization, the date of the approval of this act, June 30, 1834, is often given as the date of the establishment of the Indian Territory.

President Jackson in his message of December, 1835,

44 Act of June 30, 1834, *Statutes*, IV, 729.
45 The name Arkansas or West Arkansas was sometimes applied to the southern part of the larger Indian Territory, apparently as the result of this arrangement. Fort Towson was said to be in the Territory of Arkansas in the resolution of March 19, 1836 (*Cong. Debates*, 24 Cong. 1 sess., vol. XII, pt. iv, Appendix, p. ii), establishing new post roads. West Arkansas was used in 1853 in the report of Douglas H. Cooper, agent for the Choctaws, September 3, 1853 (*H. Ex. Docs.*, 33 Cong. 1 sess., I, i (710), 405). It appears as late as 1879 in a letter written by a Cherokee official (see below, Chapter VII, footnote 14, for citation). The perdurance of Missouri Territory as a name for the northern part of the Indian country was no doubt due in part to the similar organization of the country west of Missouri.

LARGER INDIAN TERRITORY

summed up as follows the progress of Indian consolidation to that date:

> The plan of removing the aboriginal people who yet remained within the settled portion of the United States to the country west of the Mississippi River approaches its consummation.
> . . . .The necessary measures for their political advancement and for their separation from our citizens have not been neglected. The pledge of the United States has been given by Congress that the country destined for the residence of this people shall be forever "secured and guaranteed to them." A country west of Missouri and Arkansas has been assigned to them, into which the white settlements are not to be pushed. No political communities can be formed in that extensive region, except those which are established by the Indians themselves or by the United States for them and with their concurrence. . . .[46]

This policy was continued without hint of change for several years. The report of 1844 by the Commissioner of Indian Affairs included a census of the Indians in the United States that was intended to show the progress of removal.[47] These figures may not be exact, but they can not give an entirely wrong impression. They show that sixty thousand Indians were settled south of the thirty-seventh parallel, and that these were all eastern Indians except a few Quapaws. North of that parallel the eastern Indians numbered less than five thousand. Of the western Indians between the Platte and the Cherokee line, the Osages numbered about four thousand, the Pawnees about twelve

---

46 *Messages and Papers of the Presidents*, III, 171, 172.

47 *H. Ex. Docs.*, 28 Cong. 2 sess., I (463), no. 2, p. 315. Cf. Gregg, *Commerce of the Prairies*, II, 275 (reprinted in Thwaites, *Early Western Travels*, XX, 317) and *Niles' Register*, November 30, 1844 (LXVII, 194). See below, Appendix D.

thousand, and the other tribes together about two thousand.

The Indians settled in Oklahoma except the Seneca and Quapaw bands, which together numbered about five hundred, had specific agreements that their land should never be included within the limits of an organized territory without their consent. Of the Indians north of Oklahoma, the Ottawas and the Shawnees of Ohio alone had such agreements.[48] The others had only assurances of permanent land-tenure, and the general promises in the law of 1830. The Indians of Oklahoma, in spite of internal disturbances growing out of the migrations, were successfully developing a system of self-government based on that of the states.[49] Those of Nebraska and Kansas were either scattered bands practically without civil organization, or western tribes still in the hunting stage.[50]

The law of 1830, with subsequent executive acts, set apart an Indian country extending from the Red

---

[48] Treaty with the Shawnees, August 8, 1831, *Statutes*, VII, 355 (reprinted in Kappler, II, 331); with the Ottawas, August 30, 1831, *Statutes*, VII, 359 (reprinted in Kappler, II, 335). The New York Indians were also given this promise (treaty of January, 1838, *Statutes*, VII, 550, reprinted in Kappler, II, 502), but they did not occupy their cession. A part of the Cherokee territory also lay north of the thirty-seventh parallel.

[49] Report of William Armstrong, acting superintendent of Western Territory, for 1840, *H. Ex. Docs.*, 26 Cong. 2 sess., I (382), no. 2, p. 310. These Indians were only comparatively well off, however. Gregg said in 1844 that in the whole of the Indian country there were only two places that deserved to be called villages, Doaksville and Park Hill. Gregg was "struck with the contrast between an occasional stately dwelling, with an extensive farm attached, and the miserable homes of the indigent, sometimes not ten feet square, with a little patch of corn, scarce large enough for a family garden" (Gregg, *Commerce of the Prairies*, II, 258, 259, reprinted in Thwaites, *Early Western Travels*, XX, 303, 304).

[50] Report of George W. Manypenny, commissioner of Indian Affairs, for 1853, *H. Ex. Docs.*, 33 Cong. 1 sess., I, i (710), 250, 251.

LARGER INDIAN TERRITORY

River to the Platte or beyond, but the boundary between the Cherokees and the Osages was already a very real one in 1844. The comparative density of Indian population south of this boundary and the different political status of this population, both as to tribal organizations and as to vested rights, had served to bring about such a result. The next movement divided the Indian country definitely and permanently as this line of cleavage and confined the Indian Territory to what is now Oklahoma.

CHAPTER III

THE SEPARATION OF NEBRASKA AND KANSAS FROM THE INDIAN TERRITORY

THE repeal of the Missouri Compromise and the organization of Nebraska and Kansas form as important a part of the history of Oklahoma as of those states. As a result of this action, the Indian Territory was confined to the area south of the thirty-seventh parallel, and the place of Oklahoma as the Indian state was established.

The formation of the larger Indian Territory west of Missouri and Arkansas has a marked influence on the westward migration. The Indian treaties, supplemented by the intercourse act, forbade settlement beyond a line passing through Fort Smith and the mouth of the Kansas River, and the movement into this region was stayed for many years. The stream of settlers was turned to the south and to the north, into Texas and into Iowa. As long as available land remained unoccupied elsewhere, it was not hard for the government to maintain a barrier at this line. The pressure had not become overwhelming when interest in the Pacific Coast made the larger Indian Territory for a time more important as a part of the road to the West than as a possible home for settlers.

This fact dominates the history of the movement that led to the breaking up of the larger Indian Territory. Under the conditions that had hitherto prevailed, the southern part of this area would have been subjected to greater pressure than the northern part, as the frontier line of the Southwest had always been beyond that of the Northwest. Thus, Kentucky and Tennessee were settled and admitted into the Union before Ohio, and Arkansas and Michigan were contemporary frontiers of settlement. Wisconsin, Iowa, and Texas formed the next frontier, and Oklahoma belongs geographically with this line of states. The settlers south of the Arkansas River and west of Fort Smith, who were driven out shortly after 1820 to make room for the Choctaws, were the advance guard of an invasion which, if it had not been checked, would have brought the country west of Arkansas into the Union before 1850, either as a part of Arkansas or as a separate state.[1]

After 1840 the pressure of the westward movement was shifted to the northern part of the larger Indian Territory. This region was intersected by the two great roads to the West, the Oregon trail and the Santa Fé trail; and, more important still, it controlled the only possible routes of the proposed central railroad to the Pacific. The rapidly growing states of the West and Northwest needed an open door to the coast. The small tribes whose reservations blocked the way were unable to offer serious resistance, but it is doubtful whether the more numerous and better intrenched Indians of the Five Civilized Tribes could have held

[1] It was estimated by the officer who had recently been in command at Fort Smith that two thousand persons were settled beyond the line proposed for the western boundary of Arkansas in 1823. Moreover, this line, where it crossed the Arkansas, was ten miles west of the boundary agreed upon in 1828. See W. Bradford's statement, March 25, 1824, *American State Papers, Indian Affairs*, II, 557.

THE FORMATION OF OKLAHOMA

the valley of the Platte if it had been assigned to them.[2]

The strength of the position of the southern tribes was not tested. An effort might have been made to locate a Pacific railroad in the southern part of the larger Indian Territory, as the route along the Canadian River — the thirty-fifth-parallel route — was in some respects the best one of the five or six considered;[3] but the modified southern route through Texas was acceptable to the people of the states south of Missouri. Therefore the opening of this part of the Indian Territory was hardly suggested until 1854, the year of the organization of Nebraska and Kansas.

The movement to open the northern part of the larger Indian Territory was connected from the beginning with a desire for a road to the West. The first official suggestion of an encroachment upon the country of the Indians was made in 1844. In that year William Wilkins of Pennsylvania, the secretary

---

2 It was a part of every plan for a Pacific railroad to clear the country of Indians for miles on both sides of the road. It was not only planned to secure funds for the construction of the road by the sale of this land, but it was hoped that the influx of settlers would help to make the venture profitable from the beginning. By the Pacific railroad act of July 1, 1862, the United States undertook to extinguish the Indian titles to a strip of land twenty miles wide along the proposed line, which was not yet definitely located (*Statutes*, XII, 492).

3 Five routes were ultimately given chief consideration; the northern, north of the forty-seventh parallel; the north-central, by the Platte and South Pass; the central, between the thirty-eighth and the thirty-ninth parallels; the south-central, near the thirty-fifth parallel; the southern, near the thirty-second parallel. Two important variations of the central route were sometimes counted separately. See report of the Secretary of War, February 27, 1855, *Senate Executive Documents*, 33 Cong. 2 sess., XIII, i (758), 31. For a statement of the advantages of the south-central route, see report of Lieutenant A. W. Whipple, July 3, 1854, *H. Ex. Docs.*, 33 Cong. 1 sess., XVIII, ii (737) [Division III], p. 8.

SEPARATION OF NEBRASKA AND KANSAS

of war, recommended in his annual report that a territory should be organized on both sides of the Platte. This was a plan to open the way to the Pacific, and evidently it was the result of the growing interest in Oregon. He recommended that the Indians should be pushed back to the north and to the south, and that an organized and settled district should be formed to control the passes to Santa Fé and especially to Oregon.[4]

On December 17, 1844, Stephen A. Douglas, then in Congress as a representative from Illinois, introduced a bill to organize the Territory of Nebraska, as proposed by the secretary of war;[5] and on January 22, 1845, he introduced a bill to establish a sufficient number of military posts in Oregon and Nebraska to protect commerce with New Mexico and California and the "emigration and trade to Oregon."[6]

Differences of opinion soon developed. Many thought that, in view of the recent pledges, something must be done for the Indians. On June 22, 1846, the House Committee on Indian Affairs reported a new bill to establish an Indian Territory;[7] and two years later, on June 27, 1848, this committee reported a similar bill. The latter provided for an Indian Territory ex-

---

4 *H. Ex. Docs.*, 28 Cong. 2 sess., I (463), no. 2, p. 124. Wilkins suggested that the new territory should be given the name of its chief river, the Platte or Nebraska.

5 *Cong. Globe*, 28 Cong. 2 sess., 41.

6 *Ibid.*, 173. Nebraska, as the name was first used, seems to have included only the unorganized part of the Louisiana Purchase between the fortieth and the forty-third parallels (*H. Ex. Docs.*, 30 Cong. 2 sess., I (537), map 2, between pp. 48 and 49). Later it came to mean for a time all of the unorganized part of the Louisiana Purchase north of the line of thirty-six thirty.

7 *Cong. Globe*, 29 Cong. 1 sess., 1013.

{ 33 }

THE FORMATION OF OKLAHOMA

tending from the Red River to the Platte. The superintendent of Indian affairs was designated governor of the territory, and an Indian council was to have legislative power subject to his veto. The participation of a tribe in the organization was made optional, and the right of secession and the control of all purely local affairs were reserved to the tribes.[8] Nothing came of this bill but a protest of the Indians against its consideration.[9]

The acquisition of California in 1848 made greater the demand for a road to the Pacific, and on March 15, 1848, Douglas, by this time a senator, again introduced a bill for the organization of Nebraska.[10] On December 20, 1848, he brought it up for the third time.[11] The Commissioner of Indian Affairs, W. Medill, in his annual report made at this time, announced that his department had already begun "the establishment of two colonies for the Indian tribes"—one north of the Platte, the other south of the Kansas. Between these rivers, he declared, "there would be a wide and safe passage" to the West.[12] Of course it was possible to get to Oregon by the northernmost route, but that led through the country of the Sioux and was supposed to be impracticable because of the heavy snowfall. It was possible to get to California by way of Texas, but the northern and central states wanted a route farther north. The Indian Territory proposed by the bills of

---
8 *Cong. Globe*, 30 Cong. 1 sess., 874; *House Reports*, 30 Cong. 1 sess., III (526), no. 736, p. 11.
9 *House Miscellaneous Documents*, 30 Cong. 2 sess. (544), no. 35.
10 *Cong. Globe*, 30 Cong. 1 sess., 467.
11 *Cong. Globe*, 30 Cong. 2 sess., 68.
12 *H. Ex. Docs.*, 30 Cong. 2 sess., I (537), 388-390.

SEPARATION OF NEBRASKA AND KANSAS

1834 and 1838 was a buffer between the United States and Mexico; the Indian Territory in 1848, although it had practically the same boundaries, had become a barrier through the geographical center of the United States as constituted after the war with Mexico.

It was not thought impossible to move the Indians again, as they were much in the way under the changed conditions. In January, 1849, the legislature of North Carolina petitioned Congress to give the Indians a permanent home, with the hope of their union and admission as a state.[13] This certainly meant that their home in the Indian Territory was not considered permanent. In the same month the legislature of Pennsylvania asked Congress to move the Indians of the West and Southwest to a permanent home in the Northwest Territory.[14] By this was meant what is now included in the Dakotas and Montana. The plan of settling the Indians along the Canadian border, where they would be out of the direct road to the Pacific, seems to have received consideration for some time. Two years later, in January, 1851, James Duane Doty, then in Congress as a representative from Wisconsin, urged the plan in a letter to President Filmore. He thought that the country lying between the present western boundary of Minnesota and the Missouri River was the most suitable tract for a permanent home for the northern Indians.[15]

13 *H. Misc. Docs.*, 30 Cong. 2 sess. (544), no. 39. The memorial was presented in the House on February 8.
14 *Ibid.*, no. 38. This memorial also was presented in the House on February 8.
15 Abel, "Proposals for an Indian State," *loc. cit.*, Appendix. The letter bore date of January 20.

THE FORMATION OF OKLAHOMA

The work of Asa Whitney in arousing popular interest in the construction of a transcontinental railroad was important. His plan was before the public from 1845 to 1852. It was recommended by congressional committees no less than seven times, and it was supported by petitions, resolutions of public meetings, and resolutions of state legislatures. Whitney proposed to build a railroad from Lake Michigan to the Oregon coast, and to take in exchange for it a strip of the public domain sixty miles wide "from Lake Michigan or the Mississippi River to the Pacific Ocean." He was to sell this land to settlers, pay the United States ten cents an acre for the land sold, and keep the remainder as compensation and profit. The United States of course would have had to extinguish the Indian title. The acquisition of California turned attention to a more southern route, and the interest in Whitney's plan evidently began to decline after July, 1848, when the Senate, on motion of Thomas H. Benton, senator from Missouri, refused to consider the proposition by the rather close vote of twenty-seven to twenty-one.[16]

On February 7, 1849, Benton introduced his famous bill providing for the construction by the United States of a national central highway from Saint Louis to San Francisco. This bill proposed to open the Indian country along the way, and the sum of one hundred thousand dollars was to be set aside for treating with the Indians.[17] On December 16, 1850, Benton

16 *H. Reports*, 32 Cong. 1 sess. (656), no. 101; *Cong. Globe*, 30 Cong. 1 sess., 1011. This vote was taken on July 30.

17 *Cong. Globe*, 30 Cong. 2 sess., 470. This bill proposed an appropriation of thirty thousand dollars for preliminary surveys.

{ 36 }

renewed his bill, and in a speech outlined what he thought would be the proper course for the highway. He evidently planned that it would follow the present line of the Santa Fé to Pueblo, and thence traverse the Rockies by the route of the Denver and Rio Grande.[18]

The agitation over the slavery question, about 1850, kept all other matters in the background for the time; but the settlement made by the Compromise of 1850, which it was hoped would be permanent, presently allowed other things than slavery to receive consideration. A period of railroad expansion followed. In the next four years—namely, between 1850 and 1854—the railway mileage in the United States rose from eighty-six hundred to twenty-one thousand three hundred. In 1850, under the leadership of Stephen A. Douglas, Congress entered upon a policy of making extensive land-grants in aid of railroad construction. In that year public lands were ceded to the states of Illinois, Alabama, and Mississippi, to be used to aid in constructing a railroad from the Great Lakes to the Gulf of Mexico. In July of the next year, Missouri began to build the first link of the Pacific railroad west of the Mississippi. All this again brought to the atten-

---

18 *Cong. Globe*, 31 Cong. 2 sess., 56. Because Benton in the course of his speech said that the hunter and the explorer following the trail of the Indian and of the buffalo had already marked out the great transcontinental routes, it has been said flippantly that Benton proposed to construct a road across the mountains without a survey. Nevertheless, this bill proposed an appropriation of three hundred thousand dollars to be used for making surveys and for treating with the Indians for their lands. This bill authorized the president "to employ as many citizen civil engineers" as might be necessary.

THE FORMATION OF OKLAHOMA

tion of the western states the question of the open road to the Pacific.[19]

For several years the people of these states had been asking for a better government for the country beyond them. Missouri led in this. In December, 1847, the legislature of Missouri asked Congress to create a new territory west of that state.[20] On December 12, 1851, Willard P. Hall, representative in Congress from the western district of Missouri, gave notice of intention to introduce a bill for the organization of the Territory of Nebraska.[21] In July, 1852, citizens of Parkville, just across the Missouri River from the Indian country, petitioned Congress for the organization of this territory.[22] Petitions of a similar nature could not have been uncommon at the time. Douglas, on July 13, said that during the session innumerable memorials from the western states asking for the protection of the emigrant lines had been referred to the Committee on Territories, and that scarcely a day passed without the receipt of more of them. He made this statement while he was trying to secure the passage of a bill introduced by himself for the protection of the routes to the West, a measure similar to his bill of 1845.[23]

19 McMaster, *History of the People of the United States*, VIII, 88-95; Johnson, *Stephen A. Douglas*, 169-174. For the grant of land in 1850, see act of September 20, 1850, *Statutes*, IX, 466.

20 *Cong. Globe*, 30 Cong. 1 sess., 56. The petition was presented in the House on December 20.

21 *Cong. Globe*, 32 Cong. 1 sess., 80.

22 *Ibid.*, 1666; Ray, *Repeal of the Missouri Compromise*, 82. The petition was presented in the Senate on July 7. It should be observed that in this case, as in many others, the interests of those who wished to pass through Nebraska were paramount. The settlement of Nebraska itself was only mentioned incidentally. See below, Appendix B.

23 *Cong. Globe*, 32 Cong. 1 sess., 1760, 1761. The bill mentioned was introduced by Douglas for the Committee on Territories on April 22, 1852 (*ibid.*, 1161).

SEPARATION OF NEBRASKA AND KANSAS

Since the intercourse act forbade settlement in the Indian country, the only white persons legally residing in the proposed Territory of Nebraska were officials, soldiers, missionaries, or licensed traders. They were not in a position to ask for a change, but the Indians of one tribe took up the matter. In the autumn of 1852 the Wyandottes, who lived on the Kansas River near its mouth, sent a delegate to Congress to urge the establishment of territorial government in their country.[24]

On December 13, 1852, Representative Hall renewed his bill for the organization of the Nebraska country, this time proposing the name "Territory of the Platte."[25] On February 2, 1853, William A. Richardson of Illinois, chairman of the House Committee on Territories, introduced a similar measure, possibly a committee substitute for Hall's bill, in which the name Nebraska was restored. This bill passed the House of Representatives on February 10, 1853, and was brought up in the Senate on March 2.[26]

The bill, as it passed the House, provided for the organization of a territory bounded on the north by the forty-third parallel, on the east by the states of Missouri and Iowa, on the south by the line of thirty-six thirty, and on the west by the Rocky Mountains.

---

24 The first mention of this delegate was made in the House on December 17 (*Cong. Globe*, 32 Cong. 2 sess., 85, 1127). Cf. Ray, *op. cit.*, 87. According to a statement made on May 20, 1854, by Bernhart Henn, a representative from Iowa (*Cong. Globe*, 33 Cong. 1 sess., Appendix, 885), only persons of the classes enumerated above had lived in Nebraska until a few months before, but five or six hundred others had recently been permitted to enter.

25 *Cong. Globe*, 32 Cong. 2 sess., 7, 47.

26 *Ibid.*, 474, 475, 565, 1020.

THE FORMATION OF OKLAHOMA

It was stated on the floor of the House that these limits were established in order that the new territory should control the Oregon trail and the Santa Fé trail. All lands belonging to Indians who had been specifically guaranteed permanent exclusion from the jurisdiction of a state or organized territory were expressly left out of the proposed territory until the consent for inclusion could be secured from the Indians.[27]

The opening to settlement of this area, from which slavery had been excluded, was not acceptable to the South. The member of the House who opposed the bill most vigorously was Volney E. Howard, one of the two representatives from Texas. The promise to the Indians of a permanent home in the Indian Territory was the basis of his opposition. Hall of Missouri declared angrily that the Texans wished to retain a vast, unorganized Indian country north of them so that all travel and commerce between the East and the Pacific must pass through their state. Hall also pointed out that the transcontinental railroad would not pass through the Nebraska country unless it could be opened to settlement.[28]

[27] Statements of Hall, who was the principal supporter of the bill, *ibid.*, 560-565.

[28] *Ibid.*, 556-558. Hall did not give explicit reasons for this assertion. Three reasons present themselves that may have been in his mind: A railroad passing through an unsettled country would not be supported by local traffic. If the Indian title should not be extinguished, it would not be possible to make a grant of land in aid of construction. As long as the Indian Territory remained intact, the pledges to the Indians would be a powerful sentimental argument for a different route. The first roads constructed in the diminished Indian Territory after the Civil War were located because of conditional land grants, which it was thought would be ratified soon. Bankruptcy came to them when they did not receive the expected grants. The later roads were constructed after the agricultural and mineral development of the country had begun.

SEPARATION OF NEBRASKA AND KANSAS

In the Senate the opposition to the bill was led by the two members from Texas, Sam Houston and Thomas J. Rusk. Houston urged the importance of fulfilling the recent pledges to the Indians, and Rusk declared that the wild tribes would move down upon Texas and make it uninhabitable if the Indian Territory should be opened to settlement.[29]

The attitude of the South in general toward the Nebraska bill was shown by the votes of the Southern congressmen. In the House thirty of the forty-three negative votes were from the south. Of the ninety-eight affirmative votes, eighty came from the North, seven from Kentucky and Missouri, and eleven from other Southern states. Eighty-eight members were absent or not voting. The division in the Senate on March 3 was even more significant. All the votes cast by members from the South, except the two from Missouri, a state vitally interested in the central route to the Pacific, were against the bill. With the southern senators voted five senators from the Northeast; and in spite of Douglas's efforts, the Senate rejected the bill by a vote of twenty-three to seventeen. Twenty-two members of the Senate were absent or did not vote, but the trend was unmistakable.[30]

29 *Ibid.*, 1020, 1113, 1114.
30 *Cong. Globe*, 32 Cong. 2 sess., 565, 1113-1117. If more were needed to show the sectional character of the opposition to Nebraska, the vote on Douglas's motion to take up the Nebraska bill on March 2 would suffice. Eighteen free-state senators and two senators from Missouri voted aye. Eighteen senators from slave states, six from the Northeast, and Gwin of California, a Southern man and committed at the time to the southern route to the Pacific, voted nay (*ibid.*, 1020). Wrong inferences have been drawn from the lack of consideration of the Nebraska bill in March, 1853. This vote in connection with the one of the next day indicated positively who wished to con-

{ 41 }

THE FORMATION OF OKLAHOMA

In one respect progress was made during this session of Congress. The Indian appropriation bill, which became a law on the day of the defeat of the Nebraska bill, the last day of Fillmore's administration, contained a clause authorizing the President to negotiate with the Indians west of Missouri and Iowa for the purchase of their lands.[31] Nothing, however, came of these negotiations during the year.

At the beginning of Pierce's administration, the Indian Territory still blocked the way from the Middle West to the Pacific. At one time it had seemed that the people of Arkansas and Tennessee might join with those of the states north of them to bring about the opening of the larger Indian Territory. On July 8, 1852, Solon Borland, senator from Arkansas, took a definite stand for this. Five days later John Bell, then a senator from Tennessee, wavered in his opposition to the Douglas bill for the protection of the routes to the West, and, according to Bell's analysis, this meant the opening of the country along these routes.[32] Many of the people of Arkansas undoubtedly hoped at first that the Pacific railroad would run from Memphis through their state and the southern part of the larger Indian Territory, and thence across the Rockies by way of Albuquerque. A railroad convention held at Little Rock on July 4, 1852, authorized a memorial

---

sider the Nebraska matter and who did not. The debate on Douglas's bill for the protection of the emigrant routes in July, 1852, also showed the sectional trend (*Cong. Globe*, 32 Cong. 1 sess., 1683-1686, 1756-1764).

31 *Statutes*, X, 238.

32 *Cong. Globe*, 32 Cong. 1 sess., 1685, 1763. It is worthy of note that Borland on March 3, 1853, declared against the Nebraska bill and moved to lay it on the table (*Cong. Globe*, 32 Cong. 2 sess., 117).

SEPARATION OF NEBRASKA AND KANSAS

to Congress in favor of this route.[33] About this time the people of this section began to consider another route.

On August 31, 1852, the Senate Committee on Public Lands by its chairman, Solon Borland of Arkansas, made a report submitting two plans for a railroad to the Pacific. These plans were alike in adopting a route through Texas with branches from northeastern Texas or southwestern Arkansas to Saint Louis, Memphis, Vicksburg, and New Orleans. The committee evidently sought to make a report acceptable to those who favored the central, the south-central, or the Southern route.[34]

On December 22, 1852, a bill was introduced in the Senate by William M. Gwin of California providing "for the construction of a railroad from a point on Red River, at or near the southwest corner of the State of Arkansas, on the most direct and feasible route . . . to a point on the eastern boundary of the State of California."[35] The southern road thus constructed would be as advantageous to Tennessee and Arkansas as the south-central road, and it seemed to have a better chance of success, as it would enlist the support of the

33 *Senate Miscellaneous Documents*, 32 Cong. 2 sess. (670), no. 5. The memorial was drawn up by a committee on November 1, and was presented in the Senate on December 27.

34 *Senate Reports*, 32 Cong. 1 sess., II (631), no. 344.

35 *Cong. Globe*, 32 Cong. 2 sess., 126, 339. Branches were to be constructed through the eastern part of the Indian Territory to the western border of Missouri and Iowa. On August 30, 1852, Gwin had introduced a bill providing for two roads, one from southwestern Arkansas and one from western Iowa or Missouri (*Cong. Globe*, 32 Cong. 1 sess., 2466). The branches proposed in the new bill seem to have been only a step toward the omission of all reference to Missouri and Iowa. This result was reached in the McDougall report a year later.

people of all the states south of Missouri.[36] It did not call for the opening of the southern part of the larger Indian Territory, and the retention of all the Indian country unorganized furnished a strong argument for its adoption.

An act of March 3, 1853, authorized the president to have surveys made to ascertain the most practicable and economic route for a railroad from the Mississippi to the Pacific;[37] but on March 13, 1854, before the surveys were completed, a select committee of the House of Representatives reported in favor of two roads. One was to connect "Lake Superior or the Mississippi River, in the Territory of Minnesota," with the Pacific Ocean; and the other was to be a southern road.[38] The more northern route was not thought to be practicable, and the proposal to select it was not taken seriously in the North.[39] The organization of the Nebraska country and the extinction of the Indian

[36] Jefferson Davis, secretary of war, in his report of February 27, 1855, which was based on the results of the surveys authorized by the act of March 3, 1853, recommended the adoption of this route with the eastern terminus at Fulton, Arkansas (*S. Ex. Docs.*, 33 Cong. 2 sess., XIII, i (758), 23). It is often said wrongly that Vicksburg, Mississippi, was the proposed eastern terminus of this route, and it is forgotten that the selection of the route actually recommended would have benefited equally all parts of the South. The Southern people agreed upon it as naturally as the Northern people later agreed upon the north-central route.

[37] *Statutes*, X, 219.

[38] *Cong. Globe*, 33 Cong. 1 sess., 614, 1355. Appendix, 881. The report was presented by James A. McDougall of California.

[39] Speech of Bishop Perkins, representative from New York, June 7, 1854 (*Cong. Globe*, 33 Cong. 1 sess., Appendix, 881). A glance at the map will indicate why no state of the time except Wisconsin wanted the Pacific road north of the north-central route. The southern extremity of Lake Michigan determined this.

SEPARATION OF NEBRASKA AND KANSAS

titles would remove the only objection that could be urged against a more central route.[40]

On the first day of the session of Congress beginning in December, 1853, Augustus C. Dodge of Iowa gave notice of intention to introduce a bill in the Senate for the organization of Nebraska Territory. John G. Miller of Missouri introduced a like bill in the House of Representatives a few days later.[41] The Commissioner of Indian Affairs in his annual report made at this time professed to favor the proposed opening of the Indian Territory, but he admitted that no progress had been made in the negotiations with the Indians authorized in March, 1853.[42] The task of the members of Congress from the Middle West was to secure the organization of Nebraska and thus announce that the United States intended to remove the Indians. As Douglas put it, "There are two or three points where an Indian Territory could be laid out without interfering with any of the great routes to the Pacific."[43]

Two things stood in the way of the speedy organiza-

---

40 It is necessary to remember that, while the "Northwest Territory" was still Indian country, it was not a part of the Indian Territory, that is, none of its land was held by Indians who had removed there under the pledge of the law of 1830.

41 Dodge gave notice of intention on December 7, his bill was introduced December 14, and Miller's bill was introduced December 22 (*Cong. Globe*, 33 Cong. 1 sess., 1, 44, 87).

42 *H. Ex. Docs.*, 33 Cong. 1 sess., I, i (710), 249.

43 March 3, 1853; *Cong. Globe*, 32 Cong. 2 sess., 1117. The success of the negotiations for the purchase from Mexico of the country south of the Gila, concluded on December 30, 1853 (*Treaties, Conventions*... (Malloy, compiler), I, 1121), paved the way for the removal of a serious objection to the southern route. A stretch of the southern road to the Pacific proposed in Borland's report (*loc. cit.*) ran across Mexican territory. This treaty doubtless made those interested in the north-central and the central routes more anxious for the immediate organization of the Nebraska country.

{ 45 }

THE FORMATION OF OKLAHOMA

tion of this country. The Indians of the Indian Territory had been promised that they would not be disturbed again. Many persons felt that the government was bound to leave them their reservations intact. This opinion was held especially by the older men who had some part in making the settlement in the thirties.[44] The attitude of the South toward the opening of this country was even more important. Many of the people of that section thought that the Missouri Compromise had been humiliating to them. They wished to keep the remainder of the Louisiana Purchase closed to settlement as long as possible, since they thought that it would not be open on equal terms to settlers from the North and from the South.[45]

The objections made to the organization of Nebraska because of the recent pledges to the Indians had been met as far as possible by promises to consider their interests and desires.[46] Douglas had also made an effort to meet the objections of the Southerners to the opening of Nebraska by a proposal to open the territory south of the line of thirty-six thirty.[47] As the territory to be opened north of this line was many times as extensive as the territory south of it, this plan did not prove attractive. The growing tendency of the people of the

44 See speech of Edward Everett, February 8, 1854 (*Cong. Globe*, 33 Cong. 1 sess., Appendix, 158); of John Bell, March 3 (*ibid.*, 410).

45 The desire to maintain a balance in the Senate between free and slave states was of course a great reason for the Southern objection to new territories from which slavery was excluded, for new territories soon meant new states.

46 In particular by the provision that the territorial government should not be extended over the Indians who had been promised freedom from this (*Cong. Globe*, 33 Cong. 1 sess., 222).

47 On March 3, 1853, *Cong. Globe*, 32 Cong. 2 sess., 1117.

{ 46 }

SEPARATION OF NEBRASKA AND KANSAS

states south of Missouri to unite upon a southern route for the Pacific railroad indicated that the South, on account of the Missouri Compromise, was willing to let the Indian country below the line of thirty-six thirty remain unorganized, provided the larger portion above that line also remained unorganized.[48]

This attitude had become apparent as early as April, 1838, when a body of eleven Southern senators, the most prominent of whom was John C. Calhoun, sought to secure legislation declaring that all the territory of the Louisiana Purchase to which the Indian titles had not then been extinguished should be forever closed to settlement.[49] On February 19, 1847, Calhoun denounced the Missouri Compromise and declared in favor of returning to the principles of the Constitution.[50] Other persons in the slave states announced from time to time their agreement with this position.[51] The votes in 1853, both in the Senate and in the House, proved the strength of the Southern opposition to the opening of the Nebraska country under the conditions prescribed by the Missouri Compromise. The only dem-

---

48 The total unorganized area north of the line of thirty-six thirty was nearly five hundred thousand square miles; the total area south of it was something over fifty thousand square miles. Compare statement of William C. Price, quoted by Ray (*op. cit.*, 250): "We were opposed to the opening of any part of the territory of Old Missouri Territory to settlement. . . .If slavery could not go there we wanted no one there except the Indians." Price is said to have been in close touch with all of the Southern leaders.

49 This motion was made April 28, and rejected April 30 (*Cong. Globe*, 25 Cong. 2 sess., 340, 348). This included practically all of the Louisiana Purchase north and west of the State of Missouri.

50 *Cong. Globe*, 29 Cong. 2 sess., 454.

51 In particular during the debates on the Compromise of 1850 (*Cong. Globe*, 31 Cong. 1 sess., Appendix, 988 ff.). See also *Cong. Globe*, 32 Cong. 1 sess., 1113, and the "Jackson Resolutions" given by Ray (*op. cit.*, 38).

THE FORMATION OF OKLAHOMA

ocratic senator from a slave state who voted for the Nebraska bill in 1853, David R. Atchison of Missouri, said at the time that he did so unwillingly.[52] During the summer of 1853 Atchison announced that he would not vote again for a bill to organize the Territory of Nebraska unless that bill should leave the territory open to settlement by slaveholders.[53] Evidently but one Southern senator was left who could be counted on to vote for Dodge's Nebraska bill unamended.

The introduction of Dodge's bill and its reference to the Committee on Territories, of which Douglas was chairman, placed a choice of three plans of action before Douglas: First, he could delay the consideration of the bill just when interest in Nebraska and in the Pacific railroad had become acute in the West. He had tried to press the organization of the territory before a great deal of popular interest had been aroused, and an energetic and confident man like Douglas was not likely to drop the matter under the new conditions.[54] Second, he could try to secure the passage of the Nebraska bill by a sectional vote. It is not certain that he would have succeeded;[55] but if he had succeeded,

52 *Cong. Globe*, 32 Cong. 2 sess., 1113.
53 Ray, *op. cit.*, 137.
54 The people of the East and Southeast did not realize that the Nebraska question was imminent. They believed that Douglas was forcing it on the attention of Congress. Opinions differ as to Douglas's interest in the matter, aside from politics. Johnson (*Stephen A. Douglas*, 221) says, "Nebraska became almost a hobby with Douglas." Ray (*op. cit.*, p. 18, note 134) says that Douglas's lack of genuine interest in Nebraska was surprising.
55 It is usually assumed that this would have been an easy matter. A statement asserting this made by Douglas on March 3, 1853 (*Cong. Globe*, 32 Cong. 2 sess., 1116) is sometimes quoted. This statement, however, is not to the point, as it was made before the Richardson bill had been laid on the table and before Atchison's change of position had indicated the

SEPARATION OF NEBRASKA AND KANSAS

sectional feeling would have been intensified, not only in the Democratic party but in the country as well. Lastly, he could try to find a compromise that would secure both Northern and Southern votes for the measure. But the only possible compromise was to leave the question of slavery entirely to the people of the territories.

The proposal to settle the question of slavery in the Louisiana Purchase in this way had been made before by Northern men. As early as December 2, 1847, Daniel S. Dickinson, senator from New York, had proposed resolutions asserting "that in organizing a territorial government for territory belonging to the United States . . .all questions concerning the domestic policy therein [should be left] to the legislatures chosen by the people thereof."[56] On December 24, 1847,

---

growing unity of the Southern opposition. Gwin of California voted with the Southerners on March 2, 1853, and probably would have voted with them again. Everett of Massachusetts based his opposition to the amended bill as much on his regard for Indian treaties as on his dislike for the repeal of the Missouri Compromise (*Cong. Globe*, 33 Cong. 1 sess., Appendix, 159). He would probably have voted against the establishment of the territory in any case. The free-state majority in the Senate was only two at the time.

Moreover, other senators from the Northeast had opposed the Nebraska bill, either from indifference or because of interest in another route to the West. The opposition would have taken the form that it took in 1853, or requests would have been made for postponement until the claims of the Indians had been given attention. The promises made in 1830 afforded a good pretext for opposition to the Nebraska bill, if the real motives were such that they could not be acknowledged publicly. It was stated in the New York *Evening Post* of November 15, 1853, that intrigues were on foot to keep "Nebraska out of the sisterhood of territories, and of course out of the Union as long as possible" (quoted by Ray, *op. cit.*, 181). On the whole question, see Hodder, "Genesis of the Kansas-Nebraska Act," in State Historical Society of Wisconsin, *Proceedings, 1912*, pp. 69-82.

56 *Cong. Globe*, 30 Cong. 1 sess., 54. The debate on this resolution brought up squarely the question of the right of a territory to forbid slavery within its limits. Southern men objected strongly to this settlement. They declared that any effort, either of Congress or of a territorial legislature, to legislate

THE FORMATION OF OKLAHOMA

Lewis Cass, senator from Michigan and later Democratic candidate for the presidency, declared definitely in favor of this method of settling the question of slavery in the territories.[57] It had been suggested by a Northern representative in the debate on the Nebraska bill in 1853 that the organization of Utah and New Mexico had established a precedent that might apply to Nebraska.[58] A convention held at Saint Joseph, Missouri, at the beginning of January, 1854, in which delegates from Iowa participated, demanded the organization of the Territory of Nebraska, and declared in favor of leaving the question of slavery "to be settled by the citizens of the territory when they form a state government."[59]

Douglas did not believe that slavery would ever be established in any of the new territories, regardless of the laws enacted.[60] He thought that the North was sacrificing nothing by leaving slavery to be checked by economic influences. He hoped, no doubt, that sectional hostility could be averted and that the South

---

slavery out of a territory before its admission as a state was unconstitutional (*ibid.*, 160).

57 McLaughlin, *Lewis Cass*, 235.

58 John W. Howe of Pennsylvania, February 8, 1853 (*Cong. Globe*, 32 Cong. 2 sess., 543).

59 Ray, *op. cit.*, 169.

60 "I think I am safe in assuming that each of these [territories and states to be formed from the Oregon country, the Louisiana Purchase, and the Mexican cession] will be free territories and free states, whether Congress shall prohibit slavery or not" (speech of Douglas, March 13, 1850, *Cong. Globe*, 31 Cong. 1 sess., Appendix, 371). During the debate on the repeal of the Missouri Compromise it was a part of Douglas's policy not to allude to this question, but his opinion was unchanged (Johnson, *Stephen A. Douglas*, p. 234, footnote). Douglas's chief lieutenant, Senator Dodge of Iowa, stated the same opinions freely and positively, however, in the debate on the repeal (*Cong. Globe*, 33 Cong. 1 sess., Appendix, 381).

SEPARATION OF NEBRASKA AND KANSAS

would not complain if the spread of slavery should be stopped by conditions and not by congressional action. Finally, in Douglas's opinion, the people who settled in a new territory were as capable of doing the right thing in a matter that concerned them especially as were the people of the states.[61]

Douglas misjudged conditions in two particulars. He did not realize that the North would oppose this plan as strongly as it did. Many thought that the Missouri Compromise was a compact between the sections almost as important as the Constitution, and that the South should fulfill its part of the bargain as the North had already fulfilled its part. Others did not agree with Douglas in his belief that slavery would not spread. Moreover, the great body of recent arrivals from Europe had no patience with a temporizing policy in regard to slavery. The second wrong judgment of Douglas was his failure to realize that the contest for and against slavery in a territory would also engender sectional hostility. He must have expected an outcome like the peaceable victory of the free-state men in California or the quiet progress of affairs in Oregon before 1848.[62]

61 Douglas cited Oregon as an illustration of this in his speech of March 13, 1850 (*Cong. Globe*, 31 Cong. 1 sess., Appendix, 370). See also his speech of March 3, 1854 (*Cong. Globe*, 33 Cong. 1 sess., Appendix, 336-338). Cf. Burgess, *The Middle Period*, 385.

62 Douglas could not have foreseen either the excitement in the North aroused by the repeal of the Missouri Compromise or the sectional hostility engendered by the struggle in Kansas. Either defeated any purpose, however patriotic or however selfish, that he may have had in proposing the repeal. Douglas's plan failed, but it is not certain that any other plan would have succeeded. It is often forgotten that "squatter sovereignty" was not a Southern doctrine, and that Southern men opposed it as bitterly when it was first suggested as in 1860 (see above, footnote 56). Douglas may have thought that

{ 51 }

THE FORMATION OF OKLAHOMA

On January 4, 1854, Douglas, as chairman of the Committee on Territories, reported favorably Dodge's Nebraska bill, but a section was attached which declared that in accordance with the principles established by the compromise measures of 1850, all questions relating to slavery should be left to the decision of the people of the territories and the new states to be formed.[63] This statement was hardly definite enough for the Southerners, and on January 16 Archibald Dixon, a Whig senator from Kentucky, gave notice that he would offer an amendment to the Nebraska bill specifically repealing the Missouri Compromise.[64] Douglas withdrew his report, and presented it again on January 23 with three important amendments. One provided for two territories, to be named Nebraska and Kansas, with the boundary between them at the fortieth parallel; one changed the southern boundary of the country to be organized from the parallel of thirty-six thirty to the thirty-seventh parallel; and the third asserted that the Missouri Compromise had been superseded by the Compromise of 1850.[65]

On March 3, 1854, just one year after the defeat of

---

his plan would not be more objectionable to Northerners than to Southerners. For the reception of the repeal in the North and South, see in particular McMaster, *History of the People of the United States*, VIII, 200-204.

63 *S. Reports*, 33 Cong. 1 sess., I (706), no. 15; *Cong. Globe*, 33 Cong., 1 sess., 115. The added section is given in *ibid.*, 222. Cf. Johnson, *op. cit.*, 232, 233.

64 *Cong. Globe*, 33 Cong. 1 sess., 175.

65 *Ibid.*, 221, 222. In the report of January 4 the northern boundary of Nebraska had been extended to the forty-ninth parallel. According to Johnson (*op. cit.*, 238, 239), two territories meant an equal chance for the central and the north-central routes to the Pacific. Northern Illinois and Iowa were interested in one route; southern Illinois and Missouri in the other. Douglas was therefore equally interested in both.

SEPARATION OF NEBRASKA AND KANSAS

Richardson's Nebraska bill, the Senate passed the Dodge bill, as reported by Douglas, by a vote of thirty-seven to fourteen. The senators from slave states voted twenty-three to two in favor of the bill; those from free states, fourteen to twelve.[66] Douglas had been able to secure but two Southern votes in the Senate for the Nebraska bill in March, 1853. In March, 1854, he secured all but two. There is no evidence that the change was not brought about entirely by one amendment.

The House, which had easily passed the unamended Nebraska bill in 1853, was so largely dominated by free-state men that a bitter fight ensued there over the repeal of the Missouri Compromise. On May 22, by a vote of 113 to 100, it finally passed a bill modeled closely upon the Senate bill. This was accepted by the Senate on May 25 by a vote of thirty-five to thirteen practically the same division as that by which the Dodge-Douglas bill had passed in March. The President gave his approval on May 30, and the territories of Kansas and Nebraska were established.[67]

Within a week of this, the House committee in charge of the Pacific railroad agreed to amend their measure so as to allow one of the two proposed railroads to the Pacific to run anywhere north of the thirty-seventh parallel, the southern boundary of Kansas.[68] Either this was a most extraordinary coincidence or the pas-

---

66 *Cong. Globe*, 33 Cong. 1 sess., 532.
67 *Ibid.*, 294, 1132, 1254, 1300, 1321; *Statutes*, X, 277. The bill was introduced by Richardson.
68 The agreement was made by June 7 (*Cong. Globe*, 33 Cong. 1 sess., 1355, 1381).

THE FORMATION OF OKLAHOMA

sage of the Kansas-Nebraska bill made it necessary for the committee to recognize that a more central route was practicable.

Those who urged the establishment of the territories of Nebraska and Kansas were not interested in what is now Oklahoma except so far as it was a part of the road from their states to the West. The parallel of 36° 30' had been the proposed southern boundary of the Nebraska Territory until January, 1854. The reason given for the selection of this limit was that it was needed to give the new territory control of the Santa Fé trail.[69] It is not unlikely, however, that the significance of the line of thirty-six thirty in the Missouri Compromise had something to do with the selection, and the proposed repeal of the Missouri Compromise did away with this significance. Moreover, the recognition in the Nebraska bill of the force of the Indian treaties which guaranteed certain tribes freedom from the jurisdiction of a state or territorial government added to the importance of the line between the Cherokees and the Osages. Accordingly, Douglas, in the revised bill which proposed the organization of two territories, Kansas and Nebraska, both of which should be open to slavery, made the thirty-seventh parallel, as the supposed line between the Cherokees and the Osages, the southern boundary of Kansas. The change was made at the request of William K. Sebastian, senator from Arkansas.[70]

This change in the southern boundary of Kansas was

69 By Hall, February 10, 1853 (*Cong. Globe*, 32 Cong. 2 sess., 560).
70 *Cong. Globe*, 33 Cong. 1 sess., 221.

{ 54 }

SEPARATION OF NEBRASKA AND KANSAS

a necessary part of a plan for the organization of what is now Oklahoma. The congressmen from Arkansas did not intend to leave an unorganized area on the west of their state, now that the South was no longer interested in keeping the whole of the Indian country closed to settlement. It was decided to introduce a separate measure for the organization of the territory of the Five Civilized Tribes, as it was necessary, because of their treaties, that they should receive separate consideration. Indeed, the Kansas-Nebraska act would not have applied to them without their approval, and a measure adapted to their conditions could more readily secure this approval. On February 20, 1854, Robert W. Johnson, senator from Arkansas, introduced a bill for the organization of what is now Oklahoma,[71] but this could not be taken up until the passage of the Kansas-Nebraska bill.

Thus, within a quarter of a century of the establishment of the larger Indian Territory, it was divided at the thirty-seventh parallel. The northern part was organized and opened to white settlers, while the southern part was left unorganized. This contrast in the disposition of the two parts was due chiefly to the difference between their respective situations in relation to the road to the West. The organization of the northern part was necessary to make an open road from the Northern states to the Pacific. The organization of the southern part was not equally important to the states of the South. The special promises in the treaties with

71 *Ibid.*, 449. Johnson was filling out the unexpired term of Senator Borland, who had received an appointment in the diplomatic service (*ibid.*, 1).

THE FORMATION OF OKLAHOMA

the Five Civilized Tribes, which were in addition to the general promises made to all the Indians of the larger Indian Territory, as well as the greater density of population south of the thirty-seventh parallel, contributed to this result.[72] Otherwise what is now Oklahoma would probably have been organized incidentally with Nebraska and Kansas. It is hardly questionable, however, that, if the Southern states had been trying for years to open the southern part of the Indian Territory, it would have been opened with the northern part, regardless of these treaties. In every case, the claims of Indians to the territory of the United States have yielded to determined and persistent pressure.

The repeal of the Missouri Compromise was also an important factor in the division of the larger Indian Territory. Without the repeal of this law, the nearly unanimous consent of Southern congressmen could never have been secured for the opening of that part of the Indian Territory north of the line of thirty-six thirty while the part south of it remained closed. Yet the people of the Southern states did not intend to leave the country west of Arkansas unorganized, and in the period following the passage of the Kansas-Nebraska act, efforts were made to open the territory of the Five Civilized Tribes, until the Civil War made great changes both in the Southern states and in the Southern Indian Territory.

---

[72] Two or three small tribes north of the thirty-seventh parallel, it will be remembered, had treaties like those of the Five Civilized Tribes. Their temporary exclusion from Kansas under the terms of the Kansas-Nebraska act did not affect seriously the organization of the territory.

CHAPTER IV

THE PROPOSED STATE OF NEOSHO

THE repeal of the Missouri Compromise removed the objections of the pro-slavery men to the opening of the Indian country. Before Douglas adopted popular sovereignty as a solution of the slavery question in the new territories, public opinion in the South must have been opposed to any agitation for the opening of the southern part of the Indian Territory. Such a movement in Arkansas and Tennessee would not have been in keeping with the Southern opposition to the settlement of the greater area of Indian country north of the line of thirty-six thirty. An active agitation for its opening began as soon as the repeal of the Missouri Compromise was thought to be assured. Doubtless many people in the far South still wished to keep the south-central route to the Pacific blocked so that the southernmost route might command wider support, but the people in the middle South began in 1854 to try to break through the barrier on their west.

From the first proposal to repeal the Missouri Compromise to the opening of the Civil War, repeated efforts were made to open the territory of the present state of Oklahoma, which was then for the first time a recognized unit. The need of open trade routes through this region, rather than the demand for additional agricultural land, was given as the justification of the proposed change. As the people of the South were compelled after 1854 to devote their energies more and

THE FORMATION OF OKLAHOMA

more to the defense of slavery, the movement made little progress.

On February 20, 1854, as soon as the lines were drawn in the Senate in the contest over the repeal of the Missouri Compromise, Senator Johnson introduced his bill for the organization of the country west of Arkansas.[1] Douglas had already committed himself to the opening of this country if the senators from Arkansas wished it,[2] and on July 28, 1854, the Senate Committee on Territories reported Johnson's bill favorably.[3]

The bill provided for the organization of three territories, one for each of the nations as then constituted, to be known as Chelokee, Muscogee, and Chahta,[4] with their capitals respectively at Tahlequah, Creek Agency, and Doaksville. No territory was to be established without the consent of the Indians concerned, and it was hoped that the Quapaw, Seneca-Shawnee, and Seneca bands could be induced to join the "Chelokees." The governors of the territories were to be chosen by the Indians, who were also to control their own lands and citizenship. United States courts were to be established, and were to have civil and criminal jurisdiction; but the local or Indian courts were to be left in full control of cases between Indians and other Indians. The territorial legislatures were to be authorized to provide for the punishment of white intruders.

1 See above, page 55.
2 March 3, 1853; *Cong. Globe*, 32 Cong. 2 sess., 1117.
3 *Cong. Globe*, 33 Cong. 1 sess., 1986; *S. Reports*, 33 Cong. 1 sess., II, [i] (707), no. 379. The bill is printed in full in the report.
4 Variants of Cherokee, Muskogee (i.e., Creek), and Choctaw.

PROPOSED STATE OF NEOSHO

It was proposed that the United States should pay the running expenses of the territories to be established, and no doubt it was hoped that this would prove to be a powerful inducement to secure the ratification of the plan.

This measure further provided that the Indian lands were to be surveyed on application of the local legislatures, in which case sections sixteen and thirty-six were to be set aside for common-school purposes. Provision was also to be made for college lands. Allotment in severalty and the sale of surplus lands to settlers were to be encouraged. As soon as the consent of the Indians could be secured, the three territories were to be made one, which was to be admitted into the Union as the state of Neosho.[5] The Indians must "open their country for emigration and settlement," and must demonstrate their capacity for self-government before the last step could be taken. Each Indian tribe was to retain control of its own lands in case of unification.

The object of this bill, as stated in the report of the committee, was "to persuade these Indians to open their country to emigration and settlement, to cease to hold their lands in common, to divide them out in severalty, giving to all their people the right of free sale and disposition, to intermingle with, and become an integral part of, the people of the United States, to merge their useless nationalities in that of the American

---

5 This name had been proposed for the larger Indian Territory in 1838 (*Niles' Register*, May 12, 1838, LIV, 172). The Neosho, also called Grand River below the mouth of Spring River, has been mentioned. It rises in eastern Kansas and flows south through northeastern Oklahoma into the Arkansas.

republic, and to look forward with confidence to the time when they will constitute a portion of the Union, and add another star to its flag."[6]

The proposed Territory of Chelokee is especially interesting. It was to include not only the country belonging to the Cherokees and to the minor tribes or bands, but also the country enclosed by the meridians of 100° and 103° and the parallels of 36° 30' and 37°. This area had become a part of the United States as a result of the annexation of Texas and the war with Mexico. The northern boundary of the slave state of Texas was moved back to the line of thirty-six in 1850, in deference to the Missouri Compromise. At the same time, the one hundred and third meridian was made the eastern boundary of New Mexico.[7] The establishment of the southern boundary of Kansas at the thirty-seventh parallel left this rectangle unorganized, and, although it was never ceded to the Indians, its fortunes were henceforth bound up with those of the Indian Territory. This was the first effort to attach this "public land strip," afterwards known as "No Man's Land," to the Indian Territory. According to Johnson's plan, it was to be opened at once to settlers, who were to become citizens of Chelokee Territory in all respects except that they were to be deprived of any share in the control of the lands of the Indians.

[6] Pp. 8, 31. The citizens of each tribe were to become citizens of the United States as the act became effective (*ibid.*, 28).

[7] Act of September 9, 1850 (*Statutes*, IX, 446, 447). Compare the proclamation of December 13, 1850 (*Statutes*, IX, 1005). The joint resolution of March 1, 1845, for the annexation of Texas had provided that any states formed from its territory north of the line of thirty-six thirty should be free states (*Cong. Globe*, 28 Cong. 2 sess., 171, 190-194, 362; *Statutes*, V, 798).

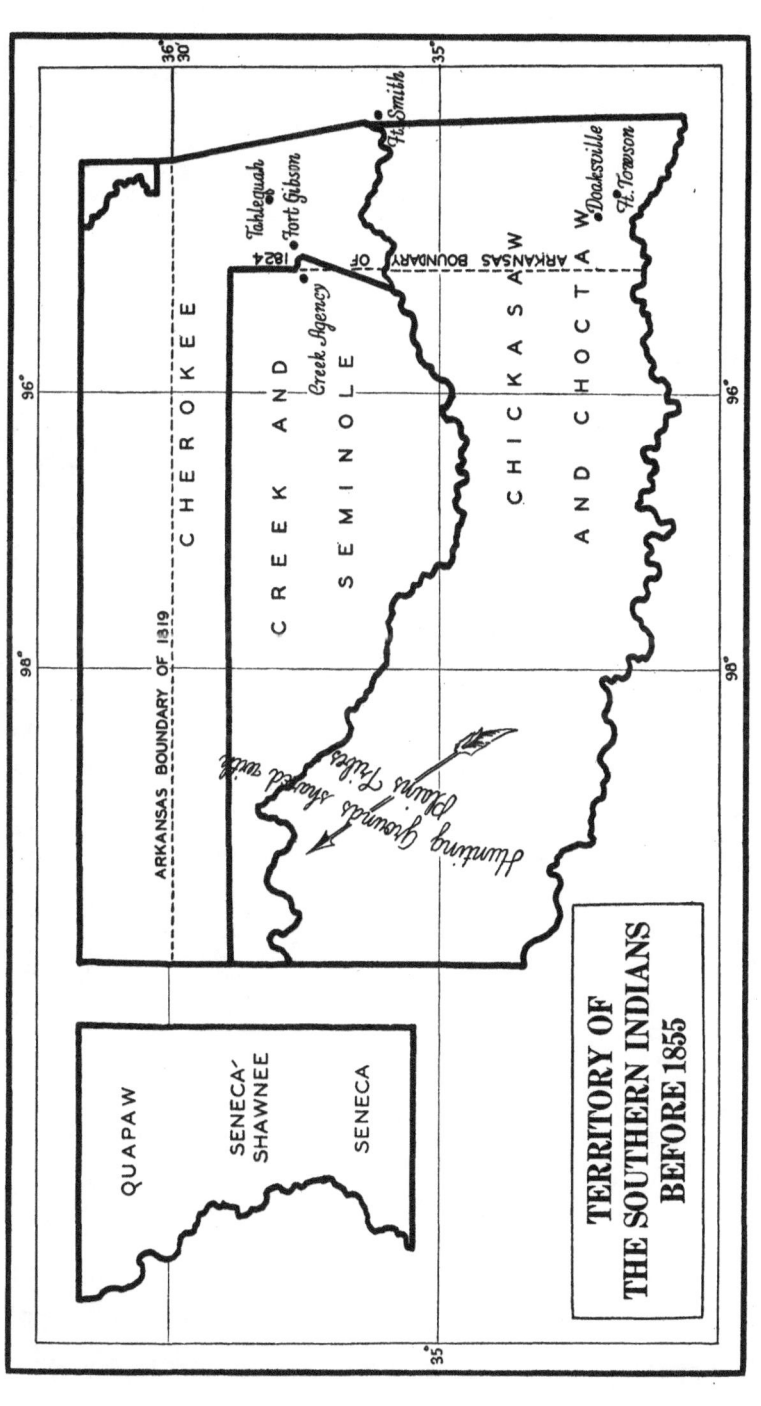

PROPOSED STATE OF NEOSHO

When the Committee on Territories made its report on July 28, the first session of the Thirty-third Congress was nearly at an end. It was agreed to make the matter a special order for December 15 following,[8] but on December 14 the Senate adjourned for four days. On December 27, on motion of Senator Johnson, the bill was recommitted to the Committee on Territories,[9] and there is no record that it received further consideration.

It is possible to dismiss this bill simply as an effort to open new land to settlement or to prepare the way for the Pacific railroad, but at least it should be noted that by its provisions the Indians were to be left in possession of their homes and not invited to move on. The plans proposed for the advancement of the Indians have fallen into two general classes. One has been based on the belief that the Indians should be removed from contact with white settlers, encouraged to retain their tribal organizations, and permitted to develop more or less in their own way under the guidance of selected teachers.[10] The other has been based on the belief that, since it has never been possible to keep the Indians entirely segregated, they should live among the settlers, that they might learn the ways of civilization from their neighbors. Unfortunately, the one or the other of these plans has been adopted in certain cases only

8 *Cong. Globe*, 33 Cong. 1 sess., 1986.

9 *Cong. Globe*, 33 Cong. 2 sess., 53, 135.

10 Cf. Walker, *The Indian Question*, 62 ff. The segregation of the Indians in detached and scattered reservations in the settled areas is a modification of this plan. Its adoption in certain cases was due at first to the opposition of the Indians to removal and later to the disappearance of the frontier.

because it fitted into the scheme of the moment for despoiling the tribesmen of their lands. Johnson's Neosho bill was the first attempt to work out a plan for the union of the whites and the Indians in the territory of the present state of Oklahoma, and probably it was the first serious and painstaking attempt ever made to work out a plan for a mixed state.[11]

The Indians of the Five Civilized Tribes were more nearly ready for the dissolution of their tribal governments in 1854 than the Indians of western Oklahoma were a generation later. By 1854 the Cherokees had recovered from the disorders arising from the migrations. Under the leadership of John Ross, the Old Settlers and the great body of recent arrivals had coalesced. The members of the Treaty party, which included a small but important part of the Cherokees, still resented the murder of their leaders, the Ridges and Elias Boudinot. Nevertheless they were quiet, and the dissolution of the tribal government would have helped to heal the breach.[12] Similar dissensions

---

[11] By acts of March 3, 1839 (*Statutes*, V, 349), and March 3, 1843 (*Statutes*, V, 645), the Brotherton and the Stockbridge and Munsee bands of three or four hundred each had been made citizens of the United States and allotted lands in severalty. These bands were of Algonquian stock and were living in Wisconsin at the time. In 1854 the government was on the eve of similar arrangements with other tribes. For a list of Indian tribes admitted to citizenship in whole or in part up to 1879, see *H. Reports*, 45 Cong. 3 sess., II (1867), no. 188, p. 27. On February 8, 1853, Representative Charles Sweetster of Ohio declared in favor of a policy of no more Indian treaties, allotment of lands in severalty, and the bestowal of citizenship upon the Indians (*Cong. Globe*, 32 Cong. 2 sess., 544).

[12] Major Ridge, John Ridge, and Elias Boudinot were the leaders of the small party of Cherokees who made the treaty of 1835 with the United States. Their part in this made them unpopular with the Ross faction, and in 1839 they were set upon and murdered. Stand Watie, the brother of Boudinot, became the leader of the Treaty party, and bad feeling persisted for

PROPOSED STATE OF NEOSHO

existed among the Creeks. Their tribal organization was primitive, and the numerous chiefs appropriated the tribal income to themselves. The Seminoles were not satisfied with their connection with the Creeks, considering it subordination. Farther south, the Chickasaws wished to separate from the Choctaws.[13] The causes of these petty quarrels would have been removed perhaps if the Indians had all united. It is probable that the Five Civilized Tribes did not recover from the effects of the Civil War and again reach their original state of order and prosperity until 1880.

The plan proposed by the Johnson bill would have been accepted ultimately by the Indians, according to the best informed officials. The opening of the northern part of the larger Indian Territory had caused a feeling of distrust among the southern Indians. They were afraid to express their approval of this bill while it was still subject to change. They feared that it would be amended during its consideration and that their approval of the original plan would be construed as an approval of the establishment of territorial government in an entirely different form. It was thought, however, by the more intelligent tribesmen that it would not be possible to secure a better arrangement than the one proposed, and it was reported by the superintendent in charge of the Five Civilized Tribes that

---

years. See Mooney, *Myths of the Cherokees*, 133, 134; Royce, *Cherokee Nation of Indians*, 293 ff., 320.

13 Report of Thomas S. Drew, southern superintendent, October 2, 1854, *S. Ex. Docs.*, 33 Cong. 2 sess., I (746), 320. For the Creek organization, see the report of Philip H. Raiford, agent for the Creeks, September 15, 1851, *S. Ex. Docs.*, 32 Cong. 1 sess., III (613), 384.

THE FORMATION OF OKLAHOMA

the measure would be accepted by the Indians and that the territorial government, or governments, would be in operation within a year or two of the enactment of the law.[14]

During the next two years, changes took place in the tribal organizations of the Indian Territory that made necessary an entirely different plan of settlement.

In June, 1855, a treaty was made with the Chickasaws and Choctaws by which these tribes, which had formed one people since 1837, were separated. By the terms of this treaty, ratified by the United States Senate in February, 1856, the territory ceded to the Choctaws in 1820 and confirmed to them in 1830 was divided into three nearly equal districts. The Choctaws and the Chickasaws were left in control respectively of the eastern and middle districts, in which distinct tribal organizations were set up. The district west of the ninety-eighth meridian was leased to the United States for the use of the Wichitas and the other Indians of the southwestern plains who had already acquired hunting rights there in 1835 and 1837. Both Chickasaws and Choctaws, however, retained the right of living anywhere within the original territory.[15]

[14] Report of Thomas S. Drew, superintendent at Fort Smith, October 2, 1854, *S. Ex. Docs.*, 33 Cong. 2 sess., I (746), 321; report of George Butler, agent for the Cherokees, September 27, 1854, *ibid.*, 323; report of Douglas H. Cooper, agent for the Choctaws, September 20, 1854, *ibid.*, 340.

[15] Treaty with the Choctaws and Chickasaws, made June 22, 1855; ratified February 21, 1856 (*Statutes*, XI, 611, reprinted in Kappler, II, 706). The line between the Choctaw and the Chickasaw districts began at the mouth of Island Bayou, ran up that stream and its eastern fork to its source, and thence due north to the Canadian.

PROPOSED STATE OF NEOSHO

Separate reservations and distinct tribal organizations were also given to the Creeks and the Seminoles by a treaty made and ratified in August, 1856. To the Seminoles was assigned the part of the original Creek territory that lay west of the ninety-seventh meridian and south of the North Fork of the Canadian.[16]

In spite of these changes, the plan of opening this country to settlement was not forgotten. In 1856 Douglas H. Cooper, the United States agent for the Chickasaws and the Choctaws, reported that the Indians in his charge aspired to become citizens of the United States. He suggested that lands should be allotted to them in severalty with restrictions on the sale of allotments for a number of years, and that the lands not needed for this purpose should be sold to white persons to be selected by the Indians and adopted by them as Indian citizens.[17] In 1857 Elias Rector, superintendent of the Indians west of Arkansas, recommended that the Johnson bill should be revised and reintroduced. In 1858 he recommended that the United States should assume control of the Five Civilized Tribes, allot them lands in severalty with the prohibition of the sale of allotments for a period of thirty years, and authorize the sale of their surplus lands.[18]

---

[16] Treaty with Creeks and Seminoles, made August 7, ratified August 16 (*Statutes*, XI, 699, reprinted in Kappler, II, 757). The eastern boundary of the Seminole reservation was just east of and parallel to the ninety-seventh meridian. Its position was fixed by the junction of Pond Creek with the Canadian.

[17] Report dated September 1, 1856; *S. Ex. Docs.*, 34 Cong. 3 sess., II (1875), 697.

[18] Reports dated September 24, 1857, *S. Ex. Docs.*, 35 Cong. 1 sess., II (919), 489; and October 26, 1858, *S. Ex. Docs.*, 35 Cong. 2 sess., I (974), 479. Rector was a citizen of Arkansas and resided at Fort Smith for many years (Utley, in Arkansas Historical Association, *Publications*, II, 274).

THE FORMATION OF OKLAHOMA

Robert J. Walker, appointed governor of the Territory of Kansas by President Buchanan, advocated the organization of the Indian Territory in his inaugural address, delivered on May 27, 1857. Walker, a Northern man who had removed to Mississippi, said that the opening of trade-routes through this country was essential for the development of Kansas and the entire Southwest. He dismissed the Indian treaties with the statement that they would "constitute no obstacle any more than precisely similar treaties did in Kansas."[19]

In December, 1858, the legislature of Arkansas petitioned Congress to adopt the south-central route for the Pacific railroad.[20] The selection of this route was out of the question unless the Indian Territory could be opened.[21]

In December, 1859, Jacob Thompson of Mississippi, the secretary of the interior, announced that the government had given up trying to remove the Indians from the frontier of settlement, and had adopted allotment in severalty as its fixed policy. As Thompson believed that the isolation of the Indians was necessary, he proposed to group their allotments in small tribal reservations.[22] He reiterated this proposal in his annual report for 1860.[23]

19 This address is printed in Gihon, *Geary and Kansas*, Appendix. The part referred to is given on pp. 341 and 342.

20 *H. Misc. Docs.*, 35 Cong. 2 sess., I (1016), no. 21. The memorial was presented in the House on January 15, 1859.

21 The Chickasaws and Choctaws agreed in the treaty of 1855, already cited, to permit a railroad to run through their territory, but no provision was made for a grant of adjacent land in aid of its construction.

22 *S. Ex. Docs.*, 36 Cong. 1 sess., I (1023), 98, 99.

23 "I am strengthened, then, in the conviction expressed in my last annual report, that the only plan that holds out any hope for the decaying aboriginal

PROPOSED STATE OF NEOSHO

Public opinion in the South, as summed up by the New Orleans *Picayune* just before the Civil War, demanded that the trade-routes to New Mexico should no longer be closed by the diminished Indian Territory. It was not thought possible that the barrier could hold much longer, and the limit of its continuation was fixed at ten years.[24]

The entire situation was altered by the Civil War. At its close the states most interested in the opening of the Indian Territory were weakened economically and politically. This did not apply to Kansas, but Kansas was chiefly interested in getting rid of the Indians within its borders, and the Indian Territory was a convenient place into which to send them. Accordingly, the plan of removal and segregation was once more adopted. When this removal had been carried out as far as possible, and when the best lands in Kansas had been occupied, the citizens began to urge the opening of the Indian Territory. In this they were aided by the people of the Southern States who had recovered prosperity and political importance by that time, and another change was soon made in the Indian policy of the United States.

---

races, is to confine them to small tribal reservations, having well-defined exterior boundaries, so that the intercourse laws can be enforced thereon, and to divide these reservations into farms of moderate dimensions, to be held in severalty by the individual members of the tribe, with all the rights incident to an estate in fee simple, except that of alienation" (*S. Ex. Docs.*, 36 Cong. 2 sess., I (1078), 35, 36).

24 Quoted by John W. Barber, *Our Whole Country*, 1475. The date of the issue of the *Picayune* is not given, but the book was copyrighted in 1861.

CHAPTER V

THE INDIAN TERRITORY DURING THE CIVIL WAR

THE territory included in the present state of Oklahoma had been set apart originally for the southern Indians, and until 1860 it had been occupied by them alone; but at the close of the Civil War, the United States deprived them of their exclusive rights within its limits. The position of the Five Civilized Tribes on the border, not their sympathy for the Southern Confederacy, caused them to take part in the war between Union and secession. The abandonment of the Indian Territory by the United States and its occupation by the Confederacy made it necessary for the Indians to recognize the authority of the Confederate government or oppose it unaided. After the war, the United States made this recognition a pretext for disregarding old agreements.

In the opening months of the Civil War, the United States after some hesitation withdrew the troops from all the posts in the Indian Territory. The attitude of the military authorities was clearly stated in a communication from Washington to Lieutenant-Colonel William H. Emory commanding on the border, "The interests of the United States are paramount to those of the friendly Indians. . . ." On April 17, 1861, the order was sent to Emory to retire to Fort Leavenworth in northeastern Kansas with all the troops that had

THE CIVIL WAR

been stationed in the Indian country.[1] In May, troops from Texas occupied without opposition the posts south of the Canadian.[2]

The attention of the Confederate government had been called to the Indian Territory in February,[3] and on March 4 the provisional congress at Montgomery authorized President Davis to send an agent to negotiate treaties with the Indian tribes west of Arkansas.[4] The Choctaws, the Chickasaws, and the Cherokees acted on the questions growing out of the war before any treaties were made.

The first formal action in the Indian Territory regarding the coming conflict was taken by the Choctaws. On February 7, 1861, carefully worded resolutions were adopted by their legislature. One sentence that was used is especially striking, "We view with deep regret and great solicitude the present unhappy political disagreement . . . portending much injury to the Choctaw government and people."[5] The resolutions expressed the hope that the Union would continue, but also the desire of the Choctaws to go with the Southern states in case of its dissolution. Finally, the Choc-

1 Townsend to Emory, March 18, April 17, 1861, *Official Records of the Rebellion*, I, i, 656, 667; Emory to Townsend, April 13, *ibid.*, 665. Townsend's letter of March 18 referred only to the friendly Indians of the Wichita reservation. (The above form is used in citing the *War of the Rebellion: a Compilation of the Official Records of the Union and Confederate Armies*. The first numeral refers to the series; the second to the volume of the series.)

2 Campbell to Emory, May 5, *ibid.*, 652; Benning to Walker, May 14, *ibid.*, 653; Emory to Townsend, May 19, May 31, *ibid.*, 648, 649.

3 *Journal of the Congress of Confederate States of America* (hereafter cited *Journal of Cong. of Confed. States*), I, 70, 80, 90. The Texas secession convention also sent commissioners to the Indian Territory in February (*Official Records of the Rebellion*, IV, i, 197, 322-325).

4 *Journal of Cong. of Confed. States*, I, 105.

5 *Official Records of the Rebellion*, I, i, 682.

THE FORMATION OF OKLAHOMA

taws assured their immediate neighbors, the people of Arkansas and Texas, that they wished to maintain friendly relations with them. On May 25 the Chickasaw legislature adopted violent resolutions which set forth that the government had deserted them and ignored their treaty rights. A sort of declaration of independence was issued, and the other Indians were called upon to assert their independence.[6] The principal chief of the Choctaws responded to this on June 14 with a proclamation declaring the Choctaws independent.[7] These declarations were preliminary to an alliance with the Confederates.

Three days later, on June 17, John Ross, the chief of the Cherokees, in a letter to General Ben McCulloch, the commander of a force of Arkansas troops, said that he and his people wished to remain neutral.[8] On August 21 the Cherokees, at a mass meeting at Tahlequah attended by nearly all of the men of the tribe, approved the policy of neutrality and declared that they were loyal first of all to the Cherokee nation. At the same time they passed a vote of confidence in the ability of the Cherokee government to look after their interests and coupled with this an admission that these interests might soon make an alliance with the Confederates "expedient and desirable."[9]

[6] *Ibid.*, I, iii, 585.
[7] *Ibid.*, 593.
[8] *Ibid.*, 596. The great council of the Indians summoned by the Cherokees in the spring of 1861 was only an effort to organize the Indians for neutrality, not a hostile movement, as it was afterwards asserted (report of Baptiste Peoria, special agent, May 1, 1862, *H. Ex. Docs.*, 37 Cong. 3 sess., II (1157), 317).
[9] Ross to McCulloch, August 24, 1861, inclosure, *Official Records of the Rebellion*, I, iii, 673. This meeting occurred just after the victory of the Con-

THE CIVIL WAR

In these actions the Indians were concerned chiefly for their own welfare. Among the Chickasaws and the Choctaws it is true that some enthusiasm was shown for the Southern cause; but as the territory of these tribes was dominated by the Confederates, it was natural that their partisans should be active. These partisans seem to have been the Indians of mixed blood;[10] but Douglas H. Cooper, a Southern man, who had been the United States agent for the Chickasaws for eight years, used his influence with the full-bloods to secure their acquiescence in the new order.[11] A few Cherokees of mixed blood of the faction opposed to Ross supported the Confederates,[12] but the great majority of Cherokees sought to remain neutral so far as this could be done without incurring the hostility of the Confederates.[13]

In pursuance of the resolution of March 4, President Davis sent Albert Pike as agent or commissioner to the tribes west of Arkansas.[14] Pike reached the Chero-

---

federates at Wilson's Creek. This accounts for the change in the attitude of the Cherokees.

10 Report of Isaac Coleman, agent for the Choctaws and Chickasaws, for 1862, *H. Ex. Docs.*, 37 Cong. 3 sess., II (1157), 284.

11 Walker to Cooper, May 13, 1861, *Official Records of the Rebellion*, I, iii, 574; Cooper to Davis, July 25, *ibid.*, 614. Cf. Cooper to Davis, August 8, 1862, *ibid.*, I, liii, 820.

12 McCulloch to Walker, June 12, 1861, *ibid.*, I, iii, 590.

13 The suspicions of the Confederates were aroused in June. McCulloch wrote to Walker, the Confederate secretary of war, "I am satisfied. . . that he [Ross] is only waiting for a favorable opportunity to put himself with the North" (June 22, 1861, *ibid.*, 595). The Confederate Congress had formally assumed the protection of the Indian Territory in May (*Journal of Cong. of Confed. States*, I, 225, 244, 263).

14 Davis to Congress, December 12, 1861, *Official Records of the Rebellion*, IV, i, 785.

kees about June 1, but Ross refused to treat with him.[15] Pike went on west, and in July and August he made treaties with the Creeks, with the Chickasaws and Choctaws, with the Seminoles, and with the Comanches and the other tribes of the leased district west of the ninety-eighth meridian and south of the Canadian.[16]

Pike then returned to Park Hill, just south of Tahlequah in the Cherokee country; and on October 2 he met delegates from the Osages and made a treaty with them.[17] Two days later at the same place he made treaties with delegates from the Quapaws and the mixed bands of Senecas and Shawnees.[18] These delegates were led by Andrew J. Dorn, agent for their tribes under the Buchanan administration. On the very day of the Osage treaty W. G. Coffin, the new Superintendent of Indian Affairs for this region, reported to Washington that the Osages, Quapaws, Senecas, and Shawnees were loyal;[19] and both Confederate[20] and Union[21] reports in 1863 agreed in saying that few

15 Pike to Toombs, May 29, 1861, *ibid.*, 359; McCulloch to Walker, June 12, *ibid.*, I, iii, 590.

16 With the Creeks, July 10, 1861, at North Fork village in the Creek country (*ibid.*, IV, i, 426-443); with the Chickasaws and Choctaws, July 12, at the same place (*ibid.*, 445-466); with the Seminoles, August 1, at the Seminole council house (*ibid.*, 513-527); with the Comanches, etc., two treaties, August 12, at the Wichita agency (*ibid.*, 542-554). William C. Young, colonel of a Texas regiment, had already entered into an agreement with the Indians of the leased district binding the Confederates to feed and protect them (Benning to Walker, May 14, *ibid.*, I, i, 653).

17 *Ibid.*, IV, i, 636-646.

18 *Ibid.*, 647-666.

19 *S. Ex. Docs.*, 37 Cong. 2 sess., I (1117), 654.

20 Report of S. C. Scott, Confederate commissioner, January, 1863, *Official Records of the Rebellion*, IV, ii, 354.

21 Report of W. G. Coffin, superintendent, for 1863, *H. Ex. Docs.*, 38 Cong. 1 sess., III (1182), 291.

THE CIVIL WAR

of these Indians except Black Dog's band of Osages had gone over to the Confederates. The Union report lauded the Osages in particular for their effective work in guarding the border, and the treaties with Pike were ascribed solely to the machinations of Dorn.

While Pike was in the West, the Confederates had won the Battle of Wilson's Creek or Oak Hills, and the Union Army in Missouri had withdrawn to Springfield. The importance of this victory was naturally overrated, and the Cherokees began to think that Confederate success was inevitable. The Ridge or Treaty faction, headed by Stand Watie, the brother of Elias Boudinot, favored the Confederates, and Stand Watie with a force of three hundred Cherokees of mixed blood had joined their army as volunteers. This party urged an alliance between the Cherokees and the Confederates, and Ross feared that Pike would make a treaty with Stand Watie recognizing him as head of the Cherokee government, as the United States had recognized Ridge and Boudinot twenty-five years before. This would have meant civil war, with the Confederates aiding Stand Watie.[22] To avoid this and to keep the Cherokees united, and no doubt partly to retain his authority, Ross consented to treat with the Confederates. Three days after the Cherokee mass meeting of August 21, Ross took the first steps toward a renewal of negotiations.[23] On October 7, at Tahle-

22 Carruth and Martin to Coffin, July 19, 1862, *H. Ex. Docs.*, 37 Cong. 3 sess., II (1157), 302; McCulloch to Walker, September 2, 1861, *Official Records of the Rebellion*, I, iii, 691, 692. Cf. Blunt to Stanton, July 21, 1862, eighteen inclosures, *ibid.*, I, xiii, 486-505.

23 Ross and others to McCulloch, August 24, 1861, inclosure, *ibid.*, I, iii, 673.

THE FORMATION OF OKLAHOMA

quah, a treaty was signed by the terms of which Cherokees became the wards and allies of the Confederates.[24]

It can never be known how far Pike's treaties met the approval of the majority of the Indians. After the war, some of the tribes were naturally anxious to make it appear that they had not approved the treaties when they were made and that deception and even force had been used.[25] It is certain that their only advisers were Confederates, and it must have seemed to them that the Confederate States had succeeded to the position recently held by the United States.

The southern Indians who wished to remain loyal to the United States received little encouragement and no support from the government during the first year of the war. The secretary of the interior, Caleb B. Smith, said in his report for 1861 that the defection of these Indians was due entirely to the abandonment of the Indian Territory by the United States.[26] None of the newly appointed Indian agents had succeeded in reaching their agencies, and they were scattered along the southern border of Kansas. The superintendent of Indian affairs in the Indian Territory had established his headquarters at Humboldt, and even the agent for the small bands on the Neosho just across the state line had stopped at Fort Scott.[27] In the beginning of November, 1861, a delegation of Creeks, Seminoles,

---

24 *Ibid.*, IV, i, 669-687.

25 Proceedings of the council at Fort Smith, *H. Ex. Docs.*, 39 Cong. 1 sess., II (1248), 505, 506, 508, 514, 519, 533.

26 *S. Ex. Docs.*, 37 Cong. 2 sess., I (1117), 447.

27 Report of the Secretary of the Interior for 1861, *ibid.*, 447; of W. G. Coffin, superintendent, *ibid.*, 654; of P. P. Elder, agent for the Quapaws, etc., *ibid.*, 652.

THE CIVIL WAR

and Chickasaws came to consult with the officials and to ask for protection.[28]

The Creeks seem to have been rather evenly divided by the war. Factional differences played a part among them as among the Cherokees. The lower Creeks approved the treaty with the Confederates, and the upper Creeks were dissatisfied with it.[29] About half of the tribe would not recognize it as valid. The leader of the Union faction was a chief named Opothleyoholo, who had been a prominent member of the tribe.[30] Ross wrote to Opothleyoholo and urged him to acquiesce in what had been done rather than bring on civil war among the Creeks;[31] but the old chief was obdurate and refused to have any relations with the Confederate authorities.

In November and December Opothleyoholo was attacked by the Treaty faction of the Creeks, who were aided by Chickasaw and Choctaw soldiers, by a few Cherokees, and by part of a Texas regiment. He held his own in the first skirmish, but he was defeated in two later engagements and driven out of the Indian Territory.[32] With him went rather more than half of

---

28 Report of George A. Cutler, agent for the Creeks, for 1862, *H. Ex. Docs.*, 37 Cong. 3 sess., II (1157), 282.

29 Gookins to Dole, April 16, 1864, inclosure, *H. Ex. Docs.*, 38 Cong. 2 sess., V (1220), 478.

30 Opothleyoholo, or Opothleyaholo, was the Creek leader who corresponded to John Ross. He opposed the removal of the Creeks to the West, but after the removal he encouraged his partisans to make the best of it. See article by George W. Grayson and Frank Huntington in Hodge, *Handbook of American Indians*, II, 141.

31 September 19, October 8, 1861, in the proceedings of the council at Fort Smith, *H. Ex. Docs.*, 39 Cong. 1 sess., II (1248), 537, 538.

32 Reports of D. H. Cooper and others, *Official Records of the Rebellion*, I, viii, 5-32; report of the Commissioner of Indian Affairs for 1862, *H. Ex. Docs.*, 37 Cong. 3 sess., II (1157), 180.

the Seminoles, as the Creek and Seminole Union factions had joined forces. The defeated Indians with their families straggled across the border in January, "famished and frozen." The United States Indian agents had plenty to do during the winter of 1861-62 in trying to care for these fugitives. In April, 1862, the records show that seven thousand six hundred southern Indians, chiefly Creeks and Seminoles, were camped in Kansas, and hundreds had died during the retreat and later.[33] The Commissioner of Indian Affairs said in his annual report for 1862: "In no part of the country have the sufferings and privations endured, and the sacrifices made by loyal citizens, on account of their fidelity in their country, exceeded those of the loyal Indians of this superintendency."[34]

The situation had changed by June, 1862. The Confederates had been defeated at Pea Ridge, in northwestern Arkansas, and had returned southward. Accordingly, an expedition was organized in Kansas with the object of recovering at least a part of the Indian Territory. This was known as the "Indian expedition" and was made up of two regiments raised from the Indians in Kansas, chiefly from the refugees, and of several regiments of other troops. This was placed under the command of William Weer, colonel of the Tenth Kansas Infantry.[35] This force met with no op-

---

33 Collamore to Dole, April 21, 1862, *ibid.*, 301; report of W. G. Coffin, superintendent, for 1862, *ibid.*, 279.

34 *Ibid.*, 180.

35 Doubleday to Blunt, June 1, 1862, *Official Records of the Rebellion*, I, xiii, 408; Doubleday to Weer, June 6, *ibid.*, 102; Weer to Doubleday, June 6, *ibid.*, 418; Salomon to Weer, June 30, *ibid.*, 418.

position in its advance, and scouting parties captured Fort Gibson and Tahlequah early in July.[36] Ross and his adherents among the Cherokees welcomed the approach of the Union troops, and a regiment of Cherokee full-bloods raised for the Confederate service went over in a body. In all, twelve or fifteen hundred Cherokees joined the Indian brigade, including the three sons of Ross. The Ross party apparently did not doubt that the Union army had come to stay, and it committed itself irrevocably to the Union cause.[37]

On July 18 the officers of the expedition then on Grand River, twelve miles north of Fort Gibson, decided that Weer was incompetent. The officer next in rank, Frederick Salomon, colonel of the Ninth Wisconsin Volunteers, arrested him and took command.[38] Salomon at once ordered a retreat.[39] He justified his action in a communication to his immediate superior, General James G. Blunt, in which he said that Weer either was insane or had become an imbecile through long-continued intemperance, and that this drastic action was necessary to save the troops.[40] The Indian

36 Weer to Moonlight, July 2, July 16, *ibid.*, 459, 160; Greeno to Weer, July 15, July 17, *ibid.*, 473, 161.
37 Weer to Moonlight, June 13, July 12, *ibid.*, 430, 487; Carruth and Martin to Coffin, July 19, *H. Ex. Docs.*, 37 Cong. 3 sess., II (1157), 302; Phillips to Henderson, January 24, 1869, *S. Reports*, 41 Cong. 2 sess. (1409), no. 113; Jones to Senate Committee on Indian Affairs, July 20, 1868, *ibid.* The contemporary evidence seems to be against the later theory that Ross was compelled by his partisans to yield to the Union forces (cf. Mooney, *Myths of the Cherokees*, 149, and Royce, *Cherokee Nation of Indians*, 330).
38 Carruth and Martin to Blunt, July 18, 1862, *Official Records of the Rebellion*, I, xiii, 478; pronunciamento of Salomon, July 18, *ibid.*, 475.
39 General orders, no. 1, *ibid.*, 476.
40 July 20, 1862, *ibid.*, 484. The context shows that Salomon was accusing Weer of violent fits of rage rather than drunkenness.

regiments, now reinforced by the Cherokees, were left behind and held the country for some time, defeating a Confederate force sent against them. They were not given support and were finally compelled to fall back into Kansas.[41]

The retreat of the Indian brigade made necessary the withdrawal of Ross and many of his friends. As a result of this ill-starred expedition, two thousand Cherokees joined the refugees in Kansas, where they camped on the neutral land.[42] Ross himself went to Philadelphia, where he remained until the close of the war. He seems to have been treated with great consideration and was practically pensioned by the United States out of the Cherokee fund.[43]

Weer and Salomon both could hardly have been suitable men to command soldiers. If Weer was a suitable officer, Salomon was simply the ringleader of a successful mutiny.[44] Nevertheless, when the troops in the Kansas military district were reorganized in three brigades a month later, Salomon was placed in command of the first brigade, and Weer of the second, and

---

[41] Furnas to Blunt, July 25, 1862, *ibid.*, 511; Phillips to Furnas, July 27, August 6, *ibid.*, 181-184; Carruth and Martin to Coffin, August 2, *H. Ex. Docs.*, 37 Cong. 3 sess., II (1157), 306.

[42] Report of W. G. Coffin, superintendent, for 1863, *H. Ex. Docs.*, 38 Cong. 1 sess., III (1182), 292; Carruth and Martin to Coffin, September 28, 1862, *H. Ex. Docs.*, 37 Cong. 3 sess., II (1157), 311.

[43] Ross to Dole, April 2, 1863, *H. Ex. Docs.*, 38 Cong. 1 sess., III (1182), 343. Compare the remarks of Senator James Harlan in *Cong. Globe*, 38 Cong. 2 sess., 1305. Royce (*Cherokee Nation of Indians*, 330), rather censures Ross for his inactivity after 1862; but only fighting was needed on the border after that date, and Ross was then seventy-two years of age.

[44] Cf. Carruth and Martin to Blunt, July 18, 1862, *Official Records of the Rebellion*, I, xiii, 478, and Phillips to Henderson, January 24, 1869, *S. Reports*, 41 Cong. 2 sess., (1409), no. 113, p. 7.

THE CIVIL WAR

the Indian troops were divided between the two.[45] This whole episode illustrates in a striking way the nature of the protection given by the United States to the Indians of the Indian Territory during the Civil War.

After the retreat of the Indian expedition, Stand Watie's faction of the Cherokees returned and took possession of Tahlequah, and Stand Watie was chosen principal chief.[46] During 1863, however, the Union forces occupied all of the country as far south as Fort Smith, Arkansas, which was captured in September of that year.[47] The Cherokees who remained loyal to the Confederates were forced to take refuge in the Choctaw country until the close of the war.[48] The Cherokees of the Ross party re-established themselves in the Cherokee country; and in February, 1863, they repudiated the Pike treaty and deposed all Cherokee officials who had been disloyal to the United States.[49]

In spite of this, order was not restored, and the Indian Territory was given over to plundering raids, many of them from the North. Although nearly all of the Cherokee men who were loyal to the United States were in the army, their country was not protected, and it was ultimately stripped bare of every-

---

45 General orders, no 4 (Blunt), *Official Records of the Rebellion*, I, xiii, 595.
46 Hudson to Dashiell, September 15, 1862, *ibid.*, I, liii, 827.
47 Blunt to Dole, February 5, 1864, *H. Ex. Docs.*, 38 Cong. 2 sess., V (1220), 466.
48 Report of W. G. Coffin, superintendent, for 1863, *H. Ex. Docs.*, 38 Cong. 1 sess., III (1182), 293; report of Isaac Coleman, agent for the Choctaws and Chickasaws, for 1865, *H. Ex. Docs.*, 39 Cong. 1 sess., II (1248), 464; report of Elijah Sells, superintendent, for 1865, *ibid.*, 438. Of the 17,000 Cherokees, 10,500 were loyal to the Union; 6,500 to the Confederates.
49 Report of the Commissioner of Indian Affairs for 1863, *H. Ex. Docs.*, 38 Cong. 1 sess., III (1182), 144. Cf. Ross to Dole, April 2, 1863, *ibid.*, 343.

thing worth taking away. The government was compelled for a time to support nearly twenty thousand loyal Indians in the Indian Territory, including the Creek and Seminole refugees, who were placed in their homes in 1864.[50]

The territory of the Choctaws and Chickasaws was held by the Confederates until practically the close of the war. No fighting of importance took place in that part of the Indian Territory, and the Indians who enlisted in the service of the Confederates remained near their homes most of the time. Consequently, they did not suffer by the destruction of their property to the same extent as the Cherokees and the Creeks.[51]

In 1864 the Indian agents tried to get the Confed-

50 Report of A. G. Proctor, special Indian agent, to Superintendent Coffin, November 28, 1863, *ibid.*, 340; report of Elijah Sells, superintendent, for 1865, *H. Ex. Docs.*, 39 Cong. 1 sess., II (1248), 444. Most of this raiding was done by "jayhawkers" from Kansas. Justin Harlan, agent for the Cherokees, said in his report for 1865 (*ibid.*, 470): "While the rebel enemies were robbing and burning their property, their Kansas friends and some others were equally busy, more numerous, with more facilities for carrying away, and equally active in stealing it. That they did three times in value the amount of stealing done by the rebels I am pretty confident." These raids did not stop with the close of the Civil War. Cattle-stealing was the chief subject discussed in the Indian reports of 1865. See, among others, the letter of Superintendent Sells to Commissioner Cooley, August 5, 1865, *ibid.*, 449-452. The government found it difficult to put a stop to this. Sells reported to Cooley, October 16, 1865: "It is utterly impossible to effectually break up this system of plunder from the Indians as long as the state [Kansas], civil, and military authorities are in sympathy with the parties engaged in this species of brokerage" (*ibid.*, 436). Compare the report of George A. Reynolds, special agent, to Superintendent Sells, July 23, 1865 (*ibid.*, 448), and the report of Lieutenant George Williams, quoted in the report of the Commissioner of Indian Affairs for 1865 (*ibid.*, 201). In March, 1865, Congress passed a law making special provisions for the punishment of those convicted of stealing cattle from the Indians (Indian appropriation act of March 3, 1865, *Statutes*, XIII, 563).

51 Report of Isaac Coleman, agent for the Choctaws and Chickasaws, for 1865, *H. Ex. Docs.*, 39 Cong. 1 sess., II (1248), 464.

THE CIVIL WAR

erate Indians to renew their allegiance to the government. These Indians held a council at Tishomingo in March, 1864, but they were not in a position to make peace.[52] It was not until the surrender of the last Confederate force that a council met at Camp Napoleon and decided to send delegates to ask peace and a restoration of harmonious relations with the United States. The officials planned at first to receive these delegates at Washington, but it was decided later to send a treaty commission to meet them on the border. In September, 1865, a peace council was held. Its most important feature was the attempt of the government to secure the ratification of a new plan for Indian consolidation.[53]

The plan of locating both northern and southern Indians in the territory south of Kansas had its inception three years before. In February, 1862, the legislature of Kansas adopted resolutions calling upon the United States to purchase and throw open to settlement the Cherokee neutral lands, the Osage, Pottawattomie, Kickapoo, Sac and Fox, Ottawa, Kansas, Iowa, Sac and Fox of Missouri, and absentee Shawnee reservations, all in that state.[54] These resolutions were

---

52 Phillips to Curtis, March 17, 1864, *H. Ex. Docs.*, 38 Cong. 2 sess., V (1220), 473; Cox to Coffin, March 16, 1864, *ibid.*, 475.

53 Report of the Commissioner of Indian Affairs for 1865, *H. Ex. Docs.*, 39 Cong. 1 sess., II (1248), 202.

54 *H. Misc. Docs.*, 37 Cong. 2 sess. (1141), no. 75. W. P. Dole, in his first annual report as Commissioner of Indian Affairs, November, 1861, recommended the settlement of the Indians on reservations "in portions of the new states" away "from the immediate vicinity of the whites" (*S. Ex. Docs.*, 37 Cong. 2 sess., I (1117), 647). In his report for 1862 he claimed that his recommendation had been the germ of the proposal to consolidate the Indians in the Indian Territory (*H. Ex. Docs.*, 37 Cong. 3 sess., II (1157), 493). In general, however, both his report for 1861 and that of the Secretary

presented in the United States Senate for the first time on March 24, and on that day Samuel C. Pomeroy, senator from Kansas, introduced a bill for the removal and consolidation of certain Indian tribes.[55] On April 16, he introduced a bill to establish the "Territory of Lanniwa," including the present state of Oklahoma and Texas north of the Red River.[56] This was obviously a scheme to secure room for the Indians of Kansas. Minnesota also had too many Indians; and Cyrus Aldrich, a representative from that state, on June 2 introduced in the House a bill with the same title.[57] The Senate Committee on Indian Affairs reported both of Pomeroy's bills on June 25, with the recommendation that they should not be considered further in that session.[58] Aldrich's bill was not reported at the time by the House Committee on Territories, to which it had been referred.

During this session Congress incidentally enacted legislation that proved to be of importance in the later negotiations with the Indians. The Indian appropria-

---

of the Interior for the same year lauded the policy that had recently been adopted in Kansas and recommended its continuance (*S. Ex. Docs.*, 37 Cong. 2 sess., I (1117), 448, 647).

55 *Cong. Globe*, 37 Cong. 2 sess., 1331.

56 *Ibid.*, 1678. Cf. Parker, *Calendar of Papers in Washington Archives relating to the Territories of the United States*, 148. The public lands of Texas belonged to that state, but it was proposed to confiscate them (report of the Secretary of the Interior for 1862, *H. Ex. Docs.*, 37 Cong. 3 sess., II (1157), 6).

57 *Cong. Globe*, 37 Cong. 2 sess., 2414, 2495. The Indian outbreak in Minnesota of August, 1862, furnished additional arguments for the removal of the Indians and their consolidation (memorial of Senator Pomeroy, November 15, 1862, *H. Ex. Docs.*, 37 Cong. 3 sess., II (1157), 491). For an able argument against Indian consolidation and in favor of the allotment of lands in severalty to the Indians in proximity to the whites, see the letter of Superintendent Coffin, September 1, 1862, *ibid.*, 312.

58 *Cong. Globe*, 37 Cong. 2 sess., 2912, 2913.

THE CIVIL WAR

tion bill which became a law on July 5, 1862, contained a clause authorizing the President to suspend wholly or in part the treaties with any tribe whose tribal organization was in revolt against the United States.[59] The ostensible purpose of this clause, as shown by the debate at the time of its adoption, was to enable the executive department to use the money due to the tribes for the benefit of the Indian refugees in Kansas,[60] but the government ultimately made use of the authority thus conferred to force concessions from the Indians.

When Congress met in December, 1862, for the short session, the plan of moving the northern Indians to the Indian Territory again received consideration. In the House of Representatives Aldrich tried to push his bill to establish the Territory of Lanniwa, but it was reported adversely on February 12.[61] In the Senate, on December 15, James H. Lane of Kansas introduced a bill to authorize the President to treat with the Indians of Kansas for their removal from that state. On January 21 Lane reported his bill from the Committee on Indian Affairs with an amendment authorizing the President to secure land in the Indian Territory by "treaty or otherwise" for the Indians of Kansas. This amendment had been suggested by the secretary of the interior, Caleb B. Smith.[62]

59 *Statutes*, XII, 528.
60 *Cong. Globe*, 37 Cong. 2 sess., 2121-2125. John Sherman, senator from Ohio, remarked during the debate, however, that the government ought to welcome the opportunity thus afforded to get rid of the treaties with the Creeks, Seminoles, and Cherokees, as they were "very harsh" and "unjust against the United States" (*ibid.*, 2125).
61 *Cong. Globe*, 37 Cong. 3 sess., 25, 915.
62 *Ibid.*, 84, 413, 505, 506. Compare the report of the Secretary of the

THE FORMATION OF OKLAHOMA

The debate upon this bill indicates clearly that the Senate Committee on Indian Affairs was considering a plan for the consolidation, in the diminished Indian Territory, of all the Indians east of the Rocky Mountains except those who wished to take allotments in severalty. The Indian Territory was to be consecrated to the Indians, and so far as possible no whites were to be permitted to come in contact with them. They were to have a territorial organization, and the possibility of an Indian state was even mentioned. Lane's bill was only the first step of this plan. It is interesting to note, in view of his later activities in bringing about further removals, that James Harlan, senator from Iowa, took a leading part in the debate.[63]

Lane's bill as amended passed the Senate on January 27. The House did not act upon it, but on February 25 the Senate attached it to the Indian appropriation bill, and on February 28 the House concurred in this action. The plan of removing the Indians of Kansas to the Indian Territory accordingly became a part of the law of the land on March 3, 1863.[64]

During 1863 the Creek refugees were induced to

Interior for 1862, *H. Ex. Docs.*, 37 Cong. 3 sess., II (1157), 11; and the report of the Commissioner of Indian Affairs, *ibid.*, 179, 180.

63 *Cong. Globe*, 37 Cong. 3 sess., 505-507. Two laws were enacted at this session for the removal of the Indians from Minnesota (acts of February 21 and March 3, 1863, *Statutes*, XII, 658, 819). It should be noted that these contained no limitation on the place to which the Indians should be removed. The one relating to the Sioux as originally proposed prescribed that the new reservation should be north of the forty-third parallel, but this provision was stricken out by the Senate Committee on Indian Affairs (*Cong. Globe*, 37 Cong. 3 sess., 528, 867). The committee apparently did not want any limitation that would prevent the removal of the northern Indians to the Indian Territory. However see below, footnote 70.

64 *Cong. Globe*, 37 Cong. 3 sess., 527, 1056, 1282, 1392; *Statutes*, XII, 793.

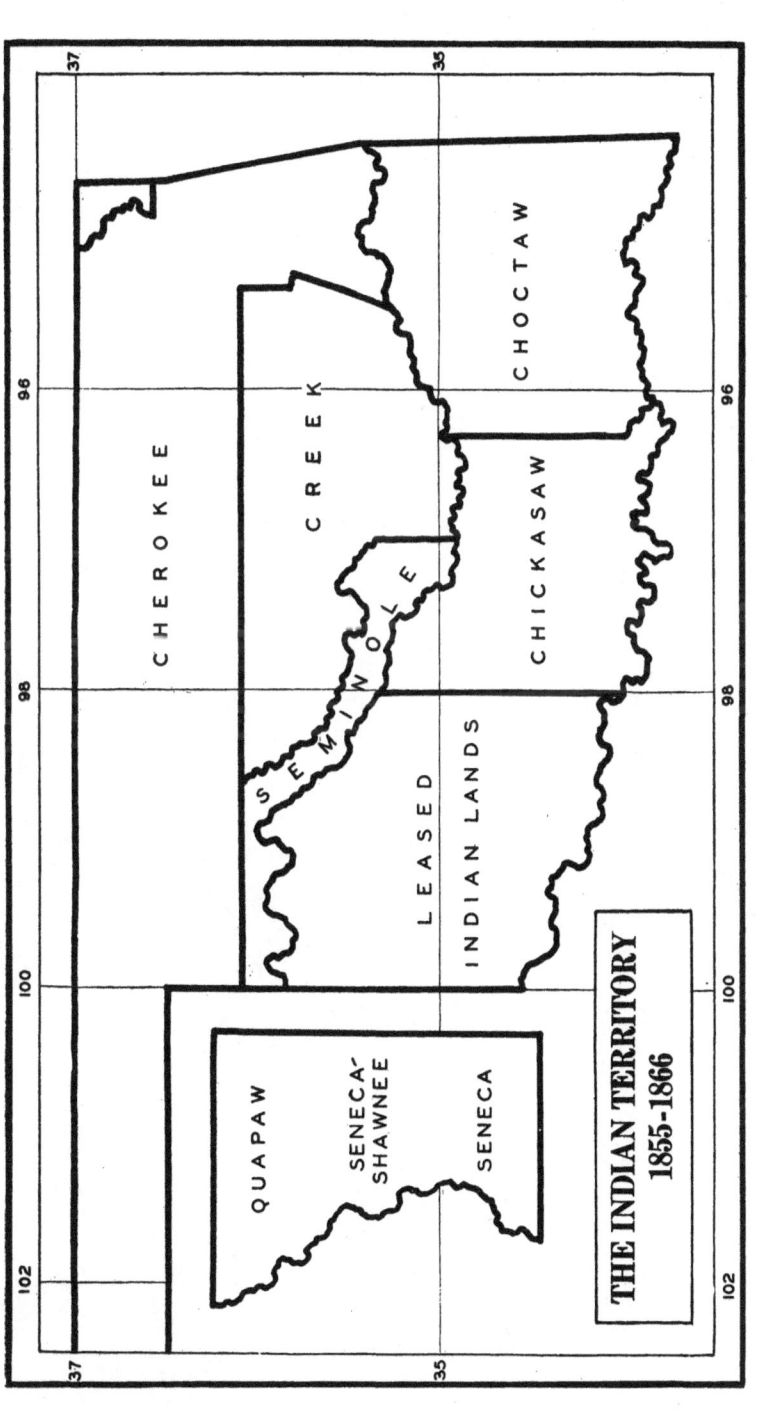

THE CIVIL WAR

cede to the United States for the use of other Indians a tract bounded on the north and east by the Cherokee country, on the south by the Arkansas River, and on the west by a north and south line forty miles west of the eastern boundary. The consideration for this cession was fixed at two hundred thousand dollars. It was said at the time that this was the country belonging to the Creeks who adhered to the Confederacy and that it included the most valuable part of the Creek territory.[65] The Senate amended the treaty of cession,[66] but the Creeks did not accept the amendment. Accordingly, the matter was dropped until the close of the war.[67] Negotiations were under way with the Cherokee refugees at the same time, and the commissioner of Indian Affairs, W. P. Dole, in his annual report for 1864 insisted that in the process of reconstruction the southern tribes should be made to provide room for other Indians.[68]

By the beginning of 1865 the war was nearly at an end, and the time for this reconstruction was at hand. On February 20 Senator Harlan introduced a bill to consolidate the Indian tribes and establish civil government in the Indian Territory. Two days later it was reported by the Senate Committee on Indian Affairs and hurriedly considered in the Senate.[69] This

---

65 Report of George A. Cutler, agent for the Creeks, for 1863, *H. Ex. Docs.*, 38 Cong. 1 sess., III (1182), 301. This included practically all the Creek country north and east of the Arkansas River.
66 Report of the Commissioner of Indian Affairs for 1864, *H. Ex. Docs.*, 38 Cong. 2 sess., V (1220), 176.
67 Proceedings of the council at Fort Smith, September, 1865, *H. Ex. Docs.*, 39 Cong. 1 sess., II (1248), 514.
68 *H. Ex. Docs.*, 38 Cong. 2 sess., V (1220), 177.
69 *Cong. Globe*, 38 Cong. 2 sess., 915, 981, 1021-1024, 1303-1310.

{ 85 }

bill was clearly intended to further the movement that had begun with the adoption of Lane's plan for the removal of the Indians from Kansas. The same senators took leading parts in the debate, the same arguments were advanced, and the same purposes were set forth in 1863 and in 1865.

The Harlan bill is noteworthy, as it furnished a model for the agreements of 1865 and 1866 with the southern Indians. The proposed territory had the boundaries of the present State of Oklahoma. The tribal organizations were to be continued, but the territory was to have a governor, a secretary, an attorney-general, and a complete system of courts. All of these offices were to be filled by executive appointment, but an elective legislative council was also to be established. Its power was "to extend to all rightful subjects and matters pertaining to the intercourse of the Indian tribes in the territory and the administration of internal justice and the punishment of crimes." While the rights of the tribes were recognized in general terms by the bill, and the courts were to enforce the tribal laws that were not inconsistent with the laws of the United States or the proposed territory, the whole proposed court system was territorial; and a liberal construction of the powers of the central government would soon have destroyed the tribal organizations. In short, the proposed territory was to be like other territories.

No tribe at peace with the United States was to be included in this territory without its consent, but it was significantly remarked that the southern tribes were

THE CIVIL WAR

still in revolt. Efforts were to be made to bring about the removal thither of the Indians of "Kansas, Nebraska, and perhaps as far north as Michigan, Wisconsin, and Minnesota."[70]

The Harlan bill passed the Senate on March 2, but it did not receive consideration in the House of Representatives, as the session of Congress ended the next day.[71] Harlan, however, was soon able to deal with the Indians as a member of the executive department.

Harlan was appointed Secretary of the Interior by President Johnson, and took charge of his office on May 15, 1865.[72] The Indian council at Camp Napoleon met on May 24,[73] and its request for a conference gave him an opportunity to lay his plans before the Indians. As has been said, it was proposed at first to permit the Indian delegates to go to Washington, but it was decided later to send a commission to meet them at Fort Smith, Arkansas, which was practically the capital of the Indian Territory, as it was the seat of the only United States court with jurisdiction within its limits, as well as the headquarters of the superintendent of Indian Affairs in charge of the southern tribes.

---

70 *Ibid.*, 1021-1024, especially the remarks of James S. Doolittle, senator from Wisconsin. It is not to be inferred that the removal to the Indian Territory of the Indians of the states on the Canadian border could have been seriously considered by many persons. The objections to such a removal, due to the differences in the climate of Minnesota and Oklahoma, were recognized too clearly (*ibid.*).

71 *Ibid.*, 1310, 1410, 1420.

72 Report of the Secretary of the Interior for 1865, *H. Ex. Docs.*, 39 Cong. 1 sess., II (1248), p. ix.

73 Reynolds to Harlan, June 28, 1865, *ibid.*, 479.

THE FORMATION OF OKLAHOMA

The council met on September 8. The commissioners representing the United States included two officials, two officers of the army, and one civilian. They were D. N. Cooley, commissioner of Indian Affairs, who was the presiding officer; Elijah Sells, superintendent at Fort Smith; Thomas Wister, "a leading member of the Society of Friends"; Brigadier-General W. S. Harney, and Colonel E. S. Parker. Parker was a Seneca Indian of mixed blood, and his participation in the negotiations gratified the Indians. During the course of the council, delegates were in attendance from all the factions of the principal tribes of the Indian Territory and from some of the tribes of Kansas.[74]

On the first day of the council, the Indians were told that they had forfeited all their rights under the old treaties, but those who had remained loyal were praised and were assured that their claims would not be forgotten.[75] On the next day it was announced that the new treaties must contain seven provisions. Five of these dealt with the abolition of slavery in the Indian Territory, the admission of the freedmen to Indian citizenship, the re-establishment of peace and order, and the enforcement of the intercourse law. The two

---

74 The annual report of the Secretary of the Interior for 1865 (*loc. cit.*) contains two accounts of the council at Fort Smith: the report of D. N. Cooley as president (480-496), and the official report (496-537), cited as the proceedings of the council at Fort Smith.

75 *Ibid.*, 498. Compare the statement made the next day: "Under the terms of the treaties with the United States, and the law of Congress of July 5, 1862, all these nations and tribes forfeited and lost all their rights to annuities and lands" (*ibid.*, 502). The commissioners did not always make clear to the Indians that the President so far had failed to exercise fully the power of suspending the treaties.

THE CIVIL WAR

most important provisions were that a part of the Indian Territory should be set aside for the use of the Indians from "Kansas and elsewhere" and that the Indians should accept the policy of the United States to unite all the tribes of this region under "one consolidated government after the plan proposed by the Senate of the United States in a bill [the Harlan bill] for organizing Indian Territory."[76]

These proposals were too drastic, and the Indians were not prepared to accept them. The delegates from the Union faction of the Cherokees relying upon the recent assurances of favor, protested against the attitude of the commission.[77] Commissioner Cooley replied to them and denounced their leader, John Ross, as the archtraitor who had betrayed the Cherokees[78] and had sought to lead astray the "pure patriot," Opothleyoholo,[79] and the Creeks of his faction. The attack on Ross had begun in the preceding February, when he ventured to protest against the Harlan bill.[80] The Union Cherokees now made a spirited reply to the charges against him.[81] The Union Creeks presented

76 *Ibid.*, 502, 503.
77 *Ibid.*, 506, 507.
78 *Ibid.*, 509, 510. According to Cooley's claims, documents had recently come to light showing that Ross had been more friendly to the Confederates than was supposed. Except the letters to Opothleyoholo, whose purpose has already been explained, these documents were of little importance.
79 Opothleyoholo was accorded extraordinary praise. Note the extravagant words used in announcing his death: "I have to record the loss of one of the principal men of the Creek nation, and probably the greatest Indian that has ever lived, Opothleyoholo, who . . .sank quietly in his grave, apparently from old age" (report of George A. Cutler, agent for the Creeks for 1863, *H. Ex. Docs.*, 38 Cong. 1 sess., III (1182), 300).
80 Speech of Senator Harlan, *Cong. Globe*, 38 Cong. 2 sess., 1305.
81 Proceedings of the council at Fort Smith, *loc. cit.*, 528.

THE FORMATION OF OKLAHOMA

a strong and dignified statement of their position.[82] The delegates from the Confederate Indians were conciliatory but not apologetic. They urged that they lacked authority to make such treaties as the commissioners wished.[83]

Commissioner Cooley was much pleased with the attitude of the leading delegate of the Confederate Cherokees, Elias C. Boudinot, son of Elias Boudinot and nephew of Stand Watie. Boudinot acted as spokesman for all the Confederate Indians and was able to establish harmonious relations between them and the commissioners. He could do this easily because he was in favor of the establishment of a territorial government for the Indians, while most of the others preferred to retain their tribal organization unimpaired.[84] The favor shown Boudinot and the bad treatment accorded Ross did not tend to improve the relations existing between the two factions of the Cherokees, especially as Cooley allowed Ross and Boudinot to engage in an altercation in the council. Cooley said in his annual report for 1865 that the ancient feuds among the Cherokees were remembered still, but that friendly relations had been established elsewhere in the Indian Territory.[85]

When the commissioners saw that they could not make treaties such as were desired with any of the

---

82 *Ibid.*, 525.

83 *Ibid.*, 504, 509, 523, 525, 533, 537.

84 *Ibid.*, 521, 522, 523, 524, 532, 535, 537. Cf. Cooley's report (*ibid.*, 495), and his annual report as Commissioner of Indian Affairs for 1865 (*ibid.*, 204, 205).

85 *Ibid.*, 524, 203.

THE CIVIL WAR

tribes, they prepared an agreement which renewed the friendship between the Indians and the United States, but left all the questions at issue to be settled later.[86] The Union Creeks objected to the wording of this agreement, but they were scolded into submission.[87] The commissioners and the Indian delegates affixed their signatures, or their marks, and peace was once more established in the Indian Territory.[88]

During the war, the officials connected with the Indian service with remarkable unanimity had pointed out in their annual reports that the southern tribes had been abandoned to the Confederates in 1861. They had also called attention to the number of Union Indians in spite of this. Even in October, 1865, Superintendent Sells reminded his superiors that two-thirds of the Cherokees, one-half of the Seminoles, and nearly one-half of the Creeks had been loyal to the United States.[89]

---

86 *Ibid.*, 512, 514.
87 *Ibid.*, 517, 518.
88 For the names supposed to have been signed to this agreement, see Kappler, *Indian Affairs*, II, 1051.
89 *H. Ex. Docs.*, 39 Cong. 1 sess., II (1248), 438, 439. The most important reports defending the Indians are as follows: report of the Secretary of the Interior for 1861, *S. Ex. Docs.*, 37 Cong. 2 sess., I (1117), 447; of the Commissioner of Indian Affairs for 1861, *ibid.*, 627; of the local superintendent for 1861, *ibid.*, 655; of the Secretary of the Interior for 1862, *H. Ex. Docs.*, 37 Cong. 3 sess., II (1157), 7; of the Commissioner of Indian Affairs for 1862, *ibid.*, 181; of the local superintendent for 1862, *ibid.*, 280, 281; of the Commissioner of Indian Affairs for 1863, *H. Ex. Docs.*, 38 Cong. 1 sess., III (1182), 142; of the local superintendent for 1863, quoted below, *ibid.*, 295; of the Commissioner of Indian Affairs for 1864, *H. Ex. Docs.*, 38 Cong. 2 sess., V (1220), 174. These were based on the reports of both regular and special agents. The reports of W. G. Coffin, the local superintendent, for 1863, referred to above, sums up the official opinion at that time: "I am fully of the opinion that if the government, at the breaking out of the rebellion, had promptly offered to the various tribes of Indians in the Indian Territory the protection provided for in existing treaty stipulations, . . . they would all

THE FORMATION OF OKLAHOMA

This statement of the conditions did not accord with the plan of action that had been adopted. It had been agreed to compel the Indians south of Kansas to cede territory for the use of the numerous small tribes that still remained in the northern part of the old Indian Territory. It was hoped also to secure the acquiescence of the former in the establishment of a territorial government. To attain these objects, it was clear that it would be necessary to threaten the Indians with the loss of all their treaty privileges in accordance with the terms of the act of July 5, 1862. A settlement could have been made more easily if Congress without further delay had assumed the right to enact legislation for the amelioration of conditions among the Indians, but this would not have been according to precedent. A statement of conditions must be made, therefore, that would be more in harmony with the accepted plan of action.

The annual report of Secretary Harlan, made in December, 1865, contained the following section that indicated the changed attitude toward the Indians:[90]

> . . . Civilized and powerful tribes, however, residing within the Indian Territory, united early in the year 1861 with the Indians of the prairies immediately west and north, for hostile operations against the United States. In flagrant violation of treaties which had been observed by us with scrupulous good faith and in the absence of any just ground of complaint, these confederated Indians entered into an alliance with the rebel authorities and raised regiments in support of their cause.[91] These organ-

---

have remained loyal. . . . But instead of doing that, the government withdrew from the vicinity of the Indian Territory all the Union forces, and thus left the Indians at the mercy of the enemy. Hence, the hostile attitude assumed by portions of the tribes referred to was the result."

90 *H. Ex. Docs.*, 39 Cong. 1 sess., II (1248), p. vii.

91 Harlan ignored the fact that the three tribes north of the Canadian

THE CIVIL WAR

ized troops fought side by side with rebel soldiers. . . . This state of things continued until the surrender of the rebel forces west of the Mississippi. Hostilities were then suspended, and, at the request of the Indians, commissioners were sent to negotiate a treaty of peace. Such preliminary arrangements were made as, it is believed, will result in the abolition of slavery among them, the cession within the Indian Territory of lands for the settlement of the Civilized Indians now residing on reservations elsewhere, and the ultimate establishment of civil government, subject to the supervision of the United States.

The perfidious[92] conduct of the Indians in making unprovoked war upon us has been visited with the severest retribution. The country within the Indian Territory has been laid waste, vast amounts of property destroyed, and the inhabitants reduced from a prosperous condition to such extreme destitution, that thousands of them must inevitably perish during the present winter, unless timely provision be made by this government for their relief.

Thus the southern Indians were accused formally of voluntary participation in the Civil War. It is true that most of the Indians of mixed blood were partisans of the Confederates from the first. They were the slave-

---

had also furnished the United States troops. According to the figures already given, the Cherokees in the Union army numbered one out of eight of the loyal population, and one out of thirteen of the total Cherokee population. According to the report of the Commissioner of Pensions for 1888, the total number of enlistments from the Indian Territory in the Union army was 3530 (*H. Ex. Docs.*, 50 Cong. 2 sess., XII (2638), chart opp. p. 1). The population of the Indian Territory at the time of the Civil War was about fifty thousand (see below, Appendix D).

92 The officials of the Department of the Interior set to work to demonstrate this perfidy in justification of the new attitude. The case against the Cherokees seemed weakest, and the Commissioner of Indian Affairs prepared a pamphlet, called *The Cherokee Question*, which contained statements regarding the disloyalty of this tribe. On June 15, 1866, he sent this as a special report to the President. Albert Pike, partly to defend his own actions, gave the commissioner whatever evidence he could of the willingness of the Indians to make treaties with the South, in a letter bearing the date of February 17, 1866. They were able to demonstrate rather conclusively that few Cherokees had been actively loyal to the United States at all times, but they were not able to present much evidence of active disloyalty.

holders, and they had appropriated the tribal property as they appropriated it from the time of Gregg to that of the Dawes Commission. A majority of the Chickasaw and the Choctaw full-bloods evidently sympathized with the South, but there is nothing to show that they wished to take an active part in the struggle. The Indians north of the Canadian were undoubtedly anxious only to be let alone. From the point of view of the tribes, since they had been recognized as treaty-making powers, all that could be asked of them was a passive acquiescence in the fortunes of war. They ought not to have been expected to oppose the Confederates unaided, in view of the promises of protection in their treaties. The manifest strength of the South in that region and the weakness of the United States at the beginning of the war awed those who were inclined to remain loyal and emboldened those who sympathized with the South. It is doubtful whether the people of Maryland or of Kentucky would have behaved better if their state had been abandoned to the Confederacy, and yet more was due from citizens of the United States than from Indian wards.

The weakness of the United States in the first years of the war compelled the Indians to make terms with the Confederates. A force in the Indian Territory sufficient to protect it probably would have kept all the tribes quiet, those north of the Canadian without doubt. As the government was so largely responsible for the terrible conditions in the territory in 1865, the Indians should have been given encouragement and help. Instead of this, they were told that their own perfidy

THE CIVIL WAR

had brought on their misery. The settlement finally made was not ungenerous, but the unfair statements concerning their part in the struggle served to create a new feeling of distrust. In the period following the Civil War, co-operation between the southern Indians and the government of the United States was more difficult than ever.[93]

[93] The work by Annie Heloise Abel, *The American Indian as Slaveholder and Secessionist* (3 vols., Cleveland, 1915-), the first volume of which appeared shortly after the above was written, is the standard account of the period covered by this chapter.

NOTE TO 1939 EDITION: The work mentioned above was published 1915-1925 under the title *The Slaveholding Indians:* Volume I, *The American Indian as Slaveholder and Secessionist;* Volume II, *The American Indian as Participant in the Civil War;* Volume III, *The American Indian Under Reconstruction.*

CHAPTER VI

THE RECONSTRUCTION OF THE INDIAN TERRITORY

AT the close of the Civil War, the government began to make definite provisions for further Indian consolidation. The scheme of removing the tribes of Kansas and Nebraska to the Indian Territory broadened into a plan for the concentration of all the Indians in two districts. The tribes of the central and southern parts of the United States were to be gathered in the present state of Oklahoma. Those of the northern part were to be given a reservation bounded on the north by the forty-sixth parallel, on the east by the Missouri River, on the south by the forty-third parallel, and on the west by the one hundred and fourth meridian.[1] Little came of the plan for a northern reservation, but some progress was made in the development of the southern district.

The history of the Indian Territory from 1866 to 1879 is the history of a struggle for the concentration of the Indians and the establishment of a territorial government. The one was partly accomplished; the other was left undone. The failure to effect a territorial organization was due chiefly to the opposition of the Indians, who believed that a change in their status would make it possible for the railroads to secure a foot-

---

1 Report of the Indian Peace Commission, January 7, 1868, *H. Ex. Docs.*, 40 Cong. 3 sess., II (1366), 505. Compare the report of E. S. Parker on Indian affairs, January 24, 1867, *H. Misc. Docs.*, 39 Cong. 2 sess. (1302), no. 37.

RECONSTRUCTION

hold in their country. In time, the Indians came to believe that all the bills for the establishment of territorial government were schemes for depriving them of their land.[2]

The first task of the government after the Civil War was to secure territory from the Five Civilized Tribes for the use of other Indians. Reports indicated that these tribes were opposed to territorial organization, but that they would consent to measures leading up to it.[3] The commission appointed to treat with them therefore sought only to have the form of territorial government accepted, and the chief feature of the treaties made in 1866 was the cession of land to the United States.[4]

The Creeks agreed that a north and south line should be surveyed through their country so as to divide it into two parts of equal size. They retained the eastern half, and ceded the United States the western half.[5] The Seminoles gave up the entire district that had been assigned them in 1856[6] and engaged to move to a

[2] See the testimony before the Senate committee in 1878, *S. Reports*, 45 Cong. 3 sess., III (1839), 134, 179, 218, 565.

[3] Cooley to Harlan, March 21, 1866, *H. Ex. Docs.*, 39 Cong. 2 sess., II (1284), 283.

[4] Treaty with the Seminoles, March 21, ratified July 19, *Statutes*, XIV, 755 (reprinted in Kappler, II, 910); with the Chickasaws and Choctaws, April 28, ratified June 28, *Statutes*, XIV, 769 (reprinted in Kappler, II, 918); with the Creeks, June 14, ratified July 19, *Statutes*, XIV, 785 (reprinted in Kappler, II, 931); with the Cherokees, July 19, ratified July 27, *Statutes* XIV, 797 (reprinted in Kappler, II, 942).

[5] The Creeks were paid thirty cents an acre for this cession. The loyal Creeks were given a large part of the sum paid, as compensation for their losses during the Civil War.

[6] The Seminoles were given fifteen cents an acre for their cession and paid fifty cents an acre for their new reservation. The loyal Seminoles were compensated for their losses out of the net proceeds of the transfer.

reservation between the Canadian and the North Fork in the territory ceded by the Creeks. The east line of the Seminoles was fixed at the new west line of the Creeks, and it was stipulated that their land should extend westward between the rivers far enough to give them two hundred thousand acres.[7] The Chickasaws and Choctaws ceded the United States the leased district west of the ninety-eighth meridian,[8] but their other districts were left as they had been established in 1855. It was understood that the United States acquired this territory only for the use of "other Indians and freedmen." This restriction on the use of the land was stated in the treaty with the Creeks, clearly implied in the treaty with the Seminoles, but not referred to in the treaty with the Chickasaws and Choctaws.

The Cherokees did not cede the United States any land in the Indian Territory at this time.[9] They agreed, however, to permit the government to settle friendly

[7] The Seminoles moved to their new reservation before it had been surveyed. They settled east of the limits proposed in the treaty. The United States finally arranged for the purchase of one hundred and seventy-five thousand acres east of the Creek dividing line. This gave the Seminoles three hundred and seventy-five thousand acres in all. See the report of the Commissioner of Indian Affairs for 1881, *H. Ex. Docs.*, 47 Cong. 1 sess., X (2018), 44; same for 1882, *H. Ex. Docs.*, 47 Cong. 2 sess., XI (2100), 44.

[8] They received three hundred thousand dollars for this district, subject to the provisions regarding the freedmen.

[9] They ceded the United States in trust their land in Kansas, both the Cherokee strip and the Cherokee neutral lands. The Cherokee strip was the part of the Cherokee country that lay just north of the thirty-seventh parallel. It was about two and one-half miles wide. It was sold to settlers in accordance with the acts of May 11, 1872, and later (report of the Secretary of the Interior for 1876, *H. Ex. Docs.*, 44 Cong. 2 sess., IV, i (1749), 20-23). When the boundary of Kansas was fixed at the thirty-seventh parallel, it was known that this was only the approximate line between the Osages and the Cherokees, but it was thought that the Cherokee country did not extend quite to the parallel (*S. Reports*, 33 Cong. 1 sess., II [i] (707), no. 379, p. 28). The name "Cherokee strip" was later applied wrongly to the Cherokee outlet.

RECONSTRUCTION

Indians in tribal reservations in any part of their country west of the ninety-sixth meridian. It was provided that these reservations should not include more than one hundred and sixty acres for each member of the tribe, and that the Cherokees should be paid for their land, when it should be taken, at a price to be fixed by the President of the United States in case of a disagreement.

The Cherokees agreed provisionally that the United States could settle civilized Indians in their country east of the ninety-sixth meridian. It was arranged that the Indians thus settled should be incorporated wholly or in part with the Cherokees. The Chickasaws and Choctaws also agreed to receive not to exceed ten thousand "Kansas Indians" into their respective districts east of the ninety-eighth meridian. About a thousand Delawares and half as many Shawnees were incorporated with the Cherokees,[10] but no serious attempt was made to settle other Indians in the tribal districts south of the Canadian.

The treaties with the Cherokees, the Creeks, and the Seminoles stipulated that the freedmen of these tribes should be made Indian citizens. The treaty with the Chickasaws and Choctaws provided that their freedmen either should be made Indian citizens by the tribes or should be removed from the tribal districts by the United States. In the latter case the tribes agreed to forfeit the sum that they had received from the sale of the district west of the ninety-eighth meridian.

10 Report of the agent for the Delawares, September 21, 1868, *H. Ex. Docs.*, 40 Cong. 3 sess., II (1366), 723; of the agent for the Shawnees, September 16, 1871, *H. Ex. Docs.*, 42 Cong. 2 sess., III, i (1505), 913.

{ 99 }

THE FORMATION OF OKLAHOMA

Provisions were made in all the treaties for the construction of railroads in the Indian Territory. The Seminoles gave the right of way for a road from the eastern to the western or southern border of their reservation, and each of the treaties with the other tribes authorized two roads. The treaty with the Cherokees, the last one completed, was made on July 19 and ratified on July 27, 1866. On July 25, 26, and 27, charters were granted to three railroads in the Indian Territory. To each road was made a grant of land to aid in its construction, but the grant was to be effective only when the Indian title should be extinguished. In accordance with these provisions, two railroads were constructed in the Indian Territory in 1871 and 1872; the Missouri, Kansas, and Texas across the territory from north to south, and the Atlantic and Pacific from the Missouri state line to a junction with the other road.[11]

The allotment of land to individuals was urged upon the Chickasaws and Choctaws in the treaty with them, and the United States agreed to survey their reservations if that should be requested by the tribal authorities.

11 For the charters, see *Statutes*, XIV, 238, 291, 294. One charter granted twenty sections for each mile of road constructed to be selected within forty miles of the right of way, whenever the Indian title should be extinguished, provided that the land should become a part of the public domain. The others granted ten sections for each mile within twenty miles of the right of way on the same conditions. For details of construction, see report of John B. Jones, agent for the Cherokees, for 1871, *H. Ex. Docs.*, 42 Cong. 2 sess., III, i (1505), 982, and the report of the Secretary of the Interior for 1873, *H. Ex. Docs.*, 43 Cong. 1 sess., IV, i (1601), p. xxvi. The Atlantic and Pacific line was only thirty-six miles long. When it became apparent that the Indian title would not be extinguished, construction stopped. See testimony of James Baker, attorney for the Atlantic and Pacific, before Senate (Patterson) committee on March 22, 1878, *S. Reports*, 45 Cong. 3 sess., III (1839), 3: "We could not build the road through a desolation of four hundred or six hundred miles. The government would not give us the land we supposed they would, and the result has been that a good many of our people have been ruined."

RECONSTRUCTION

The treaty with the Cherokees contained a similar provision. This form of allotment in severalty was only a plan for securing each Indian family a plot of ground in the tribal reservation. It was the plan of Secretary Thompson, and it was not an actual step toward the dissolution of the tribal organization.[12] The Indians, however, grouped together allotment in severalty, the railroad charters, and the proposed territorial organization. They believed that these were all designed to drive them out of the Indian Territory.[13]

The Five Civilized Tribes were induced to give their assent in these treaties to the establishment of a general council consisting of delegates elected by each nation or tribe lawfully residing in the Indian Territory. In the first council each tribe was assigned one delegate at large and one for each thousand members of the tribe. It was agreed that the United States should pay these delegates. The powers of the council were confined to the control of intertribal relations and the relations with the freedmen and white persons in the territory, but provision was made for the enlargement of these powers with the consent of the tribes and the approval

---

12 This plan was suggested, for those Indians of the Indian Territory who preferred it, in at least two treaties made soon after this; with the Kiowas and Comanches, October 21, 1867, *Statutes*, XV, 581 (reprinted in Kappler, II, 977); with the Cheyennes and Arapahoes, October 28, 1867, *Statutes*, XV, 593 (reprinted in Kappler, II, 984). It was recommended in the first annual report of the Board of Indian Commissioners, November 23, 1869, *H. Ex. Docs.*, 41 Cong. 2 sess., III (1414), 491.

13 See in particular the protests of the Indian Council, December 5, 1873, January 22, 1874, *H. Misc. Docs.*, 43 Cong. 1 sess., II (1618), nos. 85, 88; and the protest of the Cherokees, March 14, 1870, *S. Misc. Docs.*, 41 Cong. 2 sess. (1408), no. 83; and also the protests of the Cherokees and the Creeks, April 4, 1872, *H. Misc. Docs.*, 42 Cong. 2 sess., III (1526), no. 166. For a list of the principal protests, see Abel, "Proposals for an Indian State," in American Historical Association, *Annual Report, 1907*, I, 102.

THE FORMATION OF OKLAHOMA

of the President of the United States. It was stipulated that the president of the general council should be an appointee of the government of the United States, and in the treaty with the Chickasaws and Choctaws he was called the "governor of the Territory of Oklahoma." This was the first use of Oklahoma as a name for the Indian Territory. At the same time the consent of the Indians was secured for the establishment of a United States court, but it was expressly provided that the powers of the tribal courts should not be curtailed.[14]

In December, 1870, the general council instituted by the treaties of 1866 met at Okmulgee in the Creek country and drew up a plan of government for the Indian Territory. This document, known as the Okmulgee constitution, provided for a federal union of the tribes, but it did not admit the United States to a share in the government.[15] This plan was not accepted by Congress, and it was not ratified by many of the tribes.[16] The general council continued to meet annually for some time,[17] and it took a leading part in

14 This statement applies especially to the section in the treaty with the Cherokees. The treaties with the Creeks and the Seminoles each contained sections authorizing Congress to enact legislation for the better administration of justice within the Indian Territory, provided that it should not interfere with the powers of the tribal organization. The treaty with the Chickasaws and Choctaws contained this authorization in both forms.

15 Proceedings of the council with copy of the constitution, adopted, December 20, 1870, S. Ex. Docs., 41 Cong. 3 sess., I (1440), no 26; report of the Commissioner of Indian Affairs for 1870, H. Ex. Docs., 41 Cong. 3 sess., IV, i (1449), 471.

16 Report of the Secretary of the Interior for 1874, H. Ex. Docs., 43 Cong. 2 sess., VI (1639), 321.

17 Appropriations were made for their support for each year up to 1876 (act of June 20, 1878, *Statutes*, XX, 232). For a description of the general council in session, see article by A. M. Williams in *Lippincott's*, September, 1879 (XXIV, 371).

RECONSTRUCTION

opposing the plans for the organization of the territory. In 1874 the Secretary of the Interior reported that the general council was failing to accomplish its main purpose, the preparation of the Indians for territorial government.[18]

Congress meanwhile had been trying to organize the territory. As early as December, 1865, two bills were introduced for the establishment of civil government in the Indian Territory, and two similar bills were introduced later in the session before the ratification of the treaties of 1866. Numerous measures were proposed between 1866 and 1870, either for the organization of the territory or for the establishment of a better government for the Indians. During this period the name "Territory of Lincoln" was suggested in several bills. One bill provided for temporary territorial governments for the several tribal reservations and apparently was modeled on the Neosho bill of 1854.[19]

On March 17, 1870, Benjamin F. Rice, senator from Arkansas, introduced a bill for the organization of the Indian Territory under the name of "Ok-la-ho-ma." This bill was reported favorably on April 17 by Rice's colleague, Alexander McDonald, for the Committee on Territories. It was explained that the name proposed meant "home for the red man" in the Choctaw tongue and that it had been given to the Indian Territory in the treaty of 1866 with the Chickasaws and Choctaws.[20]

18 *Loc. cit.*, 321.
19 For a list of the principal bills dealing with the Indian Territory introduced in Congress during this period, see below, Appendix E.
20 *Senate Journal*, 41 Cong. 2 sess., 382; *S. Reports*, 41 Cong. 2 sess. (1409), no. 131. The name Oklahoma appears in a House bill for the first time in the bill of Robert T. Van Horn of Missouri, as reported by him with amend-

THE FORMATION OF OKLAHOMA

For the next twenty years hardly a Congress passed without the introduction of one or more bills for the establishment of the Territory of Oklahoma.

In May, 1872, in a minority report of the House Committee on Territories adverse to the establishment of the Territory of Oklahoma, George C. McKee, representative from Mississippi, declared that the real purpose of such bills was to destroy the tribal organizations and ultimately to extinguish the titles of the tribes to their lands. He pointed out that this would validate the conditional land grants made to the railroads in 1866, and that claims to twenty-three million acres of land were involved.[21]

Popular interest, moreover, was already aroused in the opening of the Indian Territory. Many persons in the surrounding states were only waiting a favorable opportunity to occupy it. The Commissioner of Indian Affairs reported in March, 1872, that hundreds of settlers had entered from Kansas and that the most desirable land had been taken up for a distance of twenty or thirty miles from the state line, from Coffeyville on the east to the Arkansas River on the west.[22] The legislature of Kansas in January, 1872, protested against the removal of these intruders and

---

ments from the Committee on Indian Affairs on January 19, 1871 (see below, Appendix E).

21 *H. Reports*, 42 Cong. 2 sess., IV (1543), no. 89. This was on the supposition that the tribal land would revert to the public domain as soon as the tribal organization should be abolished. It is still a disputed question as to how far this would have been true.

22 *S. Ex. Docs.*, 42 Cong. 2 sess., II (1479), no. 51. According to the report of the Commissioner of Indian Affairs for 1872, fifteen hundred intruders were removed in that year by a detachment of the Sixth Cavalry (*H. Ex. Docs.*, 42 Cong. 3 sess., III, i (1560), 481).

RECONSTRUCTION

asked Congress to extend the southern boundary of that state to the parallel of 36° 30'.[23] Persons engaged in commerce looked with disfavor upon this large body of unproductive land, and in December, 1872, the National Commercial Convention at Saint Louis petitioned Congress for the reorganization of the Indian Territory, and its opening to settlement.[24]

Under these conditions, the years from 1870 to 1873 were especially prolific of bills for the reorganization of the Indian Territory. Bills were introduced for the establishment of the Territory of Oklahoma, for the ratification of a judicial system, and even for the repeal of the conditional land grants. The Oklahoma bill, which had been the special object of McKee's attack, received considerable attention in the House of Representatives, but it was finally laid on the table on January 16, 1873, by a vote of ninety-five to forty-three.[25] In the Senate, on February 20, five bills dealing with the Indian Territory were laid on the table on one motion.[26] When Congress adjourned on March 3, the organization of the Indian Territory seemed further off than ever.

Meanwhile, the removal of the Indians to the Indian Territory had been partly accomplished in spite of the failure to establish a territorial government. Before 1867 the narrow strip between the Neosho

[23] The memorial was presented in the Senate on January 30 (*S. Misc. Docs.*, 42 Cong. 2 sess., I (1481), no. 49).

[24] *H. Misc. Docs.*, 42 Cong. 3 sess., II (1572), no. 42.

[25] On motion of James A. Garfield of Ohio (*House Journal*, 42 Cong. 3 sess., 184). Cf. *Cong. Globe*, 611, 616, 648-658.

[26] *Senate Journal*, 42 Cong. 3 sess., 407. For a list of bills dealing with the Indian Territory introduced during this period, see below, Appendix E.

THE FORMATION OF OKLAHOMA

River and the Missouri state line had been occupied, it will be remembered, by the Senecas of Sandusky, the Seneca-Shawnee band, and the Quapaws. The Seneca reservation of seventy thousand acres had been established by the treaties of 1831 and 1832 at the bend of the Neosho; and the other reservations, the one of the Seneca-Shawnee band of sixty thousand acres and the one of the Quapaws of one hundred and fifty sections, lay in order to the north. The north line of the Quapaw reservation was half a mile north of the Kansas state line.

By a treaty made in February, 1867, several small tribes from Kansas were placed in this district. The Senecas of Sandusky gave up twenty thousand acres on the north side of their reservation for the Wyandottes. The Seneca-Shawnee band separated, and the Senecas joined the Senecas of Sandusky. The northern half of their former joint reservation was taken for the Peorias, Kaskaskies, Weas, and Piankeshas, with whom the Miamis were now established. The part of the southern half of the old Seneca-Shawnee reservation that lay west of Spring River was taken for the Ottawas, and the remainder was retained for the Shawnee portion of the band henceforth called the Eastern Shawnees. The Quapaws ceded the United States the strip of land that lay north of the Kansas state line, and also relinquished the western part of their remaining territory to provide additional land for the Peoria and affiliated Indians. The southwestern corner of the new Quapaw reservation was fixed at a point on the old southern line three miles east of the Neosho, and all west of a line drawn from that point due north to the Kansas boundary was added to the Peoria reservation, which was thus made up of parts of the old Quapaw and Seneca-Shawnee reservations.[27]

The first reservation for Indians from Kansas that was carved out of the Creek cession was established at this time. In February, 1867, a treaty was made with the Sac and Fox Indians by which they acquired a tract of seven hundred and fifty square miles in the territory south of the Cherokees. This tract, as finally selected, extended between the Cimarron and the North Fork of the Canadian westward from the new western boundary of the Creeks as far as was necessary to make the required area of seven hundred and fifty square miles.[28]

During the same month a treaty was made with the Pottawatomies of Kansas by which they were authorized to select "a tract of land, not exceeding thirty miles square" for their tribal reservation. They selected the land lying just west of the Seminole district. Certain Indians, formerly members of the Shawnee tribe, had already settled there twenty years before. As the Pottawatomies all became citizens of the United States,

[27] Treaty of February 23, 1867, ratified June 18, 1868, *Statutes*, XV, 513 (reprinted in Kappler, II, 960). The consideration for these transfers varied somewhat, but averaged about one dollar an acre.

[28] Treaty of February 18, 1867, ratified July 25, 1868, *Statutes*, XV, 495 (reprinted in Kappler, II, 951). The reservation was selected by the Indians in accordance with the provisions of the treaty (letter of the Secretary of the Interior, March 12, 1890, *S. Ex. Docs.*, 51 Cong. 1 sess., IX (2686), no. 78, p. 17). The west line of this reservation was established on the range line between ranges three and four east of the Indian meridian, from the North Fork to a point two miles north of the line between townships twelve and thirteen north, from which line the boundary ran one mile east of the range line (*ibid.*, 18).

THE FORMATION OF OKLAHOMA

taking advantage of the choice given them in the treaty of 1867, they no longer had a tribal organization, and the part of the treaty which gave them a tribal reservation was made void. Accordingly, neither the "citizen Pottawatomies" nor the "absentee Shawnees" had any legal title to the land. Nevertheless, an act of May 23, 1872, authorized the Secretary of the Interior to allot them all lands in severalty. Their allotments were scattered over a tract bounded on the north by the North Fork of the Canadian, on the east by the Seminole country, on the south by the Canadian, and on the west by the Indian meridian.[29]

A few months later, in October, 1867, a reservation was given to the Kiowa, Comanche, and Apache Indians in the territory that had been ceded to the United States in 1866 by the Chickasaws and Choctaws. This reservation was bounded on the north by the Washita River and a line drawn from the Washita to the North Fork of the Red River, on the east by the ninety-eighth

---

[29] Treaty with the Pottawatomies, February 27, 1867, ratified July 25, 1868, *Statutes*, XV, 531 (reprinted in Kappler, II, 970); report of Francis A. Walker, commissioner of Indian Affairs, November 1, 1872, *H. Ex. Docs.*, 42 Cong. 3 sess., III, i (1560), 477; act of May 23, 1872, *Statutes*, XVII, 159. For a brief statement concerning the whole subject and the boundaries in particular, see the letter of the Secretary of the Interior, March 12, 1890, *S. Ex. Docs.*, 51 Cong. 1 sess., IX (2686), no. 78, pp. 18-21. The Indian meridian, which was only the approximate western boundary of this tract, was established during the fiscal year 1870-71 for the survey of the Chickasaw district. "The surveyors were instructed to select a suitable initial point in the center of the Chickasaw lands, or in the vicinity of Fort Arbuckle, and perpetuate it by a suitable monument, and from this point to establish a principal meridian and base line, to be known by the designation of 'The Indian Base Line and Meridian' " (report of the Commissioner of the General Land Office for 1871, *H. Ex. Docs.*, 42 Cong. 2 sess., III, i (1505), 49; cf. 329). A contract was let at once for the extension of the Indian meridian north of the Canadian River (*ibid.*, 49), and all of Oklahoma except the Panhandle has been surveyed from this meridian and base line.

RECONSTRUCTION

meridian, on the south by the Red River, and on the west by the North Fork of the Red River.[30]

In the same month a reservation, partly in the Cherokee outlet and partly in the Creek cession of 1866, was given to the southern Cheyennes and Arapahoes. This reservation was bounded on the north by the Kansas state line, on the east by the Arkansas River, and on the south and west by the Cimarron. These boundaries, however, were never of importance, as the Indians settled farther south on the North Fork of the Canadian, just west of the ninety-eighth meridian. Accordingly, the President by an executive order dated August 10, 1869, assigned them a tract bounded on the north by the Cherokee outlet, on the east by the Cimarron and the ninety-eighth meridian, on the south by the Kiowa, Comanche, and Apache reservation, and on the west by the Texas state line.[31]

By an act of May 29, 1872, the Secretary of the Interior was authorized to make an agreement with these Indians confirming them in possession of their new reservation in exchange for the one given them in 1867.

[30] Treaty with the Kiowas and Comanches, October 21, 1867, *Statutes*, XV, 581 (reprinted in Kappler, II, 977); with the Kiowas, Comanches, and Apaches, October 21, 1867, *Statutes*, XV, 589 (reprinted in Kappler, II, 982). It should be noted that these Apaches were of the Kiowa Apache tribe and were not the same as the Apaches of Arizona, a few of whom under Geronimo were afterwards settled at Fort Sill in this reservation. The line drawn from the Washita began at "a point thirty miles, by river, west of Fort Cobb, as now established," and ran due west to the North Fork of the Red River.

[31] Treaty of October 28, 1867, *Statutes*, XV, 593 (reprinted in Kappler, II, 984). The executive order is printed in the report of the Commissioner of Indian Affairs for 1882, *H. Ex. Docs.*, 47 Cong. 2 sess., XI (2100), 329. The North Fork of the Red River was always recognized as the southern boundary of this reservation west of the northwestern corner of the Kiowa, Comanche, and Apache reservation (letter of the Secretary of the Interior, March 12, 1890, *loc. cit.*, 29).

THE FORMATION OF OKLAHOMA

The office of Indian Affairs, however, decided to separate the Cheyennes from the Arapahoes; and agreements were made in October, 1872, and in November, 1873, providing for separate reservations for them. The agreements were not ratified, and the matter was dropped.[32] Meanwhile, in October, 1872, the part of the Cheyenne and Arapahoe reservation that lay south of the Canadian and east of the meridian of 98° 40' was cut off and assigned to a band of Indians composed chiefly of Wichitas, Caddos, and Delawares.[33] A reservation in the Indian Territory had been guaranteed to the Delawares by a treaty of July, 1866,[34] and other Indians had settled in this district before the Civil War.[35] The two reservations, the Cheyenne and Arapahoe and the Wichita, thus delimited by executive action, stood for many years.

Meanwhile, a part of the Cherokee country west of the ninety-sixth meridian had been assigned to the Osage and Kansas tribes. The treaty of 1865 with the Osages made certain preliminary arrangements for their removal to the Indian Territory.[36] An act of July 15, 1870, provided for the selection of a reservation for them, and in 1871 this selection was made in the Cherokee territory west of the ninety-sixth merid-

[32] Report of the Commissioner of Indian Affairs for 1872, *H. Ex. Docs.*, 42 Cong. 3 sess., III, i (1560), 489; map at the end of the letter of the Secretary of the Interior, March 12, 1890, *loc. cit.*, after p. 31.

[33] Report of the Commissioner of Indian Affairs for 1872, *loc. cit.*

[34] Treaty of July 4, 1866, *Statutes*, XIV, 793 (reprinted in Kappler, II, 937). Most of the Delawares, however, settled in the Cherokee country.

[35] Report of the Commissioner of Indian Affairs for 1872, *loc. cit.*

[36] Treaty of September 29, 1865, *Statutes*, XIV, 687 (reprinted in Kappler, II, 878).

RECONSTRUCTION

ian.[37] By an act of June 5, 1872, all the Cherokee territory between the ninety-sixth meridian and the Arkansas River was set apart for the Osage and the Kansas tribes.[38]

The plan of treating with the Indians had been changed during these removals. An act of March 3, 1871, affirmed the validity of all previous obligations, but declared that henceforth no more treaties should be made with the Indian tribes.[39] Accordingly, after that date reservations were set apart by statute or by executive order, and not by agreements with the tribal authorities ratified by the United States Senate.

Few Indians were settled in what is now Oklahoma after 1872. The Commissioner of Indian Affairs in 1876 recommended that more removals should be made and that use should be found for all the land retained in the Indian Territory. He made it clear that it would not be possible to keep a district wholly for the Indians in any other way and that the admission of white persons would soon put an end to all plans for a distinctive Indian community.[40] His successor recommended in 1877 that the Indians of Colorado and New Mexico

37 Act of July 15, 1870, *Statutes*, XVI, 362; report of the Commissioner of Indian Affairs for 1872, *loc. cit.*, 428.

38 *Statutes*, XVII, 228. The Kansas reservation, as cut off from the Osage reservation, was bounded on the north by Kansas and on the west by the Arkansas River. Its south line began at the point where the township line between townships twenty-six and twenty-seven north crosses the Arkansas River, and ran east to a point one and one-half miles east of the range line between ranges four and five east; thence north one mile; thence east two miles; thence the eastern boundary ran due north on the half-section line, three and one-half miles east of the range line between ranges four and five east, to the Kansas state line (letter of the Secretary of the Interior, March 12, 1890, *loc. cit.*, 11).

39 *Statutes*, XVI, 566.

40 J. Q. Smith, *H. Ex. Docs.*, 44 Cong. 2 sess., IV, i (1749), 385-389.

{ 111 }

THE FORMATION OF OKLAHOMA

should be removed to the Indian Territory, and in 1878 he again brought up this subject.[41] Nevertheless, in 1877, through the efforts of Roger Q. Mills, then a representative from Texas, a bill providing for the removal of certain Sioux bands to the Indian Territory was amended so as to forbid the removal of any Sioux thither,[42] and in 1879 representatives from Texas and Kansas succeeded in inserting a provision in the Indian appropriation bill forbidding the removal of the Indians of Arizona and New Mexico to the Indian Territory.[43]

These measures practically put an end to the concentration of the Indians. They were adopted ostensibly because the civilized Indians did not wish to live in proximity to savages, but it can hardly be denied that the wishes of the people of the states surrounding the Indian Territory had much to do with the outcome.[44]

Between 1874 and 1881, however, four small reservations were established in the Cherokee outlet west of the Arkansas, and a small tract east of the Neosho was set apart for the Modoc Indians. In addition, one or two small bands took up their residence in the Indian Territory without definite authorization.

In June, 1874, the Eastern Shawnees gave up to the Modocs a tract of land two and one-half miles square

---

41 E. A. Hayt, *H. Ex. Docs.*, 45 Cong. 2 sess., VIII (1800), 402; 45 Cong. 3 sess., IX (1850), 469.

42 Act of February 28, 1877, *Statutes*, XIX, 254; *Cong. Record*, 44 Cong. 2 sess., 1615-1617.

43 Act of February 17, 1879, *Statutes*, XX, 313; *Cong. Record*, 45 Cong. 3 sess., 311-318.

44 The activity of the representatives from these states in securing these laws indicates this. Compare the report made by Jordan E. Cravens of Arkansas, March 10, 1880, *H. Reports*, 46 Cong. 2 sess., II (1935), no. 474.

RECONSTRUCTION

in the northeastern corner of their diminished reserve.[45] This made seven reservations in the little strip of territory between the Neosho River and the Missouri state line; and in one of these, the Peoria tract, parts of five tribes were settled.

By an act of April 10, 1876, the Pawnees acquired a reservation between the Cimarron and the Arkansas, partly in the Cherokee outlet and partly in the Creek cession of 1866.[46] By acts of August 15, 1876, and March 3, 1877, provision was made for the removal of the Ponca tribe to the Indian Territory;[47] and by an act of May 27, 1878, their reservation was located between the Chikaskia and the Arkansas in territory purchased from the Cherokees.[48] In accordance with the terms of the act of May 27, 1878,[49] a band of Nez Percés was also removed to the Indian Territory. Four townships in the Cherokee outlet were assigned to them.[50] In 1881 it was decided to give the Otoes and

---

45 Act of March 3, 1875, *Statutes*, XVIII, 447. The agreement with the Eastern Shawnees is printed in the report of the Commissioner of Indian Affairs for 1882, *H. Ex. Docs.*, 47 Cong. 2 sess., XI (2100), 331.

46 *Statutes*, XIX, 28. The eastern boundary of the reservation was established at the range line between ranges six and seven east of the Indian meridian. The western boundary followed the range line between ranges four and five from the Cimarron to the township line between townships twenty and twenty-one north, thence ran west six miles, and thence followed the range line between ranges three and four to the Arkansas.

47 *Statutes*, XIX, 192, 287.

48 *Statutes*, XX, 76. An act of March 3, 1881, *Statutes*, XXI, 422, finally confirmed the Ponca reservation. Its northern boundary was fixed at the township line between townships twenty-five and twenty-six north, the eastern boundary at the Arkansas, the southern boundary at the township line between townships twenty-three and twenty-four north, and the western boundary at the Indian meridian (report of the Commissioner of Indian Affairs for 1882, *loc. cit.*, 332).

49 *Statutes*, XX, 74.

50 Townships twenty-five and twenty-six north in the first two ranges west of the Indian meridian (report of the Commissioner of Indian Affairs for 1882, *loc. cit.*, 51).

THE FORMATION OF OKLAHOMA

Missouris a tract in the Cherokee outlet south of the Poncas and west of the Pawnees and the Arkansas River.[51]

Between 1873 and 1875 four hundred Kickapoos, who had gone to Mexico during the Civil War and before, were brought to the Indian Territory, and were placed near the Sac and Fox agency. Just before 1880 the Iowas and other small bands from Kansas and Nebraska began to drift to the central part of the Indian Territory. These Indians all settled on the unassigned land west of the Sac and Fox country.[52]

In 1879 the Indian Territory included twenty-two separate reservations distributed among eight agencies. The members of the several tribes numbered nearly seventy-five thousand, or a few more than one to the square mile. The Chickasaw and the Choctaw freedmen, who had not been adopted in the tribes, numbered respectively twenty-six hundred and four thousand. This made a total of eighty-one thousand, but this number included thirteen thousand freedmen and two thousand five hundred white "adopted citizens."[53] In addition, sixty-two hundred white persons who had not been admitted to tribal citizenship were in the Indian Territory. Of these, twelve hundred were employees of the railroads, and five thousand were

[51] Act of March 3, 1881, *Statutes*, XXI, 380; report of the Commissioner of Indian Affairs for 1882, *loc. cit.*, 331. The southern boundary of the reservation was fixed at the township line between townships twenty-one and twenty-two, and the western boundary at the Indian meridian.

[52] Report of the Commissioner of Indian Affairs for 1875, *H. Ex. Docs.*, 44 Cong. 1 sess., IV, i (1680), 537; of the agent for the Sacs and Foxes for 1880, *H. Ex. Docs.*, 46 Cong. 3 sess., IX (1959), 212; of the agent for the Iowas for 1879, *H. Ex. Docs.*, 46 Cong. 2 sess., IX (1910), 207.

[53] See below, Appendix D.

RECONSTRUCTION

intruders.[54] Of the territory ceded to the United States in 1866 by the Chickasaws and Choctaws, all was assigned except the part west of the North Fork of the Red River, and that was claimed by Texas.[55] Of the territory ceded by the Creeks and the Seminoles in 1866, the eastern part was assigned to the new Seminole reservation and to the reservations for the Sacs and Foxes and for the Shawnees and Pottawatomies; the western part was assigned to the Cheyennes and Arapahoes; but the central part was unassigned. The entire western part of the Cherokee outlet was still in the possession of the Cherokees, and they had begun to sell grazing rights to cattlemen.[56]

The stream of Oklahoma bills continued to 1879,[57] but they were more and more identified with the movement to open the Indian country to white settlement. In January, 1875, the Indians in a series of memorials attacked the United States Board of Indian Commissioners because it favored a better government for the Indian Territory,[58] and accordingly those who were

54 Report of the Senate investigating committee, Patterson report, made February 11, 1879 (*S. Reports*, 45 Cong. 3 sess., III (1839), p. iii). At the time of this report the Missouri, Kansas, and Texas railroad ran across the territory from north to south, and the Atlantic and Pacific, soon the Saint Louis and San Francisco, was in operation from the Missouri state line to Vinita, a distance of thirty-six miles.

55 This claim grew out of a dispute as to which fork of the Red River was made the boundary by the treaty with Spain. See below, Chapter X, footnote 62.

56 See below, p. 122. For area of divisions, see below, Appendix C.

57 See below, Appendix E.

58 Protest of the Chickasaws, *S. Misc. Docs.*, 43 Cong. 2 sess., I (1630), no. 34; of the Cherokees, *ibid.*, no. 66; of the Creeks, *ibid.*, no. 71; of the Osages, *ibid.*, no. 72. These protests called attention to the fact that the chairman of the board was interested in the Atlantic and Pacific railroad. The Osage protest quoted Matthew *iv*, 8, 9, as the first conditional land

THE FORMATION OF OKLAHOMA

especially interested in the Indians practically gave up trying to effect a better organization. The House Committee on Territories in February, 1875, declared in favor of retaining the independent tribal governments as was desired by the tribes.[59] In March, 1876, this committee, to avoid the word "Territory," much disliked by the Indians, proposed to establish a "Province of Oklahoma."[60] The name "Oklahoma" was also in disfavor. It was losing its original signification, and it was no longer applied to the home of the red man, but only to the small district in the central part of the Indian Territory to which no tribe could lay claim.[61] On February 11, 1879, the Senate committee recommended that several important changes should be made in the status of the Indians, but it did not recommend a territorial government for them.[62] On March 3 the House committee presented a report adverse to territorial organization, to the allotment of lands in

---

grant on record: "Again, the devil... sheweth him all the kingdoms of the world, ... and saith unto him, All these things will I give thee, if thou wilt fall down and worship me." This board was established by an act of April 10, 1869 (*Statutes*, XVI, 40), at the suggestion of President Grant, who hoped that it might co-operate with the government in securing a better administration of Indian affairs. By the terms of the act it consisted of ten members "appointed by the president solely, from men eminent for intelligence and philanthropy, and who shall serve without pecuniary compensation." Cf. article by Merrill E. Gates, in Hodge, *Handbook of American Indians*, II, 869.

59 *H. Reports*, 43 Cong. 2 sess., IV (1659), no. 151.

60 *H. Reports*, 44 Cong. 1 sess., I (1708), no. 299. For the bill proposed, see the reprint in *Cong. Record*, 50 Cong. 1 sess., 8125.

61 The unoccupied part of the land ceded by the Creeks and the Seminoles in 1866 was called the "Oklahoma district" for the first time in the official records in the report of Major General John Pope, commander of the Department of the Missouri, for 1880 (*H. Ex. Docs.*, 46 Cong. 3 sess., II (1952), 91). The testimony in the Patterson report (*loc. cit.*), taken in 1878, affords no instance of this use of the word, but it gives evidence of the growing dislike of the Indians for the name Oklahoma (pp. 135, 136).

62 Patterson report, *loc. cit.*, p. v.

severalty, or indeed to any change of importance in the Indian Territory.[63] This report marks the end of the first series of attempts to establish the Territory of Oklahoma.

In April, 1879, an attorney for the Missouri, Kansas, and Texas railroad returned from Washington to his home in Sedalia, Missouri, after the organization of the new Congress in extra session, and announced that if Congress would not open the Indian Territory, the people would.[64] A new period had begun in the history of the Indian Territory.

63 *H. Reports*, 45 Cong. 3 sess., II (1867), no. 188.
64 "The B[ig] I[ndian] T[erritory]. Judge T. C. Sears, direct from Washington, interviewed. He say the Indian Territory will be opened up to white settlers at an early day. The Committee on Territories are in favor of prompt action. If Congress don't open it the people will" (headlines from the Sedalia *Daily Democrat*, April ?, 1879, reprinted in *S. Ex. Docs.*, 46 Cong. 1 sess., I (1869), no. 20, p. 10).

CHAPTER VII

THE BOOMERS

FOR ten years before the opening of the Oklahoma district in 1889, persistent efforts were made by settlers to occupy the unassigned land in the Indian Territory. This movement came naturally soon after the occupation of the best land in Kansas, but other events helped to shape the plan of attack and to fix the time of the first invasion.

On February 17, 1879, the Chicago *Times* published an article on the unoccupied land in the Indian Territory. The article, signed by Elias C. Boudinot, a Cherokee citizen, was copied extensively by other newspapers.[1] Boudinot prepared a letter and a map of the Indian Territory to send out in answer to inquiries about the location of this unoccupied public land. The map indicated that the Kiowa, Comanche, and Apache reservation, the area occupied by the Cheyennes and Arapahoes, and the territory in dispute with Texas, as well as the Oklahoma district, belonged to the public without incumbrance. These included nearly all of the Creek, the Seminole, and the Chickasaw-Choctaw cessions of 1866, but did not include the Cherokee outlet. Boudinot stated explicitly in the accompanying letter that the Cherokees had not ceded any land in the territory to the United States in 1866.[2]

[1] Albert to Boudinot, March 25, 1879, *S. Ex. Docs.*, 46 Cong. 1 sess, I (1869), no 20, p. 5.
[2] For letter and map, see *ibid.*, 8, 26.

THE BOOMERS

In support of his claim that there was unoccupied public land in the Indian Territory, Boudinot professed to quote from the last annual report of the Commissioner of the General Land Office. This report had contained a statement in tabular form of the total number of acres of public land, surveyed and unsurveyed in each state and territory. Boudinot gave this statement of the number of acres of surveyed public land in the Indian Territory as a statement of the number of acres of unoccupied public land. This number was 27,000,000, but Boudinot modestly scaled it down to 13,000,000 and mildly criticized the commissioner for inaccuracy. He ignored the fact that the whole of the Indian Territory had been in this report included in the public domain.[3] The report of the commissioner was quite correct in this, as the Indian country was technically a part of the territory of the United States set aside by law for the use of the Indians.[4]

Boudinot was at that time employed in Washington as clerk of the House Committee on Private Land Claims. He belonged to one of the famous Cherokee families, had been a delegate from the Cherokees to the Confederate Congress, and had played a prominent part in the negotiations at Fort Smith in September, 1865. During the period of reconstruction, he had become well known through his bitter but unsuccessful fight against the extension to the Indians of the internal revenue system without the bestowal of the correspond-

3 *H. Ex. Docs.*, 45 Cong. 3 sess., IX (1850), 222.
4 The United States *vs.* Rogers, 1846, 4 Howard 567.

ing privileges of citizenship. He was disliked by the principal Cherokees because of his advocacy of the Oklahoma bills, and he had recently been in open opposition to the Cherokee officials. He evidently hoped by an agitation about the unoccupied land in the Indian Territory to direct public attention to its condition and to bring about ultimately the chief object of the Oklahoma bills: individual instead of community ownership of land by the Indians, the organization of the Indian Territory, and its opening to white settlers.[5]

Boudinot was and had been in communication with attorneys for the Missouri, Kansas, and Texas railroad,[6] although it is not necessary to assume that he was in their pay. The Missouri, Kansas, and Texas railroad did not approach within forty miles of the area designated by Boudinot as public land, but the opening of a part of the Indian Territory, or even the growth of popular sentiment for the opening of Indian lands, was of value to it. Several railroads were in operation nearly to the territorial line, and they were probably interested in the agitation. Boudinot, in the circular letter already mentioned, had stated impartially the facilities offered by the different railroads for reaching the land described by him. Others seem

[5] Hayt to Schurz, May 10, 1879, *S. Ex. Docs.*, 46 Cong. 1 sess., I (1869), no. 20, p. 2; testimony, April 19, 1878, and arguments, January 17, 1879, of Boudinot in the Patterson report, *S. Reports*, 45 Cong. 3 sess., III (1839), 59, 181, 182, Appendix, 260-285; article by Theodora R. Jenness, in *Atlantic Monthly*, April, 1879 (XLIII, 444); Cherokee Tobacco case, 1870, 11 Wallace 616.

[6] Testimony of G. A. Reynolds, April 19, 1878, in the Patterson report *loc. cit.*, 176, 187; interview of T. C. Sears in the Sedalia *Daily Democrat* sometime in April, 1879, *S. Ex. Docs.*, 46 Cong. 1 sess., I (1869), no. 20, p. 11.

THE BOOMERS

to have been concerned in the matter. A Kansas City newspaper printed a great deal of "news" designed to arouse interest in the Indian Territory. Merchants in the border towns no doubt hoped to gain by the passage of settlers through their communities, and they may have helped to advertise the new country.[7]

The men engaged in this agitation certainly knew that the intercourse act was still in force; but the utter breakdown of the efforts to keep miners out of the Black Hills reservation in South Dakota three years before,[8] followed by the complete surrender of the government,[9] led them to hope for an equally fortunate outcome here.[10] The invasion of Indian lands at this time was not confined to the Indian Territory. The annual report of the Commissioner of Indian Affairs for 1879 contained the following statement: "Intruders have been equally troublesome on other lands. In fact, there is hardly an Indian reservation within the limits

---

[7] McNeil to Hayt, May 4, 1879, *ibid.*, 20. It was said that the *Times*, the newspaper mentioned, was in the pay of the railroads.

[8] Report of Brigadier General George Crook, Department of the Platte, for 1875, *H. Ex. Docs.*, 44 Cong. 1 sess., II, i (1674), 69, 70; for 1876, *H. Ex. Docs.*, 44 Cong. 2 sess., II, i (1742), 498, 500. He said in 1875 that very stringent measures had been taken to keep the miners out of the Black Hills. He showed, however, a very decided sympathy for them. His statement of their point of view is interesting, as it gives the opinion on the frontier of the government's Indian policy: "The settlers who develop our mines and open the frontier to civilization are the nation's wards no less than their more fortunate fellows, the Indians, who are fed, clothed, and maintained in utter idleness by the government they, the settlers, help to support." In Crook's report for 1876, he admitted that the Black Hills were occupied by miners.

[9] The Black Hills district was ceded to the United States in February, 1877 (report of the Secretary of the Interior for 1877, *H. Ex. Docs.*, 45 Cong. 2 sess., VIII (1800), 241).

[10] General Sherman said that Boudinot's map and the weakness of the government in the Black Hills matter were the prime causes of the attempt (*S. Ex. Docs.*, 46 Cong. 1 sess., I (1869), no. 20, p. 27).

of the United States which has not been subject to their encroachment."[11] In at least two reservations, the Malheur reservation in Oregon, and the Pyramid Lake reservation in Nevada, the invaders appear to have been quite successful.[12] As the Indian Territory was the most important reservation in the United States, C. C. Carpenter, the leader of the Black Hills invaders, came to organize the attack on it. He was reported to be in Kansas City early in April, and later in the month he went on to Independence and Coffeyville on the border of the Cherokee country.[13]

The Cherokee officials were greatly alarmed by the threatened invasion. In particular, the officer connected with the collection of rent from the cattlemen took fright,[14] and a very urgent call for aid reached Washington before the end of April. The President responded on April 26 with a proclamation[15] warning all persons that the law would be enforced, even if military power had to be employed. Early in May reports reached the Department of Justice that the movement was widespread and that preparations for invasion were being made along the entire border of Kansas.[16] The agent at the Sac and Fox agency in the heart of the Indian

11 *H. Ex. Docs.*, 46 Cong. 2 sess., IX (1910), 104.
12 Report of the agent at the Malheur reservation for 1879, *ibid.*, 236; report of the Commissioner of Indian Affairs for 1880, *H. Ex. Docs.*, 46 Cong. 3 sess., IX (1959), 93.
13 *Missouri Republican*, sometime in April, 1879, report from Vinita dated April 11, *S. Ex. Docs.*, 46 Cong. 1 sess., I (1869), no. 20, p. 12; McNeil to Hayt, May 4, 1879, *ibid.*, p. 20.
14 L. B. Bell, to "Dear Bill" (apparently W. P. Adair), April 19, 1879, *ibid.*, 5.
15 *Ibid.*, 1.
16 Devens to McCrary, May 3, *ibid.*, 26.

THE BOOMERS

Territory reported, in a letter bearing the date of April 30, that twenty or more wagons, containing chiefly men but also some women and children, had just passed that place.[17] On May 6 the United States attorney at Topeka telegraphed that large numbers of citizens had crossed the border from Baxter Springs and had taken possession of the Quapaw reservation. He said that there was a continued passage of intruders and much excitement, which seemed to be spreading.[18] A day or two later, reports reached the War Department that miners were going into the Wichita Mountains, in which it was said that gold had been discovered.[19]

The situation was met promptly and effectively by the military authorities.[20] A show of force was all that was needed. The squatters on the Quapaw reservation returned to Kansas after staking off their claims,[21] and it is clear that comparatively few had crossed the line at any other place. On May 11 General John Pope reported that the squatters were certainly obeying the law. He stated that in his opinion the whole movement had been organized for the purpose of testing the attitude of the government.[22] If he had added that it was also an effort to arouse popular interest in the Indian Territory, he would have been entirely right. In some quarters the response to this effort was immediate.

17 Woodward to Hayt, *ibid.*, 12.
18 Peck to Devens, *ibid.*, 28.
19 Sheridan to Sherman, May 9, *ibid.*, 32.
20 The orders and resulting activities are given, *ibid.*, 24-31.
21 Sheridan to Townsend, May 9, inclosure, *ibid.*, 33.
22 *Ibid.*, 34.

THE FORMATION OF OKLAHOMA

On April 21, 1879, R. Graham Frost, representative from Missouri, presented to the House a resolution of the Missouri state legislature calling for a better organization of the Indian Territory, and on the same day he introduced a new bill to organize it as the Territory of Oklahoma.[23] On May 5, while the excitement on the border was at its height, James R. Waddill, also a representative from Missouri, introduced a bill directing the Secretary of the Interior to open the unoccupied land in the Indian Territory to settlement under the homestead laws.[24]

As early as January 30, 1878, the Senate had asked for information regarding the unoccupied land of the Indian Territory.[25] On May 14, 1879, the Senate adopted a resolution introduced by George G. Vest of Missouri renewing this inquiry with an added question as to the use that the government expected to make of the land in the Indian Territory not occupied by Indians.[26] In the brief debate upon the resolution, Senator Vest announced that it was his intention soon to introduce a bill to make the Indian Territory a state, and that he would do this in obedience to the instructions of the legislature of Missouri. He declared that the Southwest would not willingly permit this territory to continue as a bar to intercourse and an asylum for vicious and dangerous tribes from other parts of the United States. Accordingly, he gave it as his

23 *Cong. Record*, 46 Cong. 1 sess., 634.
24 *Ibid.*, 1061.
25 *Cong. Record*. 45 Cong. 2 sess., 666.
26 *Cong. Record*, 46 Cong. 1 sess., 1273, 1315.

THE BOOMERS

opinion that it was time to take the preliminary steps leading toward reorganization.[27]

Although General Pope had said that the invasion was checked before the middle of May, activities were reported later. A detachment of cavalry, sent out from Arkansas City, Kansas, on May 26, found several traces of intruders and warned individuals here and there to leave the territory.[28] In particular, this detachment on May 28 arrested James M. Bell, who had established a settlement of fifteen or twenty persons on the Chikaskia River thirty-five miles south of Arkansas City. Bell was a Cherokee citizen, and half of his band were Cherokees. They had started from Vinita[29] in the Cherokee country, but they were acting nominally under the auspices of an organization at Chetopa, Kansas, calling itself "The Indian Territory Colonization Society."[30] Bell and Boudinot belonged to the same faction of the Cherokees, and they were evidently close friends, for shortly after this date they were partners in business.[31]

Persons from Baxter Springs, Kansas, petitioned Congress in the spring of 1879 for a law authorizing them to settle on the Quapaw reservation.[32] These

27 *Ibid.*, 1314.
28 Report of Sergeant J. M. Warren, May 30, *S. Ex. Docs.*, 46 Cong. 1 sess., I (1869), no. 29, p. 3. Compare Bell's testimony before the Senate committee on January 28, 1885, *S. Reports*, 49 Cong. 1 sess., VIII (2362), pt. i, p. 265.
29 L. B. Bell to "Dear Bill," April 19, *S. Ex. Docs.*, 46 Cong. 1 sess., I (1869), no. 20, p. 4.
30 Barrett to Morse, May 29, *ibid.*, 4.
31 Boudinot's testimony before the Senate committee, January 10, 1885, *S. Reports*, 49 Cong. 1 sess., VIII (2362), pt. i, p. 102.
32 The petition was presented in the House on April 5 (*Cong. Record*, 46 Cong. 1 sess., 271; *H. Reports*, 46 Cong. 1 sess., I (1934), no. 13).

petitioners were probably the squatters who staked off claims in the reservation. The local agent of the Quapaws reported on August 27 that the persons who had tried to pre-empt homesteads in the spring had not yet given up hope, but continued to steal in by night to look over their claims and renew their stakes.[33]

Another and less desirable class of settlers had gone into the unoccupied land to stay as long as possible. Late in 1879 the agent in charge of the Pottawatomies and Kickapoos, who were on the eastern border of the Oklahoma district, reported[34] that the Indians were annoyed by a band of at least one hundred lawless men, many of them fugitives from justice. They drove the live stock off the reservations and supplied the Indians with whiskey. It should be added that this gang was captured and deported by a company of soldiers during the following year.[35]

General Philip H. Sheridan, commanding the division, reported[36] on July 28, 1879, that he had had to establish five or six new camps along the border of the Indian Territory to keep out squatters and that these camps would have to be made permanent posts unless Congress should take action. General John Pope, commanding the department, recommended in his annual report for 1879 that the government should consider seriously the reorganization of the Indian Territory on the ground that it could not remain

33 Report for 1879, *H. Ex. Docs.*, 46 Cong. 1 sess., IX (1910), 184.
34 Report of the agent for the Sacs and Foxes for 1879, *ibid.*, 186.
35 Report of the agent for the Sacs and Foxes for 1880, *H. Ex. Docs.*, 46 Cong. 3 sess., IX (1959), 215.
36 *S. Ex. Docs.*, 46 Cong. 2 sess., I (1882), no. 10.

THE BOOMERS

much longer as it was. He added that the attempted invasion of May, 1879, had been easily checked, but that pressure would henceforth become greater all the time.[37]

In February, 1880, information reached Washington that bands were forming in southern Kansas to renew the invasion of the Indian Territory.[38] The promoters represented that the President had changed his mind about the legal status of the Oklahoma district and would not authorize the military authorities to interfere again with prospective settlers. To meet this claim, President Hayes on February 12 issued a second proclamation[39] similar in purport to the one of April, 1879. Carpenter, who had been characterized by an inspector in the Indian service as a "bragging, lying nuisance,"[40] did not appear again, but the movement had found a new and more persistent leader.

This new leader was David L. Payne,[41] who had first appeared in the history of the Indian country as a captain in the Eighteenth Kansas Volunteer Cavalry, summoned in 1867 to assist the regulars in clearing western Kansas of hostile Indians of the Plains Tribes. This regiment of four companies had served for only four months; but a new Indian war began in October, 1868, and Payne became a captain in the Nineteenth

---

37 *H. Ex. Docs.*, 46 Cong. 2 sess., II (1903), 79.
38 Report of the Commissioner of Indian Affairs for 1880, *H. Ex. Docs.*, 46 Cong. 3 sess., IX (1959), 97.
39 *Ibid.*, 97, 323.
40 McNeil to Hayt, May 4, 1879, *S. Ex. Docs.*, 46 Cong. 1 sess., I (1869), no. 20, p. 20.
41 Payne was born near Fairmont, Indiana, in 1836, came to Kansas in 1857, and served in the Union army during the Civil War (Abbott, *History and Civics of Oklahoma*, 169, 170).

THE FORMATION OF OKLAHOMA

Kansas Volunteer Cavalry, which was called into service at that time. This regiment, in company with a regiment of regular cavalry, pursued the Indians nearly across the western part of the Indian Territory in the winter of 1868-69.[42]

In 1878, Payne was in Washington, where he had a place as assistant doorkeeper of the House of Representatives and messenger for the House Committee on Invalid Pensions. During the year he filed two petitions for more pay,[43] and he also secured the introduction in the Senate of a bill[44] to grant him a pension for his services as a volunteer soldier. Success did not attend these efforts, and, to make matters worse, on December 1, 1878, his name was dropped from the list of the employees of the House. He secured permission from the clerk of the committee to continue at his old place with the hope of ultimate reinstatement. He persisted in this plan for four months;[45] but the chance of reinstatement grew less, and Boudinot's agitation regarding the unoccupied land of the Indian Territory, carried on from a near-by committee room, offered a new field for persistency such as his.

On April 1, 1879, just when Carpenter was organizing the first invasion of the Indian Territory, Payne gave up his attempt to be reinstated. He did not neglect, however, to file a claim for four months' services as committee messenger on the strength of his

---

42 Crawford, *Kansas in the Sixties*, 260, 281, 317-336, 405, 431.
43 February 27; June 5 (*Cong. Record*, 45 Cong. 2 sess., 1394, 4170).
44 January 27, 1879 (*Cong. Record*, 45 Cong. 3 sess., 754).
45 *H. Reports*, 46 Cong. 2 sess., I (1934), no. 29.

THE BOOMERS

understanding with the clerk of the committee.[46] Likewise, he had a new private pension bill[47] introduced in the Senate for his benefit. Neither of these attempts was destined to secure results. It is interesting to note, however, that if Payne had succeeded in remaining in the employ of the House of Representatives, he would never have acquired a place in the history of the Southwest as the prince of boomers, nor would an Oklahoma county have borne his name.

Payne's first appearance as leader of a band of settlers was in the spring of 1880. On May 15 he was arrested with eleven companions at a camp forty miles east of Fort Reno and one and one-half miles south of the North Fork of the Canadian River, in the heart of the Oklahoma district;[48] or, according to his theory, he was driven by soldiers from his home in section fourteen, township eleven north, range three west of the Indian meridian.[49] The squatters were discharged as soon as they were removed across the state line. Payne used his freedom to return to his "home" as soon as possible. He was arrested again on July 15 with twenty companions.[50] On this occasion he was turned over to the United States district court at Fort Smith, Arkansas, which according to the law of June 30, 1834, had jurisdiction in the matter.

46 *Ibid.*
47 April 16; *Cong. Record*, 46 Cong. 1 sess., 469; *S. Reports*, 46 Cong. 2 sess., VI (1898), no. 665.
48 Report of the Commissioner of Indian Affairs for 1880, *H. Ex. Docs.*, 46 Cong. 3 sess., IX (1959), 98.
49 *S. Reports*, 49 Cong. 1 sess., IX (2363), Appendix, 61. Payne claimed erroneously that it was within forty miles of the Missouri, Kansas, and Texas railroad.
50 Report of the Commissioner of Indian Affairs for 1880, *loc. cit.*

THE FORMATION OF OKLAHOMA

Payne's case was set for trial at the November term of court, but it did not receive final consideration until May, 1881. The real question at issue was the status of the Oklahoma district. The particular point was the status of the part included in the Seminole cession of 1866, since Payne had squatted south of the North Fork of the Canadian, the boundary between the Creek and the Seminole cessions. Payne claimed that this land was a part of the public domain and open to settlers, while the government claimed that it was still a part of the Indian country and that Payne was an intruder and subject to a fine of one thousand dollars for returning to it after removal. The court decided that the Seminole cession of 1866, because of the implied restrictions in the treaty of conveyance, remained Indian country, although a part of it had not yet been assigned to any Indian tribe. This settled the status of the entire Oklahoma district, since the restrictions implied in the Seminole treaty were stated clearly in the Creek treaty. Accordingly, a penalty of one thousand dollars was assessed against Payne;[51] but, as the method of collecting it had to be by civil action and as he had no property that could be levied upon, this plan of enforcing the law had no terrors for him, and he returned at once to his self-imposed task.[52]

Before the end of 1880, while his case was still undecided, Payne was back on the Kansas border. He ad-

---

51 *Federal Reporter*, VIII, 883.

52 Price to Kirkwood, March 13, 1882, *H. Ex. Docs.*, 47 Cong. 1 sess., XXII (2030), no. 145; report of the Commissioner of Indian Affairs for 1883, *H. Ex. Docs.*, 48 Cong. 1 sess., XI (2191), 18. For a more detailed discussion of this case, see below, Chapter VIII.

THE BOOMERS

vertised extensively that he intended to cross into the Oklahoma district. He was able to assemble a following of several hundred persons on the Kansas line between Arkansas City and Caldwell. Soldiers patrolled the border constantly with orders to shoot the horses of intruders who ventured across the line. This threat held the intruders in check, and the cold weather caused them to disperse early in January. In the summer and fall of 1881 it became apparent that Payne was at the head of an organization of considerable importance. Moreover, a new report of the discovery of precious metals in the Wichita Mountains furnished added attractions for the intruder.[53]

Payne's efforts during 1882 were much like those of the preceding years, but he was evidently not very successful. In that year he brought suit for damages against General John Pope, commander of the Department of the Missouri, and about the same time he brought a similar suit against an officer who had escorted him to Fort Smith.[54] He must have been very active in 1883, for Pope reported that the whole affair had become simply a series of processions to and from the Kansas line.[55] A large expedition left Arkansas City in February of that year for the Oklahoma district. According to the official reports[56] to the War Department, this company included two hundred and fifty persons,

53 Pope's report for 1881, *H. Ex. Docs.*, 47 Cong. 1 sess., II (2010), 114.
54 Pope's report for 1882, *H. Ex. Docs.*, 47 Cong. 2 sess., II (2091), 98 See also the brief of papers showing action of the War Department (*S. Ex. Docs.*, 48 Cong. 2 sess., II [i] (2263), no. 50, p. 5).
55 *H. Ex. Docs.*, 48 Cong. 1 sess., II (2182), 130.
56 Cited by the Commissioner of Indian Affairs in his annual report for 1883, *H. Ex. Docs.*, 48 Cong. 1 sess., XI (2191), 19.

THE FORMATION OF OKLAHOMA

twenty of them women and children, with about one hundred wagons filled with provisions, tents, furniture, and farming tools. Companies from Coffeyville and Caldwell started at the same time to join the main body. There were indications that many of these persons were quiet, well-to-do farmers, but all were supplied with arms, chiefly rifles and carbines.

This colony, numbering in all four or five hundred persons, settled on the Deep Fork, in what is now Lincoln County, but the colonists were left alone for only a few days. They were taken across the Kansas line to Arkansas City and Caldwell and released.[57] In June, Payne applied to the United States circuit court at Topeka for an injunction restraining military interference with his entrance into and possession of the Oklahoma district.[58] In July a new company was collected at Arkansas City, and in August one hundred and fifty persons crossed the line, but they were arrested at Camp Russell on the Cimarron River. At least two other invasions were attempted later in 1883.[59]

By this time the enterprise had been organized as Payne's Oklahoma Colony. Payne was president, and there were also a secretary and a treasurer. During the greater part of the time the membership fee was fixed at two dollars and a half. Payne retained two dollars of this for the colony, and the remainder went to the secretary "for recording claims." The form of certificate of membership was as follows:

57 W. L. Couch's testimony before the Senate committee, June 6, 1885 (*S. Reports*, 49 Cong. 1 sess., IX (2363), 437-440).
58 Report of the Commissioner of Indian Affairs for 1883, *loc. cit.*, 19.
59 Couch's testimony, *loc. cit.*, 437-440.

THE BOOMERS

[Captain D. L. Payne, president; Hon. J. M. Steele, treasurer; W. H. Osburn, secretary.]

CERTIFICATE OF MEMBERSHIP

Office of Payne's Oklahoma Colony

Wichita, Kans.,............, 188....

This certifies that........................, having paid the fee of two dollars, is a member of Payne's Oklahoma Colony, is entitled to all the benefits and protection of said colony and an equal voice in all matters pertaining to and the formation of its local government.

In testimony whereof the official signatures of the president and secretary are hereto subscribed, and the seal of the colony attached.

....................., ...,[60]
      Secretary   *President*

This certificate of membership in Payne's colony was supposed to secure for the holder the protection of that body in retaining his homestead. No member of the colony would be permitted to settle on a claim already staked off by another member, and it was understood that persons who were not members would be allowed to settle only on land that had not been chosen by or for those who had paid for it. In other words, the colony was to become a vigilance committee to protect the rights of its members in an extra-legal, not to say illegal way. It was of course understood that the holder of a certificate must go through the usual process to secure the title for his land from the government as soon as the country had been opened to settlement under the homestead law.

[60] For the facts concerning the Oklahoma Colony, see the report of the Commissioner of Indian Affairs for 1883, *loc. cit.*, 19; and Couch's testimony, *loc. cit.*, 438, 440, 441, 453-457. Both Couch's testimony and Hatch's statement, cited below, indicate that an organization had existed as early as 1880.

THE FORMATION OF OKLAHOMA

Some evidence exists that a person who did not wish to go across the border line until the country was regularly opened to settlement arranged with the colony to select a farm or town lots for him. The colony agreed to protect this selection from other claimants until the one for whom it had been made found it convenient to take possession of it. The fee in this case was said to have been as much as twenty-five dollars. Some such plan must have been in use, as Payne's successor said that, although he had been an active member of the colony only since February, 1883, he had been financially interested in the Oklahoma enterprise since 1880.

The income from these sources must have been fairly large, especially as the fee for active membership was raised for a time to six dollars.[61] Colonel Edward Hatch, in command of the new military district of Oklahoma, estimated that Payne had collected one hundred thousand dollars in fees of one sort or another between 1880 and 1884. Hatch declared that Payne and the other leaders did not want the Oklahoma district opened to settlement because that would put an end to their profits.[62]

Payne made his last and perhaps most stubborn attempts in 1884. He collected a band of five or six hundred persons at Hunnewell on the Kansas line. By this time the men were not only well armed, but they were threatening to resist arrest. In May a party of fifty succeeded in getting as far south as the Cimarron,

---

61 Couch's testimony, *loc. cit.*, 438, 453. Couch said that the money was spent for "attorney's fees, stationery, postage, printing, and in carrying our mail when we are in the [Oklahoma] country."

62 Brief of papers showing action of the War Department, *loc. cit.*, 5.

THE BOOMERS

but they were driven back by the cavalry. The main invasion came in June, and settlements were made at Rock Falls on the Chikaskia, four or five miles south of the state line, and on the Bois d'Arc. Many of the colonists returned to Kansas when warned by Colonel Hatch, and the others were arrested on August 7. The women and children and most of the men were released as usual, but Payne and a few other old offenders were turned over to the United States court. Payne was released, apparently on his own recognizance, and was back in Hunnewell reorganizing his colony before the soldiers who had taken him to Fort Smith could return. By the beginning of October, the colonists, or "boomers,"[63] as they were called in the official reports from this time, were parading with banners inscribed, "On to Oklahoma," "Oklahoma forever," "We go this time to stay." It was even said Payne made incendiary speeches. In these it was claimed that he advised "burning the country" and "bushwhacking" if the opposition continued. Payne died suddenly in November, but the boomers went on with the expedition which he had organized.[64]

---

[63] Brigadier General Wesley Merritt, commanding the Department of the Missouri thus explained this word in his report for 1889 (*H. Ex. Docs.*, 51 Cong. 1 sess., II (2715), 165): "These movements have been attended by much agitation in various ways, 'booming,' in the parlance of the day, the country—exaggerating its advantages as an agricultural and as a mining country. Persons engaged in the agitation, as well as those who entered the territory, were known as 'boomers.' " The term "boomer," however, finally came to include only those who sought to enter the territory.

[64] Report of Brigadier General C. C. Augur, Department of the Missouri, for 1884, *H. Ex. Docs.*, 48 Cong. 2 sess., II (2277), 118; report of the Commissioner of Indian Affairs for 1884, *H. Ex. Docs.*, 48 Cong. 2 sess., XII (2287), 3; Couch's testimony, *loc. cit.*, 441; the brief of papers showing action of the War Department, *loc. cit.*, 5.

THE FORMATION OF OKLAHOMA

W. L. Couch, one of Payne's lieutenants, was selected as the new leader;[65] and in December, 1884, armed bands began to cross into the Indian Territory. Several groups of stragglers were captured and deported by the cavalry on December 1, 2, 3, 4, and 7, but the larger part of the invaders succeeded in reaching the northeastern corner of the Oklahoma district. By the end of the month it was officially reported to the War Department that the intruders numbered four hundred, including a very few women and children, and that they were sheltered in small excavations in the sand hills on the north side of the Cimarron. Their principal camp was on Stillwater Creek, and a detachment of thirty soldiers under a lieutenant was sent to arrest Couch and take him from this camp. The detachment found itself confronted by two hundred determined men armed with rifles and double-barrelled shotguns, and a retreat was hastily ordered.

By the middle of January three hundred and seventy-five men were gathered at the boomer camp known as Stillwater. Opposed to the boomers were three hundred and fifty soldiers of the Ninth Cavalry under Colonel Hatch. They were stationed at Camp Russell on the Cimarron a few miles west of Stillwater, near the mouth of Ephraim Creek. On January 20 orders were sent from Washington to arrest the intruders even if it should be necessary to shed blood. Three hundred additional soldiers were ordered to the border from Fort

---

65 Couch's testimony, *loc. cit.*, 441. Cooper, Miller, and Eichelberger are mentioned as other leaders (report of the Commissioner of Indian Affairs for 1884, *loc. cit.*, 3).

THE BOOMERS

Leavenworth, in order that the hopelessness of resistance might become apparent to the boomers. A communication was sent to Couch notifying him of these preparations. He replied that he had four hundred men and they expected to fight. Thus it seemed for a few days that a contest could not be avoided; but snow and cold weather made the transportation of reinforcements difficult, and Colonel Hatch adopted a plan that was better than fighting. He ordered his troops to move into position north of the camp of the boomers, that is, between it and the Kansas line. This cut off supplies and stopped new arrivals, and in a very few days the boomers were starved out and compelled to surrender.[66]

This was the last serious invasion of Oklahoma. On March 3, 1885, Congress took action that meant the ultimate opening of the unoccupied land of the Indian Territory. The Indian appropriation act passed on that day contained a section that authorized negotiations with the Creeks, the Seminoles, and the Cherokees for the purchase outright of the unoccupied lands to which they had claims.[67] The real work of the boomers was done, although their activities did not cease altogether until the opening of Oklahoma in April, 1889.

[66] Brief of papers showing action of the War Department, *loc. cit.*, 7, 8; report of Brigadier-General Nelson A. Miles, Department of the Missouri, for 1885, *H. Ex. Docs.*, 49 Cong. 1 sess., II (2369), 155; Couch's testimony, *loc. cit.*, 441.
[67] *Statutes*, XXIII, 384.

CHAPTER VIII

HOW THE BOOMERS WON

THE incorporation in the Indian appropriation act of March 3, 1885, of a section authorizing the purchase of the Oklahoma district and the Cherokee outlet was the first victory of the boomers. To understand the conditions that made this victory possible it is necessary to study the peculiarities in the law dealing with intruders on Indian lands and to examine the popular and political support that the boomers had in their campaign.

The government failed to stop the invasion of the Oklahoma district because the statutes intended to protect the Indian country, as interpreted by the courts, were found to be practically without a penalty for their violation. In spite of the efforts of the executive department, Congress did not strengthen the statutes to meet the conditions. The course of the boomer agitation can not be understood without a knowledge of the difficulties that had to be met in the enforcement of the law.

A clause in the act of June 30, 1834, the intercourse act, had provided that intruders should be removed from the Indian country by military force if necessary. In order to strengthen this law, a section in the Indian appropriation act of 1856 provided that an intruder who returned to the Indian country after removal should be subject to a penalty of one thousand dollars. In the compilation of the revised statutes in 1873, this

HOW THE BOOMERS WON

section was placed under "Title XXVIII, Indians," together with the act of 1834 and other laws relating to the Indians and their lands. One section under Title XXVIII, taken from the law of 1834, reads as follows: "All penalties which shall accrue under this Title shall be sued for and recovered in an action in the nature of an action of debt."[1] In Payne's case the court decided that the penalty for returning to the Indian country after removal could be collected only by civil action.

Judgment in a civil suit was given against Payne for the first time at Fort Smith in May, 1881. As he had no property that could be levied upon, and as he could not be imprisoned for debt, he was practically immune from civil action.[2] On January 6, 1883, Congress amended the section in the act of 1834 by which the whole of the Indian Territory had been administered as a part of the western district of Arkansas. The territory set apart for and occupied by the Five Civilized Tribes remained under the jurisdiction of the court at Fort Smith, but the country lying west of the territory occupied by these tribes was divided between the district of Kansas and the northern district of Texas, with the Canadian as the boundary between them.[3] As this transferred the area known as Oklahoma to the

---

[1] Sections 2147 and 2148 of the *Revised Statutes* are from the intercourse act of 1834, whose passage has been discussed above, in Chapter II; section 2124 is from the act of August 18, 1856, *Statutes* XI, 80. Section 2118 under Title XXVIII, taken from the act of 1834, provided for a penalty of one thousand dollars for making a settlement in the Indian country. This would have authorized a suit against a boomer on his first intrusion, but, as will appear, no effort was made to enforce this section alone.

[2] Price to Kirkwood, March 13, 1882, *H. Ex. Docs.*, 47 Cong. 1 sess., XXII (2030), no. 145. Cf. *Nation*, June 1, 1882 (XXXIV, 453).

[3] *Statutes*, XXII, 400.

district of Kansas, an effort was made to prosecute the boomers as criminals in the United States district court at Wichita. Payne and others were charged with conspiring together to return to the Indian country after they had been removed from it. The court quashed the indictment on December 11, 1884, and decided that civil suit only could be brought against the boomers.[4]

The United States district court at Fort Smith still claimed jurisdiction over the Cherokee outlet, on the ground that it was a part of the territory set apart for and occupied by the Five Civilized Tribes.[5] This accounts for the fact that boomers were sometimes taken to Fort Smith after January, 1883. Apparently, if they were apprehended on their way through the Cherokee outlet, the court at Fort Smith still claimed jurisdiction over them; but if they succeeded in reaching the Oklahoma district before arrest, their cases had to be heard at Wichita. Couch admitted in 1885 that at Fort Smith there were three hundred and sixty-five judgments against the boomers, with eight hundred suits still pending at Wichita.[6]

It was not the fault of the executive department that the law relating to trespass on Indian lands was not amended. As early as 1880, the acting commissioner of Indian affairs, E. M. Marble, recommended in his

4 *Federal Reporter*, XXII, 426.

5 United States *vs.* Rogers, 1885, *Federal Reporter*, XXIII, 658. The United States circuit court decided in 1887 (United States *vs.* Soule, *Federal Reporter*, XXX, 918) that the Cherokee outlet, while it had been set apart for the Cherokees and was owned by them, was not occupied by them in the sense meant by Congress, and that it was therefore within the jurisdiction of the district of Kansas.

6 Couch's testimony before Senate committee, June 6, 1885; *S. Reports*, 49 Cong. 1 sess., IX (2363), 460.

annual report that the law should be revised, as it had become "practically a dead letter."[7] In his messages of March 29, 1882, and December 10, 1883, President Arthur recommended the passage of an act that would authorize the criminal prosecution of trespassers on Indian land.[8] Two bills embodying the recommendation passed the Senate—one on April 24, 1884, and one on February 24, 1885[9]—but neither of them passed the House of Representatives. During the Cleveland administration the boomer raids were not so serious, but the President on December 21, 1885, and again on January 4, 1888, recommended a bill similar to the one asked for by his predecessor.[10] The Senate on February 17, 1886, complied with this recommendation,[11] but, as in previous years, the House did not act. On March 3, 1888, after President Cleveland's second message requesting action, the House Committee on Indian Affairs went so far as to report favorably[12] upon a bill drawn to meet the wishes of the executive department; but the bill got no further, and congressional action in the matter was never taken.

It is a noteworthy fact that, except in the application of the law to the Indian Territory at this time, the courts have held that intruders who return to the Indian country after removal are subject to criminal

---

7 *H. Ex. Docs.*, 46 Cong. 3 sess., IX (1959), 93.
8 *H. Ex. Docs.*, 47 Cong. 1 sess., XXII (2030), no. 145; *H. Ex. Docs.*, 48 Cong. 1 sess., XIII (2193), no. 17.
9 *Cong. Record*, 48 Cong. 1 sess., 3283, 3334; 2 sess., 2063.
10 *S. Ex. Docs.*, 49 Cong. 1 sess., I (2333), no. 14; *S. Ex. Docs.*, 50 Cong. 1 sess., I (2504), no. 41.
11 *Cong. Record*, 49 Cong. 1 sess., 1556.
12 *H. Reports*, 50 Cong. 1 sess., III (2600), no. 839.

prosecution. In 1883, in the midst of Payne's activities, the United States circuit court in an Oregon case decided[13] that the inclusion of the law of 1856 under Title XXVIII did not prevent the enforcement of its provisions by criminal action; and, in a case heard in 1898 in the United States district court for the district of Montana, the court reaffirmed this decision and established it by facts and arguments that seem conclusive.[14]

The members of Payne's colony found it easy to believe that Payne really had justice on his side, as the courts always failed to hold him. The military authorities in their reports called attention to the respect of the would-be colonists for the law, and, according to contemporary opinion, the rank and file of the boomers thought that they were acting within their rights. Complaints were heard on the floor of the United States Senate regarding the wrong impressions created by garbled reports of the judicial decisions.[15] To aid in confirming these wrong impressions, Payne boldly brought suit against the officers of the army and even applied for an injunction to protect him and his colony in their rights.[16] Couch, the successor of Payne, according to his statement to a congressional committee,

---

13 United States *vs.* Howard, *Federal Reporter*, XVII, 638.

14 United States *vs.* Stocking, *Federal Reporter*, LXXXVII, 857.

15 Pope's report for 1880, *H. Ex. Docs.*, 46 Cong. 3 sess., II (1952), 91; same for 1881, *H. Ex. Docs.*, 47 Cong. 1 sess., II (2010), 114; report of the Commissioner of Indian Affairs for 1884, *H. Ex. Docs.*, 48 Cong. 2 sess., XII (2287), 32; *Cong. Record*, 48 Cong. 2 sess., 916-920, 2063.

16 Pope's report for 1882, *H. Ex. Docs.*, 47 Cong. 2 sess., II (2091), 98, 99; report of the Commissioner of Indian Affairs for 1883, *H. Ex. Docs.*, 48 Cong. 1 sess., XI (2191), 19.

ignored the President's proclamation because the courts, which were above the President, had decided that the Oklahoma district was not Indian country. He claimed also that he was ready to go before a court at any time.[17] This latter assertion was probably true so far as a civil case was concerned. Couch had sold several farms in Kansas and disposed of all his live stock before or just after joining the boomers in February, 1883, and these transfers undoubtedly helped him to face with equanimity a civil judgment in favor of the United States.[18]

Many of the boomers understood that their position was technically illegal; but they professed to believe that this was true only because the Oklahoma district had not been opened to settlement by the formal action of Congress, and they tried to justify themselves by claiming that much of the Western country had been settled in technical violation of the law.[19] They thought that the government ought to be able to stop the invasions if they were really illegal. As Couch put it, "the trifling of the authorities" convinced them "that the government did not have a good case."[20]

The boomers were neither ordinary lawbreakers nor idlers. Most of them were farmers who wanted free land, and as a rule they were industrious, well-meaning people. They had religious services in camp, and drunkenness among them was practically unknown. It

17 Couch's testimony, *loc. cit.*, 441, 442; cf. 460.
18 *Ibid.*, 438.
19 See below, Appendix F. first petition. For evidence that these claims had some basis, see below, Appendix G.
20 Couch's testimony, *loc. cit.*, 460.

THE FORMATION OF OKLAHOMA

was not altogether clear at the time how they supported themselves on the border; but they were willing to work between expeditions, and many of them found employment in Caldwell and Arkansas City. As each head of a family was equipped with a pair of horses and a stout wagon, the men could engage in hauling; and in particular some were occupied in transporting supplies for the soldiers whose presence on the border they themselves made necessary.[21]

The belief that the cattlemen were wrongly enjoying the use of unoccupied Indian lands brought popular support to the boomer agitation. The Cherokees had sold grazing rights on the Cherokee outlet for several years, and in July, 1883, they leased the whole tract, in all six million acres, to a company called the Cherokee Strip Live Stock Association, which in turn sublet to smaller companies. This lease was for a term of five years, and the annual rental agreed upon was one hundred thousand dollars. This rental was so low that it lent support to the charge in the Cherokee legislature of bribery in awarding the contract. Other Indian lands were leased for grazing purposes for an annual rental of two or three cents an acre.[22] The power of the Indians to grant leases was ill defined, and the Secretary of the Interior refused either to

[21] Lieutenant Colonel N. A. M. Dudley's testimony before the Senate committee, June 6, 1885, *S. Reports*, 49 Cong. 1 sess., IX (2363), 461; Lieutenant Gonzales S. Bingham's testimony at the same time, *ibid.*, 463; Couch's testimony, *loc. cit.*, 444.

[22] Testimony and documents in the report of the Committee on Indian Affairs, June 6, 1886, *S. Reports*, 49 Cong. 1 sess., VIII (2362), pt. i, pp. 98, 130, 277-308, 312, 313. See also letter of the Secretary of the Interior regarding leases, January 3, 1885, *S. Ex. Docs.*, 48 Cong. 2 sess., I [i] (2261), no. 17, pp. 12-15.

HOW THE BOOMERS WON

approve or disapprove the contracts. The position of the leaseholders was somewhat uncertain, but they at least were presumed to have the consent of the Indians to remain in the Indian country.[23] It is easy to see that these agreements placed the claims of the cattlemen on a different basis from those of the boomers, but to many persons at the time an annual payment of a cent or two an acre was an insufficient margin of difference.

The occupation of the Oklahoma district by cattlemen was a special cause of complaint. The district belonged to the United States, subject only to certain restrictions upon its use, and no Indian tribe had the right to lease or otherwise utilize any part of it. The government of course did not lease it to any company, but the cattlemen who pastured their herds on its borders took possession of the whole district at times.[24] This occupation was quite different from the right of permanent settlement claimed by the boomers, and the government naturally viewed it with less alarm. The Secretary of the Interior in July, 1883, advised the military authorities not to concern themselves about temporary encroachments of this character.[25] The boomers declared that the soldiers made no effort to

[23] Teller to Fenlon, April 25, 1883, *S. Ex. Docs.*, 48 Cong. 1 sess., IV (2165), no. 54, p. 99.
[24] Tufts to Price, March 5 and May 21, 1884, *S. Ex. Docs.*, 48 Cong. 2 sess., I, [i] (2261), no. 17, p. 90. Cattle were driven slowly from range to range or to the railroad or market, as they had to pasture on the way. It is easy to understand that the cattlemen lingered as long as possible in the Oklahoma district, or indeed that on the pretext of passing through it they virtually made it a part of the range.
[25] Teller to Lincoln, July 10, *S. Ex. Docs.*, 48 Cong. 1 sess., IV (2165), no. 54, p. 30.

THE FORMATION OF OKLAHOMA

restrain the cattlemen; but this statement was hardly true, as efforts were made to keep the Oklahoma district clear of all intruders. It was even more difficult, however, to control the cattlemen, who had some rights in the Indian Territory, than the boomers, who had no rights across the state line.[26]

On the whole, public opinion in the Middle West ran strongly in favor of the boomers. A resolution of the Illinois legislature adopted in February, 1885, asked Congress to interfere in the strife between the cattlemen and the people who wanted homes in that part of the Indian Territory known as Oklahoma and to open the land in question to homestead entry. When this memorial was read in the Senate, the chairman of the Committee on Indian Affairs, Henry L. Dawes of Massachusetts, declared that he received newspapers every day from Illinois, Missouri, and Kansas complaining because Congress did not act.[27] The military authorities, it should be noted, were still convinced that the agitation was given financial aid by "interested corporations," and such an expression could refer only to the railroads.[28] Thus accusation was met with accusation. Those who tried to safeguard the rights of the Indians were charged with aiding the cattlemen, and those who sympathized with the boomers were

26 Couch's testimony, *loc. cit.*, 445-448; Lieutenant Bingham's testimony, *loc. cit.*, 463.

27 This memorial was presented on February 24 (*Cong. Record*, 48 Cong. 2 sess., 2062). Numerous petitions were received by Congress asking for the opening of the unoccupied land in the Indian Territory; some of them opposed the use of the army to keep out the boomers (*Cong. Record*, 48 Cong. 1 sess., 331, 650, 906, 1639, 1884, 4494; 4094, 2 sess., 348, 792, 1072, 1191, 1244, 1447). For a sample petition, see below, Appendix F, second petition.

28 Sheridan's report for 1885, *H. Ex. Docs.*, 49 Cong. 1 sess., II (2369), 60.

HOW THE BOOMERS WON

said to be in the pay of the railroads. The growing strength of the boomers was reflected in Congress, and those who wished to retain the Indian Territory intact were soon in the minority. The contest in Washington for the opening of the unoccupied Indian lands ran parallel with the boomer agitation on the border.

As has been seen, efforts were made in 1879 by Senator Vest and others of the Missouri delegation in Congress to secure a reorganization of the Indian Territory. The Senate Committee on Territories on March 4, 1880, reported a bill by Vest that gave any Indian in the Indian Territory the right to become a citizen of the United States, in which case he could demand his share of the tribal property. This bill proposed a system of United States courts in the Indian Territory and contained provisions for the allotment of lands in severalty and the abolition of Indian citizenship. It failed to receive serious consideration in either house, although Representative Frost succeeded in having it reported on April 6, 1880, by the House Committee on Territories as a substitute for his bill to organize the Territory of Oklahoma.[29]

The boomer agitation brought forth a number of bills proposing the allotment in severalty of Indian lands. Five or six such bills were introduced in the Forty-Sixth Congress. One of them was reported favorably by the House Committee on Indian Affairs on May 12, 1880, and the Senate committee a week later reported a similar bill, which, however, did not

---

29 *Cong. Record*, 46 Cong. 2 sess., 1298; *H. Reports*, 46 Cong. 2 sess., III (1936), no. 755.

THE FORMATION OF OKLAHOMA

apply to the Indian Territory.[30] Vest succeeded in having the Senate bill amended to apply to all Indians except those of the Five Civilized Tribes.[31] This bill did not become a law, and none of the others met with better success. For some time after this, no special legislation was proposed for the Indian Territory except a new bill to establish the Territory of Oklahoma, which was introduced on January 9, 1882.[32]

During the next few years attempts were made to find a use for the unoccupied Indian lands without sacrificing the integrity of the Indian Territory. The Secretary of the Interior had announced on May 26, 1879, in answer to the Vest resolution of inquiry, that it was the settled policy of the government to maintain the Indian Territory intact.[33] The settlement of the Oklahoma district by freedmen was seriously considered. It was even proposed to bring in negroes from the surrounding states, as the treaties that restricted the use of this district to Indians and their freedmen were supposed by some to allow its occupation by any freedmen.

In 1881 a "Freedmen's Oklahoma Association" had

30 Senate Bill 423, by William B. Allison of Iowa, April 15, 1879, *Cong. Record*, 46 Cong. 1 sess., 434; House Bill 354, by Alfred M. Scales of North Carolina, April 21, *ibid.*, 615; Senate Bill 584, by Algernon S. Paddock of Nebraska, May 12, *ibid.*, 1238; Senate Bill 989, by Alvin Saunders of Nebraska, January 12, 1880, *Cong. Record*, 46 Cong., 2 sess., 274; House Bill 5038, by Scales for the Committee on Indian Affairs, March 8, *ibid.*, 1394, reported May 12, *ibid.*, 3278 (cf. *H. Reports*, 46 Cong. 2 sess., V (1938), no. 1576); Senate Bill 1773, by Richard Coke of Texas for the Committee on Indian Affairs, May 19, *Cong. Record*, 46 Cong. 2 sess., 3507.

31 January 24, 1881; *Cong. Record*, 46 Cong. 3 sess., 779, 875.

32 Senate Bill 761, by Edward H. Rollins of New Hampshire; *Cong. Record*, 47 Cong. 1 sess., 265.

33 Carl Schurz; *S. Ex. Docs.*, 46 Cong. 1 sess., I (1869), no. 26.

been formed similar to Payne's Oklahoma Colony, and perhaps it had similar objects. Boudinot's circular of 1879 was quoted by the originators of this scheme as evidence of the existence of land suitable for colonization.[34] In 1882 petitions reached Congress from negroes living in "Kansas and other states" asking that they should be allowed to settle in the unoccupied land of the Indian Territory and form organized communities of their own.[35]

On June 13, 1882, Henry W. Blair, senator from New Hampshire, addressed a communication to the Secretary of the Interior requesting information as to the land in the Indian Territory available for occupation by negroes.[36] Without waiting for a reply to his inquiry, he introduced on June 16 a bill to authorize freedmen to enter certain unoccupied land in the Indian Territory.[37] In July, however, he received a letter from the Secretary of the Interior stating that only the freedmen of the Five Civilized Tribes were entitled to the use of this land and that freedmen in general had no more right in the Indian Territory than other citizens of the United States.[38] This opinion was supported by the decision of the court in the case against Payne in May, 1881, as, in passing on one of the claims of Payne, the court had passed on the meaning

---

34 Holcomb to Kirkwood, April 25, 1881, *S. Ex. Docs.*, 47 Cong. 1 sess., V (1990), no. 111.

35 Blair to Teller, June 13, 1882, *S. Misc. Docs.*, 47 Cong. 1 sess., IV (1996), no. 117.

36 *Ibid.*

37 *Cong. Record*, 47 Cong. 1 sess., 4994.

38 Teller to Blair, July 8, inclosure, *S. Misc. Docs.*, 47 Cong. 1 sess., IV (1996), no. 117.

of the term "freedmen" as used in the treaties of 1866. Accordingly, Blair's bill did not receive further consideration.

The plan of using the unoccupied land of the Indian Territory for the colonization of the freedmen of the Five Civilized Tribes met the approval of the secretary of the interior, Henry M. Teller of Colorado, and his commissioner of Indian Affairs, H. Price. The freedmen of the Chickasaws had been promised in 1866 that either they should be made Indian citizens or they should be removed to land of their own. This promise had not been kept. The other freedmen in the Indian Territory also had grievances.[39] It was hoped that the removal of these freedmen to the Oklahoma district would satisfy them and at the same time afford a use for the unoccupied land in the Indian Territory in keeping with treaty stipulations. It may be assumed that it was also planned to foil the boomers in this way.[40]

Commissioner Price and Secretary Teller succeeded in getting President Arthur to send a special message to Congress recommending an appropriation to enable them to place the freedmen of the Five Civilized Tribes and their descendants in the "Oklahoma district in the Indian Territory." This message, sent on January 14, 1884, simply renewed a recommendation that the department had already made directly to Congress on February 28, 1883. The message gave some details of

---

[39] Report of the Committee on Indian Affairs, June 4, 1886, *S. Reports*, 49 Cong. 1 sess., VIII (2362), p. xxv. The Choctaw freedmen were made citizens in 1883 (report of the Commissioner of Indian Affairs for 1884, *H. Ex. Docs.*, 48 Cong. 2 sess., XII (2287), 36).

[40] Report of the Commissioner of Indian Affairs for 1883, *H. Ex. Docs.*, 48 Cong. 1 sess., XI (2191), 45.

the plan. One hundred and sixty acres of land were to be alloted to each head of a family, eighty acres to each single man over twenty-one, and eighty acres to each minor orphan. Congress did not act upon this recommendation, and accordingly the possibility of a negro state in the heart of the Indian Territory passed away.[41]

Meanwhile, the unoccupied land had been diminished by executive action. For several years about four hundred Kickapoos, known as the Mexican Kickapoos, had been camped in the eastern part of the Oklahoma district. Just north of them across the Deep Fork were eighty-five or ninety Iowas. These Indians asked for definite reservations. The President, by two executive orders dated August 15, 1883, set aside for them the area bounded on the north by the Cimarron, on the east by the Sac and Fox reservation, on the south by the North Fork of the Canadian, and on the west by the Indian meridian. The Deep Fork was made the boundary between the new reservations.[42]

In this year Granville H. Oury, delegate from Arizona, introduced a bill providing for the removal of the Indians of his territory to the Indian Territory. As Congress had already decided against this, his proposition did not receive consideration.[43]

In January, 1884, the Senate Committee on Indian

41 The message appears in *S. Ex. Docs.*, 48 Cong. 1 sess., IV (2165), no. 51. It was proposed in 1888 to remove the Chickasaw freedmen to the Oklahoma district (*S. Ex. Docs.*, 50 Cong. 1 sess., X (2513), no. 166, pp. 7, 9). Cf. *Cong. Record*, 50 Cong. 1 sess., 4663.

42 Report of the Commissioner of Indian Affairs for 1883, *loc. cit.*, 45, 142-145, 281.

43 December 11, 1883, *Cong. Record*, 48 Cong. 1 sess., 121.

THE FORMATION OF OKLAHOMA

Affairs brought in a report adverse to the opening of the Oklahoma district to homestead entry. This report was not made on any pending measure, but was in answer to the numerous petitions from the West and especially from the boomers. Although it was a conservative statement of the restrictions on the title of the United States to the unoccupied land, it seems to have been the last report made in Congress assuming that the integrity of the Indian Territory could be maintained.[44]

The first indication that Congress was becoming interested again in the Indian Territory was the adoption by the Senate on December 4, 1883, of a request for information regarding leases of Indian lands.[45] From the information furnished by the Secretary of the Interior, it was apparent that many Indians were dissatisfied with the leasing system, and each house authorized its Committee on Indian Affairs to investigate the whole matter. The Senate later extended the powers of its committee to enable it to investigate conditions in general in the Indian Territory. Time was given for a thorough study of the conditions, and a report was not asked for until the first session of the Forty-ninth Congress, beginning in December, 1885.[46]

[44] The report was made on January 22 (*S. Reports*, 48 Cong. 1 sess., I (2173), no. 64)

[45] *Cong. Record*, 48 Cong. 1 sess., 19, 370, the information is given in a letter of the Secretary of the Interior, January 12, 1884, *S. Ex. Docs.*, 48 Cong. 1 sess., IV (2165), no. 54.

[46] The Senate committee was authorized on February 26, 1884; the House committee on May 31; the Senate committee's powers were increased and its time extended by resolutions of June 11 and December 3, 1884, and February 23, 1885 (*Cong. Record*, 48 Cong. 1 sess., 1341, 1377, 4711, 4998; 2 sess., 11, 35, 2004).

HOW THE BOOMERS WON

Meanwhile certain congressmen were trying to make specific changes in conditions. On May 2, 1884, Preston B. Plumb of Kansas introduced a bill in the Senate to open to homestead entry certain unoccupied Indian lands.[47] When Congress met in December, 1884, for the short session, those who desired to authorize the settlement of whites in the Indian Territory were more outspoken. On December 8, just when Couch and his men must have been reaching Stillwater, Thomas Ryan of Kansas introduced Plumb's bill in the House of Representatives.[48] On January 20, 1885, when the country was excited by the news that Colonel Hatch's soldiers were facing an armed band of boomers, equal to them in numbers and possibly in fighting strength, Senator Plumb introduced a resolution requesting the President to state his views and his purposes in opposing the occupation of land that was believed by many to be public land.[49]

The next day Senator Vest proposed to substitute for the Plumb resolution a resolution authorizing negotiations for the purchase of the Oklahoma district free from restrictions. In the debate that followed, a difference of opinion regarding the status of this district became apparent. Plumb defended the right of the United States to extend the homestead law over it without further negotiations, while Vest declared that the government was bound, morally at least, to negotiate with the Indians for the removal of the restrictions

---

47 *Cong. Record*, 48 Cong. 1 sess., 3689.
48 *Cong. Record*, 48 Cong. 2 sess., 81.
49 *Ibid.*, 848; cf. 916.

THE FORMATION OF OKLAHOMA

on its use.[50] It was decided that Plumb's resolution was a proper one in any case, and it was agreed to by the Senate on January 22.[51] Vest's resolution was introduced separately; and on January 23, after it had been amended to include the Cherokee outlet, it was referred to the Committee on Indian Affairs.[52] In the House of Representatives Ryan accepted Vest's plan, and on January 22 he was able to incorporate in the Indian appropriation bill an amendment authorizing negotiations for the Oklahoma district and the Cherokee outlet. This bill had been introduced on January 16 by the Committee on Appropriations, and on January 22 it passed the House as amended and went to the Senate. Here Ryan's amendment was stricken out on February 16, chiefly on the ground that it was legislation not properly included in an appropriation measure. Two days later the Senate Committee on Indian Affairs, to which the Vest resolution had been referred, reported a substitute for it. The first section of this substitute was the resolution as referred, and the second section authorized the criminal prosecution of intruders on Indian land. This measure passed the Senate on February 24.[53]

Both the House of Representatives and the Senate had voted to authorize negotiations for the purchase of the Oklahoma district and the Cherokee outlet, and in the meantime the executive department had gone on record as favoring negotiations. The President on

50 *Ibid.*, 877, 916-920.
51 *Ibid.*, 916, 921.
52 *Ibid.*, 921, 943-947.
53 *Ibid.*, 767, 935, 938, 1748, 1829, 2063.

HOW THE BOOMERS WON

January 30 sent a message in answer to the Plumb resolution. This message included Secretary Teller's statement of the purpose of the department in opposing the boomers, and in this statement Teller seized the opportunity to declare in favor of the purchase of the unoccupied land. Public opinion demanded it, he declared, and there was no good reason why the Indian claims should not be bought out.[54]

The military authorities on the border had recommended for some time that this land should be opened for settlement unless Congress could be induced to change the law relating to the punishment of intruders. On January 10, 1885, Colonel Hatch urged in the strongest terms that action should be taken. He added that his force would "be entirely insufficient to arrest the movement that would be sure to take place in the spring from the hordes coming from Kansas, Missouri, and Arkansas, an estimate from reliable sources placing the number who will attempt the settlement of Indian lands in the territory as not less than twenty thousand people."[55] Efforts to secure legislation for the punishment of intruders had failed. Efforts to find some use for the land in keeping with treaty restrictions had also failed. The executive authorities accordingly agreed that a change of attitude was necessary.

---

54 *S. Ex. Docs.*, 48 Cong. 2 sess., II [i] (2263), no. 54. The answer to the Plumb resolution was sent in two messages. In addition to the one just mentioned, one was sent to the Senate on January 28 (*ibid.*, no. 50). It contained a letter of Robert T. Lincoln, secretary of war, and its chief feature was a brief of papers showing action taken by the War Department in protecting the Indian Territory from invaders from April, 1879, to January, 1885.

55 Brief of papers showing action of the War Department, *ibid.*, 8.

THE FORMATION OF OKLAHOMA

The refusal of the Senate to insert in the Indian appropriation bill the Ryan amendment authorizing negotiations with the Indians led to a revival of the plan of settlement without further negotiations. Ryan on February 16 reintroduced his bill in the House declaring certain unoccupied land in the Indian Territory open to settlement. A week later Bishop W. Perkins, a representative from Kansas, introduced a bill providing for negotiations with the Cherokees for the purchase of the outlet but declaring the Oklahoma district open to homestead entry.[56]

It was probably useless to push either of these plans, and the moderate proposal was taken up again. The Indian appropriation bill, as amended, passed the Senate on February 16 and was sent to the Conference Committee on the next day. After several days of wrangling, the points of difference were settled except the disposition of the Ryan amendment. The Senate conferees offered to accept it if the House conferees would accept with it a section authorizing the criminal prosecution of intruders on Indian land. The latter refused to do this, however. The conferees of both houses were equally insistent, but on March 3 the Senate receded from its position and accepted the House plan by a vote of thirty-three to twenty-seven. On the same day the President signed the bill, and the government was finally committed to the breaking up of the Indian Territory.[57]

56 *Cong. Record*, 48 Cong. 2 sess., 1856, 2033.
57 *Ibid.*, 1750, 1791, 2466-2468, 2569; *Statutes*, XXIII, 384. The motion to recede was made by Senator Vest, and it was carried over the protest of the conferees.

HOW THE BOOMERS WON

The boomers had won their point because they were supported by public opinion in the Middle West. It was still necessary to bring pressure to bear on the Indians to secure their acquiescence; but they understood that Congress had the power, whether it had the moral right or not, to take their land and pay them as much or as little as it pleased. The boomers henceforth had only to see that the government did not neglect to press the matter to a successful conclusion.[58]

58 Cf. Couch's testimony, *loc. cit.*, 450, 458.

CHAPTER IX

FOUR YEARS OF WAITING

THE authorization of the purchase of the Cherokee outlet and of the Oklahoma district meant that the United States had abandoned the policy of maintaining the Indian Territory intact. The consent of the Indians had to be secured, however, before the land could be occupied, and many of the boomers remained on the border waiting until this could be done. When the government's interest in the matter seemed to wane, the boomers and their friends in Congress and elsewhere became active. Finally, after four years, the consent of the Creeks and the Seminoles was obtained, and the Oklahoma district was at last ready for settlers.

When Couch and his friends were starved out at Stillwater early in 1885, they declared that they would return in the spring.[1] They knew that they were winning a political victory in the closing days of the Forty-eighth Congress, and they exaggerated its immediate effects. They received information that the official attitude toward the settlement of the Indian Territory was changing, and they interpreted this to mean that they would be allowed by the incoming administration to move in without the consent of the Indians. Accordingly, Couch and the other leaders, who had been arrested and indicted on the really serious charges growing out of their resistance to the army of the

---

1 Speech of John J. Ingalls, senator from Kansas, March 2, 1885, *Cong. Record*, 48 Cong. 2 sess., 2393.

FOUR YEARS OF WAITING

United States, secured bail and began to make preparations to cross the border after March 4.[2]

President Cleveland was informed of their plans, and on March 13, 1885, he issued a proclamation of the usual sort.[3] This was the fourth presidential proclamation against the boomers, as President Arthur had issued one in July, 1884.[4] Couch was surprised and dissatisfied with the turn of affairs, and he decided to go to Washington to ascertain the real intentions of the government. Apparently he was told by the Secretary of the Interior that the whole matter would be investigated, and that neither boomers nor cattlemen would be allowed in the Oklahoma district until the investigation was completed. At a meeting on April 23, the boomers, in accordance with Couch's advice, decided to make no further attempts to enter the Indian Territory for a reasonable time. Several hundred of them went home; but about two hundred, who had no particular place to go, remained in camp near Caldwell. For several months they made no demonstrations, and the authorities were persuaded that the trouble was over. Accordingly, the United States District Attorney was instructed to dismiss the charges against Couch and the other leaders.[5]

---

[2] Couch's testimony before the Senate committee, June 6, 1885, *S. Reports*, 49 Cong. 1 sess., IX (2363), 442; report of the Commissioner of Indian Affairs for 1885, *H. Ex. Docs.*, 49 Cong. 1 sess., XII (2379), 58, 59.

[3] *Ibid.*, 59, 509. Cf. report of the Secretary of the Interior for 1885, *H. Ex. Docs.*, 49 Cong. 1 sess., XI (2378), 32.

[4] For the four proclamations, see *Messages and Papers of the Presidents*, VII, 548, 598; VIII, 224, 303.

[5] Report of the Commissioner of Indian Affairs for 1885, *loc. cit.*, 59, 60; Couch's testimony, *loc. cit.*, 442-445.

THE FORMATION OF OKLAHOMA

In October, 1885, Couch again led the boomers across the line. This time they reached the Canadian and camped near Council Grove, but in November they were removed by soldiers. They evidently wished only to remind the government of their existence. The Oklahoma district was still closed to them, and they desired to bring this to the attention of Congress, which would meet in December. They did not offer to resist the soldiers, either because they thought that resistance would not further their objects or because the leaders did not care to risk another indictment.[6]

From their point of view, the boomers had occasion to be dissatisfied with the executive department. It had not negotiated with the Indians to secure the relinquishment of their claims to any part of the Indian Territory.[7] While the Nez Percés had been removed from their reservation in the Cherokee outlet, the Tonkawas, recently brought back from Texas, had been assigned to the area thus left vacant.[8] The Attorney-General had ruled in July, 1885, that the system by which the Indians were leasing their lands was illegal and that all leases were voidable; but only the leases of the Cheyennes and Arapahoes had actually been declared void by the President.[9] A plan was forming, however, designed to provide a permanent solution of the Indian question. The old policy of fostering

[6] Report of the Commissioner of Indian Affairs for 1886, *H. Ex. Docs.*, 49 Cong. 2 sess., VIII (2467), 121.

[7] Report of the Secretary of the Interior for 1885, *loc. cit.*, 34, 35.

[8] Report of the Commissioner of Indian Affairs for 1885, *loc. cit.*, 57, 322, 324. The Nez Percés were taken to their old home in the Pacific Northwest in accordance with the act of March 3, 1885 (*Statutes*, XXIII, 378).

[9] Report of the Commissioner of Indian Affairs for 1885, *loc. cit.*, 18, 19.

tribal organizations was to be abandoned forever.[10] The boomers were not informed of this, as the executive department did not wish to open the central part of the Indian Territory to settlers until a new policy had been adopted.

The military authorities had decided that a part of the Indian country ought to be allotted to the Indians individually, and some of them thought that the remainder ought to be purchased for settlers. General Nelson A. Miles, commander of the Department of the Missouri, in which the Indian Territory lay, made very specific recommendations in his report for 1885. He recommended that the Indian Territory should be abolished as "a block in the pathway of civilization" and "a dark blot in the center of the map of the United States." He proposed that a commission of three members should be authorized by law to take up and complete as rapidly as possible the work of allotting lands in severalty to the Indians. General Sheridan, in his report for that year as commander of the army, disapproved the plan to do away with the Indian Territory, but he, too, recommended the allotment of lands in severalty to the Indians, with the disposal of the surplus to settlers.[11]

Secretary of the Interior L. Q. C. Lamar and Commissioner J. D. C. Atkins saw that something of the sort must be done, but they wished to keep the Indian allotments in a body, preferably in the eastern part of the Indian Territory. The part of Lamar's report

10 Report of the Secretary of the Interior for 1885, *loc. cit.*, 13.
11 *H. Ex. Docs.*, 49 Cong. 1 sess., II (2369), 63, 152-155.

for 1885 dealing with this question was evidently prepared while he was angered by Couch's invasion of October, for he declared that nothing would "postpone the change in the use of these lands longer" than attempts to take possession of them in defiance of the law.[12]

The effect of these opinions was shown in the message of the President submitted to Congress in December, 1885. He recommended the passage to Congress in December, 1885. He recommended the passage of a law providing for the appointment of a commission of six members, three of whom should be detailed from the army. So far as the duties of this commission were worked out in the message, it was to be authorized to study the Indian question and to determine upon an Indian policy. In particular, it was to consider the further concentration of the Indians in the Indian Territory, the purchase of their surplus lands for settlement, the allotment of lands in severalty, and the bestowal of citizenship upon the Indians with the abolition of tribal citizenship. The President recommended that this commission "should, in conjunction with the Secretary of the Interior, be given all the authority to deal definitely with the questions presented, deemed safe and consistent."[13]

When the Forty-ninth Congress met in December, 1885, five sorts of measures applying to the Indian Territory were introduced. These measures presented

[12] Report of the Secretary of the Interior for 1885, *loc. cit.*, 35; of the Commissioner of Indian Affairs for 1885, *loc. cit.*, 13.
[13] *Messages and Papers of the Presidents*, VIII, 355-357.

FOUR YEARS OF WAITING

plans for the reform of the judicial system, the opening of the unoccupied land, the organization of the Territory of Oklahoma, the concentration of the Indians in the eastern two-thirds of the Territory, and the allotment of lands in severalty.

The reform of the judicial system was the object of several bills. Some of these proposed in cases between whites and Indians to confer civil jurisdiction on the United States courts, which had only limited criminal jurisdiction at the time. Others set forth plans for recasting the whole court system of the territory. None of these bills made much progress.[14]

The bill to declare the unoccupied land in the Indian Territory open to homestead entry was renewed by Senator Plumb at the beginning of the session, and a like bill was introduced in the House of Representatives. Neither of these bills received further consideration.[15]

---

14 Bill to establish a court (Senate Bill 102), by George G. Vest of Missouri, December 8, 1885 (*Cong. Record*, 49 Cong. 1 sess., 128); to create the judicial district of north Texas and the Indian Territory (Senate Bill 997), by Richard Coke of Texas (by request), January 11, 1886 (*ibid.*, 569); to give the existing United States courts civil jurisdiction in the Indian Territory (Senate Bill 1025), by James K. Jones of Arkansas, January 12 (*ibid.*, 604); to attach parts of the Indian Territory to the eastern and northern districts of Texas (Senate Bill 1026), by Samuel B. Maxey of Texas, January 12 (*ibid.*, 604); to give existing courts additional criminal jurisdiction (Senate Bill 1506), by Henry L. Dawes of Massachusetts (by request), February 15 (*ibid.*, 1427); same title as Senate Bill 102, House Bill 748, by Bishop W. Perkins of Kansas, December 21, 1885 (*ibid.*, 389); same title as Senate Bill 997, House Bill 2462, by James W. Throckmorton of Texas, January 6, 1886 (*ibid.*, 488); same title as Senate Bill 1025, House Bill 3211, by John H. Rogers of Arkansas, January 11 (*ibid.*, 579); same title as Senate Bill 1025, House Bill 5545, by Rogers, for the Committee on Judiciary, February 13 (*ibid.*, 1346).

15 Senate Bill 393, December 10, 1885, *ibid.*, 154; House Bill 749, by Perkins, December 21, *ibid.*, 389.

THE FORMATION OF OKLAHOMA

Five or six bills were introduced in this Congress providing for the organization of the Territory of Oklahoma, which was to include the whole of the Indian Territory and the public land strip.[16] These bills proposed incidentally to allot land in severalty to the Indians, but their chief purpose was to provide for the opening of the unoccupied land to settlement as quickly as possible. One of these measures had been drawn up by the Committee on Territories, and it was reported favorably on April 15, 1886. According to its terms, the reservations of the Five Civilized Tribes were to be included nominally in the Territory of Oklahoma, but actually they were to be attached to the territory only for judicial purposes. It was proposed that the public land strip and the Oklahoma district should be opened to settlement at once. A commission provided for in the bill was to determine whether the Creeks and the Seminoles should be given additional compensation on account of the failure of the United States to observe the restrictions in the treaties ceding the Oklahoma district. It was proposed further that

---

16 Senate Bill 717, by Charles H. Van Wyck of Nebraska, December 21, 1885, *ibid.*, 345; House Bill 315, by Richard W. Townshend of Illinois, December 21, *ibid.*, 375; House Bill 584, by James B. Weaver of Iowa, December 21, *ibid.*, 384; House Bill 4842, by Weaver, January 28, 1886, *ibid.*, 956; House Bill 7217, by William D. Hill of Ohio, for the Committee on Territories, March 25, *ibid.*, 2752. During this session a flood of petitions reached Congress asking for the opening of this land to settlement. These petitions were from all parts of the United States except the far west, but in particular from Illinois, Iowa, Kansas, and Missouri. More than half of them came from the Knights of Labor. See *Cong. Record*, 49 Cong. 1 sess., *Index*, 322. The far-western states probably still preferred to retain the Indian Territory as a place of refuge for their Indians. On January 13, 1886, Thomas M. Bowen of Colorado brought up once more in the Senate the plan of removing all the Indians to the Indian Territory (*Cong. Record*, 49 Cong. 1 sess., 621).

FOUR YEARS OF WAITING

the Cherokee outlet should be transferred to settlers if this commission and the Cherokees could agree upon the terms of transfer. One section of the bill authorized the commission to treat with other Indians for any land in excess of their requirements. All sales of grazing rights was to be forbidden in the future, and all current leases were to be cancelled. These provisions would have made much of the unoccupied land, including the Cherokee outlet, worthless to the Indians for the time, and doubtless were intended to induce them to dispose of their surplus lands. This bill was debated earnestly, but it did not come to a vote during the session.[17]

The bills to establish a Territory of Oklahoma were designed chiefly to furnish additional land for home-seekers, but the other bills to be considered were designed first of all to provide for the formation of an Indian policy. A subcommittee of the House Committee on Appropriations had been authorized in the closing days of the Forty-eighth Congress to investigate expenditures for the Indians. This subcommittee prepared a report, and with it presented a bill drawn up by the Secretary of the Interior in conformity with the recommendations in the President's message of December, 1885. The report and the accompanying bill were presented on March 16, 1886. The bill proposed a commission of six members, three of them officers detailed from the army, with power to negotiate with the Indians and to make any disposition of them or of their

---

[17] *Ibid.*, 3514, 4063, 5214, 8035-8038; *H. Reports*, 49 Cong. 1 sess., VI (2440), no. 1684.

lands, not contrary to law or to previous treaties, without reference to Congress. The special task of the commission was to be the formation of an Indian policy.[18]

The majority report of the subcommittee, presented by its chairman, William S. Holman of Indiana, reflected accurately the desire of the administration for a gradual concentration of the Indians of the Indian Territory in its eastern two-thirds and the opening of the remainder to settlement. The allotment of lands in severalty was to be urged upon the Indians, but nothing was to be done without their consent. The minority report, signed by Joseph G. Cannon of Illinois and Thomas Ryan of Kansas, criticized this plan. It urged a policy in which rapid development was possible, and objected to the further concentration of the Indians as contrary to the interests of the Indians themselves.[19]

The chief opponents of the Holman bill were the friends of the immediate opening of the Oklahoma district, led by James B. Weaver of Iowa.[20] They feared unnecessary delay in accomplishing results, and in particular some of them feared that the commission, acting in harmony with the known wishes of the Commissioner of Indian Affairs, would move some of the Indians of the western part of the Indian Territory and establish them in the Oklahoma district. By the terms

---

18 House Bill 6973; *Cong. Record*, 49 Cong. 1 sess., 2414, 3197, 8035; *H. Reports*, 49 Cong. 1 sess., IV (2438), no. 1076.

19 *Ibid.*

20 *Cong. Record*, 49 Cong. 1 sess., 3641-3643, 4550-4561. Weaver was the third-party candidate for the presidency in 1880 and again in 1892. At this time he represented an Iowa district in Congress.

FOUR YEARS OF WAITING

of the bill this would have been possible—at least in the case of the Cheyennes and Arapahoes, as they occupied their reservation only by executive order. The bill was not allowed to come to a vote during the session.[21] Holman made an effort during the second session of this Congress, the Forty-ninth, to obtain a hearing for it, but he did not succeed.[22]

Meanwhile, a plan for the allotment of lands in severalty to the Indians was receiving favorable consideration. This plan had been brought to the attention of Congress many years before.

Soon after the Civil War, suggestions had been made for the extension of the policy of assigning the Indians separate holdings within a tribal reservation. The United States Board of Indian Commissioners in their first report, made in 1869, had recommended that the Indians as individuals should be given patents, and in their report for 1876 they had made this recommendation even more definite. In 1878 they presented a draft of a bill to carry out their proposals.[23] Carl Schurz, secretary of the interior during the Hayes administration, accepted this policy and urged it upon Congress in his reports.[24] The board proposed that

[21] *Ibid.*, 4554, 4559, 4560, 8035-8038.
[22] *Cong. Record*, 49 Cong. 2 sess., 121. Holman also introduced this bill in the next Congress and secured a favorable report from the House Committee on Indian Affairs (*Cong. Record*, 50 Cong. 1 sess., 211, 1760).
[23] For a brief discussion of the part played by the Board of Indian Commissioners, the Indian Rights Association, and the Lake Mohonk Indian Conference in bringing about allotment in severalty, see articles by M. K. Sniffen, S. M. Brosius, and Merril E. Gates in Hodge, *Handbook of American Indians*, I, 608, 928; II, 869.
[24] Report of the Secretary of the Interior for 1877, *H. Ex. Docs.*, 45 Cong. 2 sess., VIII (1800), p. xi; for 1878, *H. Ex. Docs.*, 45 Cong. 3 sess., IX (1850),

allotment should be followed by the breaking up of the tribal reservations and the dissolution of the tribal organizations, but Schurz seems not to have been prepared to take this step. He proposed to settle other tribes in the Indian Territory, which he wished to keep intact for the Indians.

The adoption of allotment in severalty to the Indians would inevitably free a part of the lands held by them as tribes. Many of the reservations were large in proportion to the number of occupants, and it was not desired to give the Indian sufficient land to make him a landlord. On the contrary, it was hoped that he would acquire habits of industry by the possession of only so much land as he could utilize. If further removals of tribes to the Indian Territory could not be made, some of it must be opened to settlement; and persons who were not interested in the Indians advocated allotment in severalty in order that a part of their country might be secured for settlers. Accordingly, the first stream of bills for allotment came with the agitation for the use of unoccupied Indian lands beginning in 1879. While these bills were ostensibly designed for the benefit of the Indians, their evident purpose was to release land for settlement.

As has been said, five or six bills providing for allotment in severalty were introduced in the Forty-sixth Congress.[25] Similar bills were introduced in the Forty-

---

p. i; for 1879, *H. Ex. Docs.*, 46 Cong. 2 sess., IX (1910), 12; for 1880, *H. Ex. Docs.*, 46 Cong. 3 sess., IX (1959), 11.

25 See above, Chapter VIII, footnote 30.

FOUR YEARS OF WAITING

seventh, Forty-eighth, and Forty-ninth Congresses.[26] One of these passed the Senate on March 26, 1884, and it was reported favorably by the House Committee on Indian Affairs on January 9, 1885, but it failed to pass the House at this session. By the terms of this bill, the consent of two-thirds of the men of the tribe had to be secured before allotment could take place.[27]

On December 8, 1885, Henry L. Dawes of Massachusetts introduced a new bill in the Senate for the allotment of lands in severalty to the Indians. It passed the Senate on February 26, 1886, and the House of Representatives on December 16. After the houses had wrangled over the details of the measure in conference, an agreement was finally reached, and the President approved it on February 8, 1887. This act was drawn so that it did not apply to the Osage, Peoria, Miami, or Sac and Fox Indians, or to the Indians of the Five Civilized Tribes. These latter were the most advanced and most nearly ready of all for such a policy, but they were known to be bitterly opposed to any change in their organization. In spite of these omissions, the Dawes act was a distinct step toward the solution of the Indian question.[28]

By the terms of this act the President could authorize the allotments of lands in severalty to the Indians of any tribe whenever he thought that such allotment

---

26 *Cong. Record*, 47 Cong. 1 sess., Index, 217; 48 Cong. 1 sess., Index, 226; 49 Cong. 1 sess., Index, 322.

27 Senate Bill 48, by Coke, December 4, 1883, *Cong. Record*, 48 Cong. 1 sess., 13; passed Senate, *ibid.*, 2280; reported favorably, 2 sess., 580 (cf. *H. Reports*, 48 Cong. 2 sess., I (2328), no. 2247).

28 Senate Bill 54; *Cong. Record*, 49 Cong. 1 sess., 123, 1558, 1764; 2 sess., 226, 772, 882, 972, 1577; *Statutes*, XXIV, 388 (reprinted in Kappler, I, 33).

THE FORMATION OF OKLAHOMA

would be for their benefit. Each head of a family was entitled to one hundred and sixty acres of land; half as much might be assigned to each single person over eighteen and to each orphan under that age. Other persons under eighteen were entitled to forty acres each. The holder of an allotment could not sell or mortgage it for twenty-five years, and this period of restriction could be extended by the President. Finally, this was in effect a naturalization law for the Indian, since he became a citizen of the United States as soon as the patent to his land was made.[29] The President was authorized to negotiate with the tribe for any surplus land left after the allotment had been completed. It was provided that land secured in this way should be sold, in tracts of one hundred and sixty acres each, to actual settlers, who could secure title only after five years' residence.

This act applied to the western half of the Indian Territory, although it did not apply to the greater part of the eastern half. Arrangements were made at once to allot land to the members of the Pottawatomie and the absentee Shawnee bands. This work had been done once, but its results had been lost. Authority was given to prepare for the allotment of individual holdings to the Quapaw, Shawnee, Seneca, Wyandotte, Ottawa, Modoc, Kiowa, Comanche, and Wichita Indians.[30]

---

29 This provision was made necessary by a decision of the Supreme Court on November 3, 1884, Elk *vs.* Wilkins, 112 U. S., 94. According to this decision, an Indian who had severed his tribal relations to take a homestead did not become thereby a citizen of the United States. An act of March 3, 1875 (*Statutes*, XVIII, 420), amended by an act of July 4, 1884 (*Statutes*, XXIII, 96), had extended the privileges of the homestead law to Indians who severed their tribal relations.

30 Report of the Secretary of the Interior for 1887, *H. Ex. Docs.*, 50 Cong.

FOUR YEARS OF WAITING

The proposal to establish a Territory of Oklahoma did not receive much attention during the second session of the Forty-ninth Congress, which ended in March, 1887.[31] During this session, however, the public land strip extending west of the hundredth meridian was first given serious consideration.

Until 1869 this strip had been designated on official maps as a part of the Indian Territory, but since that time it had appeared as a separate division. The first legislation regarding it, which authorized a partial survey, was enacted on March 3, 1881.[32] In accordance with the provisions of this act, the Cimarron meridian was established on the one hundred and third meridian of longitude, and a base line was established on the parallel of thirty-six thirty. During the next biennial period these lines were surveyed, as well as the exterior lines of the townships.[33] Before 1884 the cattlemen apparently were in undisturbed possession; but in that year settlers began to come in, and serious rivalry ensued.[34] Since this area was not opened legally to settlement and was not even attached to any judicial

---

1 sess., X (2541), 27. For a statement regarding the previous allotments mentioned, see the report of Charles W. Kirk, agent, for 1886, *H. Ex. Docs.*, 49 Cong. 2 sess., VIII (2467), 361.

31 House Bill 7217. The committee bill was considered on three occasions (*Cong. Record*, 49 Cong. 2 sess., 269, 334-347, 1737). A few petitions were received (*ibid.*, 791, 870, 969, 1029, 1173, 1425).

32 *Statutes*, XXI, 451.

33 Letter of the commissioner of the General Land Office, William A. J. Sparks, January 29, 1886, *S. Reports*, 50 Cong. 1 sess., II (2520), no. 353; Donaldson, *The Public Domain*, 462, 1167, 1187. The Cimarron meridian received its name, of course, from the Cimarron River.

34 Report of the Commissioner of the General Land office for 1884, *H. Ex. Docs.*, 48 Cong. 2 sess., XI (2286), 14.

THE FORMATION OF OKLAHOMA

district, it became known popularly as "No Man's Land."

During the first session of the Forty-ninth Congress a bill was introduced in the House by Thomas Ryan of Kansas which provided for the extension of the jurisdiction of the United States district court for the district of Kansas over No Man's Land and for the opening of it to settlement under the homestead law.[35] The commissioner of the General Land Office, William A. J. Sparks, in response to a request for information in January, 1886, recommended the civil organization of this strip if the Ryan bill should become a law. The House of Representatives passed this bill on December 11, 1886, and the Senate passed it on March 3, 1887;[36] but the President did not sign it,[37] evidently because no provision had been made for the civil organization of the territory which it was proposed to open to settlement.

In December, 1887, a person appeared in Washington claiming to be the duly elected delegate of the people of No Man's Land, which they had organized as "Cimarron Territory." According to the memorial presented to Congress at this time, the first steps toward organization were taken at a convention which met at Beaver on November 29, 1886. The first election was held on February 22, 1887, and the first legislature, a council of nine members, met on March 4. The

35 House Bill 679, December 21, 1885; *Cong. Record*, 49 Cong. 1 sess., 387, 1347.
36 *Cong. Record*, 49 Cong. 2 sess., 86, 2611. For the Sparks letter, see above, footnote 33.
37 *Cong. Record*, 50 Cong. 1 sess., 39.

FOUR YEARS OF WAITING

second election was held on November 8, and at that time a delegate to Congress was chosen, as well as a new legislature composed of an upper house of nine and a lower house of fourteen members. A population of ten thousand was claimed in the memorial, and Congress was asked to recognize their government. The House of Representatives rejected the claims of this delegate at once.[38]

Unsuccessful efforts were made in the Fiftieth Congress to provide an organization for this strip separate from the Indian Territory. Secretary Lamar had suggested in November, 1887, that it should be annexed to New Mexico,[39] and bills to enact this recommendation into law were introduced, one in each house.[40] A proposal to incorporate this troublesome area with Kansas seemed to offer the best solution of the problem, and a bill to extend the borders of Kansas to include it, subject of course to the consent of the legislature of that state, passed the Senate without debate or division on March 29, 1888.[41] A companion measure to open the

[38] This memorial, signed by Owen G. Chase, who claimed to have been chosen delegate, was presented in the House on December 12 (*Cong. Record*, 50 Cong. 1 sess., 38, 40). It is interesting to note that a contesting delegate submitted his claims on January 25, 1888 (*ibid.*, 718). The area of this strip is 5761 square miles. The estimate of the population in 1887 given in the memorial was undoubtedly far too large. The population of Beaver County, Oklahoma, which was then coextensive with the old public land strip, was only 2674 in 1890, and it was only 3051 in 1900. The opening of land farther east in 1889, however, may have drawn some of the settlers away.

[39] *H. Ex. Docs.*, 50 Cong. 1 sess., X (2541), 23.

[40] Senate Bill 790, by James Z. George of Mississippi, December 14, 1887, *Cong. Record*, 50 Cong. 1 sess., 58; House Bill 6168, by Antonio Joseph of New Mexico, January 30, 1888, *ibid.*, 806.

[41] Senate Bill 1633, introduced by Preston B. Plumb of Kansas, January 24, 1888, *ibid.*, 649, 1402, 2479. Cf. *S. Reports*, 50 Cong. 1 sess., II (2520), no. 353.

THE FORMATION OF OKLAHOMA

land to homestead entry had been passed by the Senate on February 23.[42] When these bills reached the House their further progress was blocked by the friends of the Oklahoma bill, chief of whom at the time was William M. Springer of Illinois, chairman of the Committee on Territories.[43] A satisfactory adjustment of affairs in No Man's Land would have deprived the friends of the Territory of Oklahoma of their most telling argument for its immediate organization.[44] Moreover, the people of this strip, so far as can be determined from their memorials to Congress, did not wish it to be separated from the Indian Territory, and their self-constituted authorities petitioned on two occasions for the passage of the Oklahoma bill.[45]

The people of No Man's Land did not intend to pay taxes until they were given some form of civil organization. Four distilleries were said to be in operation there in April, 1888, the owners refusing to pay the taxes imposed by the internal revenue laws. It was impossible to compel payment, not because the law failed to include this area in a collection district, but because no court had jurisdiction within its limits.[46]

A more serious result of this condition became apparent in the summer of 1888. Four citizens of Kansas

---

42 Senate Bill 1080, introduced by Daniel W. Voorhees of Indiana, December 22, 1887, *Cong. Record*, 50 Cong. 1 sess., 164, 784, 1405.

43 *Ibid.*, 1446, 2570, 6739, 8906-8909. Weaver also actively opposed the passage of this bill.

44 See *H. Reports*, 50 Cong. 1 sess., VIII (2605), no. 2857, p. 11.

45 *Cong. Record*, 50 Cong. 1 sess., 718, 1467, 1807, 1891, 2367; 2 sess., 1880, 1965.

46 Letter of C. S. Fairchild, secretary of the treasury, May 1, 1888, inclosures, *H. Ex. Docs.*, 50 Cong. 1 sess., XXIX (2561), no. 292.

FOUR YEARS OF WAITING

were murdered just across the border in this strip, and it was not possible even to institute a judicial inquiry concerning the matter.[47]

Finally, in the closing days of the Fiftieth Congress a plan was agreed upon for the inclusion of the public land strip with the Indian Territory under the jurisdiction of a separate court, the sessions to be held at Muskogee. By an act of March 1, 1889, the Indian Territory was established as a partially organized unit, with boundaries identical with those of the present state of Oklahoma. Provision was made at last for the enforcement of the laws of the United States in No Man's Land, but its settlers were still unable to enter homesteads or to set up a local government.[48]

Renewed efforts had been made during the sessions of the Fiftieth Congress to organize the Territory of Oklahoma. Three bills planned to accomplish this result were introduced early in the first session. The Committee on Territories on February 7, 1888, and again on July 11, reported favorably a bill introduced by its chairman. The Territory of Oklahoma proposed by this bill included only the districts west of the reservations of the Five Civilized Tribes. These reservations and the small ones northeast of them were excluded from the territory, in name as well as in fact. This was the new feature of importance in the Springer bill, and it was the first time that the name Oklahoma was used with the special application that it had during the

---

47 H. B. Kelly, "No Man's Land," February 11, 1889, Kansas State Historical Society, *Collections*, IV, 324.

48 *Statutes*, XXV, 783.

THE FORMATION OF OKLAHOMA

period just before the admission of the state. The passage of the Dawes act providing for the allotment of lands in severalty had made it unnecessary to include certain sections of the preceding Oklahoma bills, but in general this bill closely followed its predecessors.[49]

Numerous petitions for the organization of Oklahoma reached Congress during this session, most of them from Kansas and Nebraska. On February 8, 1888, there met at Kansas City a convention that claimed to represent the people of all the states bordering on the Indian Territory. It prepared a memorial setting forth that only the "chiefs, squawmen, and half-breeds" were in favor of retaining the Indian Territory as it was. It was declared that a change would be a benefit to the real Indians. Complaint was made that lawless conditions existed in the territory and in particular that no court had jurisdiction in civil cases between citizens of the United States and Indians. The real significance of the memorial was contained in the statement, "The Indian Territory lies in the center of Southwestern civilization, an obstacle to trade development and an injury to every state which borders upon it." The resolutions adopted by the convention called for the opening of the Indian Territory, or at least of its western part, to settlement, with payment to the Indians for

---

49 House Bill 1277, by Springer, January 4, 1888, *Cong. Record*, 50 Cong. 1 sess., 209; House Bill 1285, by Townshend, January 4, *ibid.*, 209; House Bill 1350, by Weaver, January 4, *ibid.*, 212; *H. Reports*, 50 Cong. 1 sess., II (2599), no. 263; VIII (2605), no. 2857; *Cong. Record*, 50 Cong. 1 sess., 1025, 5540, 6143, 6741-6757, 6869-6880, 7272, 8050, 8054, 8082, 8116, 8121, 8587. The bill reported on July 11 was House Bill 10614, introduced by Springer on June 25. This bill was practically the same as House Bill 1277. The object of the second introduction in the same session was said to be only to provide a convenient way of incorporating minor amendments.

their lands. Finally, the resolutions asked that these lands should be disposed of in small holdings to actual settlers and that no leases or other forms of monopoly should be tolerated. Eighteen delegates were selected to present the memorial and resolutions to Congress. One of these delegates was W. L. Couch, the chief of the boomers.[50]

The boomers had remained quiet for some time after the invasion of October, 1885. The officer in command on the border reported in 1886 that the leaders had promised to let the government develop its policy regarding the Indian Territory without interference from them. Railroad construction through the Cherokee outlet and the Oklahoma district gave many of them employment, and the unhindered flow of settlers into No Man's Land afforded an outlet for the more impatient. In spite of this, a movement from the south across the Chickasaw country began to assume importance for the first time in 1886, and in that year soldiers were required to dislodge a band that had camped on the Canadian.[51] A patrol of the border was needed in 1887,[52] and by the winter of 1888-89 the soldiers were kept as busy as ever. The character of

[50] For the petitions, see *Cong. Record*, 50 Cong. 1 sess., Index, 553. Two Kansas communities sent in petitions against the organization of the Territory of Oklahoma (*Cong. Record*, 50 Cong. 1 sess., 1720, 1763, 2243). For the memorial of the convention, see *ibid.*, 1382.

[51] Report of Captain Price, quoted in the report of Major General Alfred H. Terry, commander of the Division of the Missouri, for 1886, *H. Ex. Docs.*, 49 Cong. 2 sess., II (2462), 119; report of the Commissioner of Indian Affairs for 1886, *H. Ex. Docs.*, 49 Cong. 2 sess., VIII (2467), 122; report of Robert L. Owen, union agent, for 1886, *ibid.*, 375.

[52] Report of General Sheridan for 1887, *H. Ex. Docs.*, 50 Cong. 1 sess., II (2533), 72.

the invasion had changed, however, and boomers crossed the lines singly and in small bands. They did not offer to resist arrest.[53]

In the second session of the Fiftieth Congress, which met in December, 1888, the Springer bill was kept to the front in the House of Representatives. George T. Barnes of Georgia, a member of the Committee on Territories, endeavored to substitute for this bill the plan of concentrating the Indians of the Indian Territory east of the ninety-eighth meridian. This plan, which had been proposed originally by the Commissioner of Indian Affairs in 1885, had strong support in the House; but it was finally defeated by a vote of 119 to 124.[54] On February 1, 1889, the Springer bill passed the House by a vote of 147 to 102.[55]

Thereupon the contest was shifted to the Senate. Petitions for the organization of Oklahoma continued to reach Congress. The legislature of Kansas in January, 1889, had called for the immediate opening of the Indian Territory to settlement. Among other memorials of similar import were several from organizations of business men interested in the Southwest. The "council of Cimarron Territory" made its last public appearance in February in a petition of the Senate for

[53] "During the months of January, February, and March detachments were constantly engaged in scouting Oklahoma . . . removing intruders" (report of Brigadier-General W. Merritt, commander of the Department of the Missouri, for 1889, *H. Ex. Docs.*, 51 Cong. 1 sess., II (2715), 163).

[54] *Cong. Record*, 50 Cong. 1 sess., 1577; 2 sess., 1387, 1388. The vote was taken on January 31, 1889. For the recommendations of the Commissioner of Indian Affairs, see report for 1885, *H. Ex. Docs.*, 49 Cong. 1 sess., XII (2379), 13; for 1886, *H. Ex. Docs.*, 49 Cong. 2 sess., VIII (2467), 88.

[55] *Cong. Record*, 50 Cong. 2 sess., 1402.

FOUR YEARS OF WAITING

the passage of the Oklahoma bill.[56] On February 18 the House bill to establish the Territory of Oklahoma was reported favorably by the Senate Committee on Territories. Several members of the Senate clearly wished to urge its consideration, but the session was drawing to a close, and the appropriation bills demanded attention.[57] Above all, a sudden change in the attitude of the Creeks and the Seminoles made a different plan of action possible.

Representatives of the Five Civilized Tribes had agreed in June, 1886, to reject all offers from the government for the purchase of land for the use of citizens of the United States. This action had been ratified by the legislature of each tribe, but sentiment among the Creeks at the time was far from unanimous.[58]

The Creeks decided that it would not be well to wait too long if they wished to negotiate with the government. The Springer bill proposed a commission to determine whether the Creeks and the Seminoles were entitled to additional compensation for the Oklahoma district, but it did not provide for negotiations with them. In January, 1889, a delegation headed by Pleasant Porter came to Washington and offered to relinquish to the United States the Creek claims to the land in question. William F. Vilas, who had succeeded

[56] The memorial from the Kansas legislature was presented in the Senate on January 30 (*ibid.*, 1324). The petition from No Man's Land reached the Senate of February 16 (*ibid.*, 1965). For other petitions, see *ibid.*, 58, 1544, 1765, 1880, 1918, 1965, 1999, 2371, 2426. Two more petitions from Kansas against the Oklahoma bill were presented during this session (*ibid.*, 413, 633).

[57] *Ibid.*, 1501, 2010, 2287.

[58] Report of Robert L. Owen, union agent, for 1886, *H. Ex. Docs.*, 49 Cong. 2 sess., VIII (2467), 376-378.

THE FORMATION OF OKLAHOMA

Lamar as Secretary of the Interior, received the delegation under the authority conferred by the law of March 3, 1885. An agreement was signed on January 19, 1889, in which the Creeks for a consideration of two million two hundred and eighty thousand dollars released the United States from all restrictions on the use of the entire Creek cession of 1866. This agreement was ratified by the Creek legislature on January 31, and on February 6 it was submitted to Congress by the President.[59]

The Senate on February 15 passed a bill approving this agreement and making the appropriation necessary to conclude the matter. Senator Dawes succeeded in attaching to the bill a section designed to put an end to the invasions of the Oklahoma district. This section provided that a person who entered the Creek cession prior to its opening by law forfeited his right to make a homestead entry within its limits. The House on February 23 passed the bill as it came from the Senate, and the President signed it on March 1.[60]

Secretary Vilas had hardly completed the negotiations with the Creeks before two Seminole delegates presented themselves. On February 15 they submitted a formal communication asking the government to enter into an agreement with them concerning their cession of 1866, similar to the agreement just made with the Creeks. Vilas did not think that the cases were

---

59 *Cong. Record*, 50 Cong. 2 sess., 1543, 1563, 2244, 2368; *S. Ex. Docs.*, 50 Cong. 2 sess., III (2612), no. 98. For details of this agreement, see below, Appendix H.

60 Senate Bill 3920, introduced by Dawes, for the Committee on Indian Affairs, February 7; *Cong. Record*, 50 Cong. 2 sess., 1590, 1919, 2244, 2598; *Statutes*, XXV, 757.

parallel, since the restrictions in the Seminole treaty were implied and not expressed as in the Creek treaty. He transmitted their proposals to the President, who in a special message placed the whole matter before Congress on February 19.[61]

The Senate Committee on Indian Affairs by its chairman promptly introduced a bill to accept the offer of the Seminoles and to make an appropriation of one million nine hundred and twelve thousand dollars as additional compensation for the land ceded by them in 1866.[62] This bill also contained a section denying the right of homestead entry in this cession to persons who entered it prior to its opening by law.

As the adjournment of Congress was at hand, the passage of this as a separate measure through both houses seemed hardly possible. Accordingly, the members of the House Committee on Indian Affairs agreed to try to attach it as an amendment to the Indian appropriation bill, and with it they agreed to include an additional section of importance. This section authorized the President to open the Oklahoma district to settlement immediately, in accordance with the terms of the homestead law. On February 26, Samuel W. Peel of Arkansas, chairman of the committee, offered the amendment as it had been agreed upon in committee, and it was adopted by the House on the next day. At the same time Representative

[61] *S. Ex. Docs.*, 50 Cong. 2 sess., III (2612), no. 122 (cf. *Cong. Record*, 50 Cong. 2 sess., 2368). The leading Seminole delegate was John F. Brown. For the difference in the wording of the treaties, see below, Appendix H.

[62] Senate Bill 3984, by Dawes, February 21; *ibid.*, 2139. For details of this agreement, see below, Appendix H.

THE FORMATION OF OKLAHOMA

Ryan secured the insertion of a section authorizing the President to establish two land offices in the district to be opened. The Indian appropriation bill thus amended passed the House on February 27, and in a slightly modified form it passed the Senate on March 2. The bill was sent to a conference committee, was reported by this committee carrying the sections relating to Oklahoma essentially as they had been adopted by the House, was passed finally by both houses on March 2, 1889, and was approved by President Cleveland on the same day.[63]

This agreement was still to be ratified by the Seminole legislature; but as this ratification was only a formality under the conditions, the Oklahoma district was practically ready for settlement. The amendments to the Indian appropriation bill providing for the opening were adopted so hastily that no thought was given to the organization of the country. In the Senate, it is true, an unsuccessful effort was made to secure an amendment to establish the Territory of Oklahoma.[64] The failure to set up the machinery of government really nullified part of the work that Congress had done. As will appear later, the statutes relating to town sites on the public lands were inoperative without the aid of county and municipal officials.

A great change had been brought about in the western half of the Indian Territory by the passage of the Dawes act and by the adoption of provisions for

---

63 House Bill 12578, introduced by Peel, for the Committee on Indian Affairs, February 13; *Cong. Record*, 50 Cong. 2 sess., 1858, 2367, 2368, 2399-2403, 2411, 2414, 2595, 2633, 2698, 2724; *Statutes*, XXV, 1004.

64 By Charles B. Farwell of Illinois, *Cong. Record*, 50 Cong. 2 sess., 2602.

FOUR YEARS OF WAITING

opening of the Oklahoma district. Another change was in prospect, as Representative Springer had secured the insertion in the Indian appropriation act of a section authorizing a commission to treat directly with the Indians of this region for their surplus lands and with the Cherokees in particular for the outlet.[65] These were the accomplishments of the four years of the Cleveland administration, and the boomers had only to wait for President Harrison's proclamation, to occupy the country from which they had so many times been driven.

[65] February 27, *ibid.*, 2407; *Statutes*, XXV, 1004.

CHAPTER X

THE SETTLEMENT OF OKLAHOMA TERRITORY

BETWEEN 1889 and 1901 the western half of the Indian Territory, organized as the Territory of Oklahoma, was opened to settlement. Beginning with the Oklahoma district on April 22, 1889, the reservations in this area one after another were divided into freeholds for citizens of the United States. By September, 1901, practically all of the land west of the districts belonging to the Five Civilized Tribes had been occupied.

The most striking feature of the settlement of Oklahoma was the rush that occurred on the opening of each tract. The Indian Territory had become a wedge of the frontier embedded in the cultivated and inhabited area. The proximity of this unoccupied country to the railroads made it available for settlement, and the comparative scarcity of free land enhanced its value. The ten years of the boomer agitation had made known its existence and exaggerated its attractiveness. Many indeed took part in the rushes from mere curiosity or from love of adventure. As notice of the opening of each tract was given in advance, and as efforts were made to keep everyone out until the appointed day had arrived, all the prospective settlers entered at the same time. The settlement of the Oklahoma district, which took place in one afternoon, was a typical rush.

The opening of Indian lands with a race or a lottery

SETTLEMENT OF OKLAHOMA TERRITORY

was not confined to Oklahoma. Similar openings took place from time to time in other parts of the West, as reservations were disposed of in accordance with the newly adopted policy of allotment in severalty and the sale of the surplus lands to settlers. Nevertheless, the first and most noteworthy rushes took place in Oklahoma, and it was the only commonwealth formed at this time from the Indian country.[1]

On March 16, 1889, the Seminoles formally agreed to the removal of any restrictions on the use of their cession of 1866. This, according to the terms of the act of March 3, left President Harrison free to open the Oklahoma district, and on March 23 he issued a proclamation declaring that it would be ready for settlers at noon on April 22. The President called attention to the provision in the law curtailing the rights of persons entering prior to the formal opening. He gave notice that this provision would be enforced.[2]

The Oklahoma district, the settlement of which was thus authorized, was a heart-shaped area in the center of the Indian Territory. To reach it from Kansas it was necessary to pass through the Cherokee outlet. The

---

[1] The most detailed account of the growth of Oklahoma from 1889 to 1901 is that of Solon J. Buck, "The Settlement of Oklahoma," in *Wisconsin Academy of Science, Arts, and Letters, Transactions*, XV, 343-379. For openings outside of Oklahoma, see among others the report of the Commissioner of the General Land Office for 1895, *H. Docs.*, 54 Cong. 1 sess., XIV (3381), 119; and same for 1907, *H. Docs.*, 60 Cong. 1 sess., XXVI (5295), 92.

[2] *Statutes*, XXV, 1544; *Messages and Papers of the Presidents*, IX, 15. President Harrison said in his first annual message that he was constrained to open the land to settlement, in spite of the failure of Congress to provide a government, because of the numbers who were waiting on the border (*ibid.*, 47). It will be remembered that this land was opened under the provisions of the homestead law, which made it free to settlers who could satisfy the conditions of the law.

THE FORMATION OF OKLAHOMA

Chickasaw district separated it from Texas, and several reservations lay between it and Arkansas. Its southern and southwestern boundary was the Canadian, a wide shallow stream flowing from the mountains of New Mexico to join the Arkansas River. Two streams crossed the district from east to west, the Cimarron and the North Fork of the Canadian. The latter is little more than a creek, but the Cimarron closely resembles the main Canadian. A line of the Atchison, Topeka, and Santa Fé Railroad had recently been constructed through the district from north to south a little east of its center, and a stage line ran parallel to the railroad about thirty miles farther west.[3] The area of the land included in the President's proclamation at this time was a little less than three thousand square miles. In other words, the Oklahoma district was about three-fifths as large as Connecticut.[4]

Between the middle of March and the middle of April several thousand persons gathered in the neighboring states ready to make the race for homesteads or town lots.[5] Before the day set for the opening they were allowed to pass through the intervening Indian country and form on the borders of the district to be opened.[6]

---

3 See map at the end of letter of John W. Noble, secretary of the interior, March 12, 1890, *S. Ex. Docs.*, 51 Cong. 1 sess., IX (2686), no. 78. The map given above, frontispiece, is based on this map.

4 According to the report of the Secretary of the Interior for 1889, 1,887,-796.47 acres (*H. Ex. Docs.*, 51 Cong. 1 sess., XI (2724), p. iv). It will be remembered that the area of the district had been diminished by executive action in 1883.

5 *Ibid.*, p. v.

6 Merritt to Cook, April 8, 1889, *S. Ex. Docs.*, 51 Cong. 1 sess., IX (2686), no. 72, p. 2; Proctor to Crook, April 11, *ibid.*

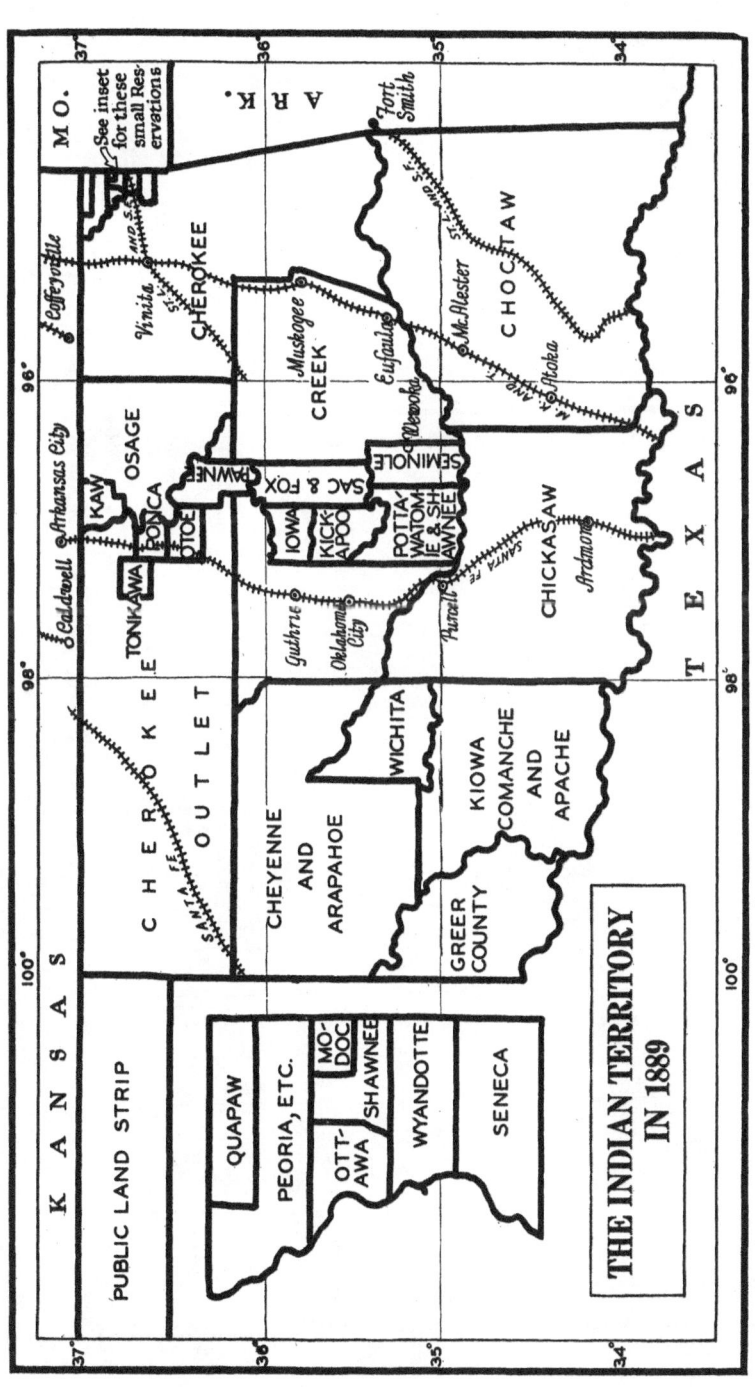

SETTLEMENT OF OKLAHOMA TERRITORY

Additional soldiers were placed on guard as a precautionary measure. On April 22 a force equal to two regiments was in the field. The cavalry, nearly half of the total force, was stationed along the border to hold the settlers back until noon. The infantry was stationed at important points in the district, especially at the two places where land offices had been established.[7] These were Guthrie, where the Santa Fé Railroad crossed the Cimarron, and Kingfisher, a stage station thirty miles west of Guthrie.[8]

Promptly at noon the settlers were given the signal to start, and the run began. Men raced on horseback, in carriages, and in wagons. Five trains entered the district from the north. The first of these reached Guthrie, twenty miles south, at one-thirty in the afternoon, but the passengers found that United States deputy marshals, together with settlers who had slipped by the border patrol, had already staked out a town site. Other persons had been busily engaged since noon making entries for adjacent farms.[9] Those who entered in this way before the appointed time were

---

7 Report of Brigadier-General Merritt, commander of the Department of the Missouri, for 1889, *H. Ex. Docs.*, 51 Cong. 1 sess., II (2715), 163.

8 Report of the Commissioner of the General Land Office, for 1889, *H. Ex. Docs.*, 51 Cong. 1 sess., XI (2724), 113. The line between the two original land districts was the line between ranges three and four west of the Indian meridian.

9 Report of the Secretary of the Interior for 1889, *loc. cit.*, p. vi; MacBride and Pickler to Noble, April 27, 1889, *S. Ex. Docs.*, 51 Cong. 1 sess., V (2682), no. 33, p. 1; "The Opening of Oklahoma," by Hamilton S. Wicks, an eyewitness, *Cosmopolitan*, September, 1889 (VII, 460). Compare also *S. Ex. Docs.*, 51 Cong. 1 sess., XXXI (2746), no. 209. The signal was a blast of the bugle— at least this was true at the place where the Santa Fé trains entered from the north.

known as "sooners."[10] Purcell, where the Santa Fé Railroad crossed the Canadian, was the starting-place for most of the settlers entering from the south. Many of these reached Oklahoma station, where the Santa Fé crossed the North Fork of the Canadian, midway between Purcell and Guthrie.[11] Rivalry between Guthrie and Oklahoma City began at once. Other towns were staked out and occupied, and by nightfall many of the homesteads had one or more claimants.[12]

Brigadier-General Wesley Merritt, personally in command of the troops in the district, reported on April 23 that the settlers who had entered numbered ten or twelve thousand. According to this communication, three thousand of these were at Guthrie, as many at or near Kingfisher, and three or four thousand at Oklahoma City and in the country between Oklahoma City and Purcell.[13] It must be remembered that nearly all of these were men. They represented a much larger prospective population. Merritt's estimate must have been extremely conservative, as other observers tripled or even quadrupled the numbers given by him.[14]

10 Report of the Governor of Oklahoma for 1891, *H. Ex. Docs.*, 52 Cong. 1 sess., XVI (2935), 450.

11 Merritt to Crook, April 23, 1889, *S. Ex. Docs.*, 51 Cong. 1 sess., IX (2686), no. 72, p. 11. Sooners surveyed Oklahoma City also (Pickler to Noble, May 8, inclosures, *S. Ex. Docs.*, 51 Cong. 1 sess., V (2682), no. 33, p. 7).

12 Report of the Secretary of the Interior for 1889, *loc. cit.*, p. vi.

13 Merritt to Crook, April 23, *S. Ex. Docs.*, 51 Cong. 1 sess., IX (2686), no. 72, p. 11.

14 D. F. Stiles, captain of a company of infantry stationed at Oklahoma City, reported, later in the year, it is true, that "over twelve thousand people" were camped at Oklahoma City on April 23 (Stiles to Sanger, November 7, *S. Ex. Docs.*, 51 Cong. 1 sess., IX (2686), no. 72, p. 35). Wicks (*loc. cit.*, 468) estimated that ten thousand persons were at Guthrie on April 23. He said that there were fifteen thousand there three months later, thirteen thousand of whom were men. Newspaper accounts of the time placed the number who

SETTLEMENT OF OKLAHOMA TERRITORY

The opening in April, 1889, had certain features that were peculiar to it. Congress had adjourned on March 3 without providing for the government of the Oklahoma district apart from the Indian Territory, and the settlers were thus left largely to their own devices. The failure to establish a government led incidentally to a remarkable situation in the towns. As the sections in the statutes which authorized the plotting of town sites on the public land could be placed in operation only by the action of local and civil officials, it was decided that no towns could be established legally.[15] The farmer could take the first step toward the acquisition of a title to his farm under the homestead law, but the dweller in one of the new towns was unable to acquire a legal claim to the lot on which he proposed to settle. The situation was further complicated by a provision that no town site should contain more than three hundred and twenty acres, an area too small for a city of three thousand or more men.[16]

The inhabitants of the towns at once organized temporary or provisional governments. The first steps

---

took part in the rush at fifty thousand, but many of these did not remain long (*Nation*, May 2, 1889, XLVIII, 360). Fifty thousand is also the traditional number accepted in Oklahoma.

15 Stockslager to Vest, April 5, 1889, *H. Ex. Docs.*, 51 Cong. 1 sess., XI (2724), 61. The law provided that the plat of a town established on public land must be filed with the register of the land office by the corporate authorities of the town, if incorporated; if not, by the judge of the county in which it was situated (*Revised Statutes*, secs. 2387, 2388).

16 This was a special provision in the law which authorized the opening of the Oklahoma district (*Statutes*, XXVI, 1005). The general law graduated the number of acres allowed according to the number of inhabitants in town, and the limit was fixed at twelve hundred and eighty acres (*Revised Statutes*, sec. 2389).

toward organization were taken at Guthrie on the evening of April 22, and shortly afterwards D. B. Dyer was elected mayor.[17] At Oklahoma City a call was issued on April 26 for a mass meeting on the next day.[18] At this meeting W. L. Couch, recently leader of the boomers, was chosen temporary mayor, and on May 1 he was elected for a term of one year.[19] Two factions made their appearance after the election. One, the Seminoles, supported Couch; the other, the Kickapoos, demanded a reorganization. The military authorities had to interfere to preserve order.[20] By the end of April local governments were established in the smaller towns.[21]

The settlers at once began to make improvements. Portable houses were brought in on the first afternoon and set up as soon as possible. Guthrie and Oklahoma City grew into typical western towns as rapidly as materials for building could be transported.[22]

In November, according to the annual report of the Secretary of the Interior, sixty thousand persons were in the Oklahoma district. Twenty thousand of these lived in the towns that had been established. Guthrie was said to contain eight thousand inhabitants; Okla-

[17] Wicks, *loc. cit.*, 470.
[18] The call is reprinted in *S. Ex. Docs.*, 51 Cong. 1 sess., IX (2686), no. 72, p. 28.
[19] Minutes of meeting of April 27, copy of records of Oklahoma City relating to the election of May 1, *ibid.*, 29, 30.
[20] Report of J. P. Sanger, inspector-general, November 7, 1889, *ibid.*, 24; Snyder to Sanger, October 26, 1889, *ibid.*, 37.
[21] Williams to Adjutant-General, United States army, April 30, 1889, repeating message of Merritt, *S. Ex. Docs.*, 51 Cong. 1 sess., IX (2686), no. 72, p. 12.
[22] Wicks, *loc. cit.*, 468-470; Pickler to Noble, May 8, 1889, inclosures, *S. Ex. Docs.*, 51 Cong. 1 sess., V (2682), no. 33, pp. 7-11.

SETTLEMENT OF OKLAHOMA TERRITORY

homa City five thousand; and Kingfisher, including Lisbon, three thousand. The settlers supported twenty-nine schools, thirty-eight churches, and twenty-two newspapers.[23]

During the rush and for some time afterward no serious disorder occurred.[24] The first violence reported was at Oklahoma City on June 14, when the newly appointed city marshal of South Oklahoma was shot and killed by the man whom he had supplanted.[25] A general feeling of unrest became apparent in Oklahoma City and probably sprang up in the other towns before the close of the summer, due to the insufficiency of titles and the absence of a properly constituted government.[26]

The town sites had been surveyed by so-called companies. The members of the company took possession of the land as soon as the survey had been completed. Those who came afterwards were required to purchase claims to lots, either from the former occupants or from the company as a whole. In some instances town-site companies clashed. The Seminoles and the Kickapoos of Oklahoma City were originally the partisans of rival companies. One of the chief functions of the provisional town governments was to

23 For 1889, *loc. cit.*, p. vii.
24 Williams to Adjutant-General, United States army, April 30, 1889, repeating message of Merritt, *S. Ex. Docs.*, 51 Cong. 1 sess., IX (2686), no. 72, p. 12.
25 Stiles to Sanger, November 6, 1889, *ibid.*, 31; Snyder to Sanger, October 26, 1889, *ibid.*, 37.
26 Report of J. P. Sanger, inspector-general, inclosures, *loc. cit.*, 22-47 (cf. memorial of a convention of delegates from the town sites in Oklahoma, November 19, 1889, *S. Misc. Docs.*, 51 Cong. 1 sess., II (2698), no. 74).

THE FORMATION OF OKLAHOMA

provide a means of arbitrating disputes between claimants.[27]

The settlers observed the regulation that no town site should contain more than three hundred and twenty acres. Although they were proceeding in an extra-legal manner, they did not wish to do anything that was clearly illegal. To conform to the letter of the law, the larger towns were made up of two or more contiguous town sites, each with its distinct municipal organization. Kingfisher and Lisbon have already been named as forming one town, and South Oklahoma has been mentioned as a part of Oklahoma City. Guthrie finally included five town sites: East Guthrie, South Guthrie, West Guthrie, Capitol Hill, and Guthrie proper or "Dyer's Guthrie."[28]

Towns expanding in this way encroached on land that was claimed for homestead entry. In fact, nearly all of the town sites were contested by persons who had selected them for homesteads.[29]

These complications afforded many opportunities for disputes, and it is remarkable that comparatively good order was maintained. Doubtless it was due in great measure to the presence of the soldiers that serious disturbances were avoided, but General Merritt in his report gave the settlers full credit for their part in this work.[30]

[27] Report of J. P. Sanger, *loc. cit.*, 22-26; Pickler to Noble, May 8, 1889, inclosures, *S. Ex. Docs.*, 51 Cong. 1 sess., V (2682), no. 33, pp. 7-11; same to same, June 21, *ibid.*, 28.

[28] *H. Reports*, 51 Cong. 1 sess., I (2807), no. 4; Pickler to Noble, June 21, 1889, *loc. cit.*, 29.

[29] Memorial of convention of delegates from town sites in Oklahoma, *loc. cit.*

[30] For 1889, *H. Ex. Docs.*, 51 Cong. 1 sess., II (2715), 165, 166.

SETTLEMENT OF OKLAHOMA TERRITORY

When Congress met in December, 1889, the organization of the Territory of Oklahoma was proposed at once. In the Senate the chairman of the Committee on Territories, Orville H. Platte of Connecticut, introduced a bill on December 9 for the establishment of a territory including only the Oklahoma district. The committee reported this bill favorably on January 20, 1890, and on February 13, the Senate passed it with an amendment which brought in No Man's Land.[31] Meanwhile, four or five plans had been proposed in the House of Representatives.[32] The House Committee on Territories on February 15 reported favorably a bill that had been proposed by Bishop W. Perkins of Kansas, and two days later the committee reported the Senate bill amended by the substitution of the Perkins bill. On March 13 the House passed the Senate measure thus amended. It provided for a Territory of Oklahoma which should include all of the Indian Territory except the districts occupied by the Five Civilized Tribes and the seven small reservations northeast of them. The conference committee, yielding to the claims of the Cherokees, who were supported by their friends in Congress, agreed to exclude also the Cherokee outlet. The exclusion of this area was only nominal, however, as it was attached to Oklahoma for judicial purposes. The report of the conference

---

[31] Senate Bill 895, *Cong. Record*, 51 Cong. 1 sess., 123, 688, 1083, 1157, 1274, 1279.

[32] House Bill 6, by William M. Springer of Illinois, December 16, 1889, *ibid.*, 193; House Bill 7, by Charles S. Baker of New York, December 16, *ibid.*, 193; House Bill 224, by Springer, December 18 (bill for State of Columbia; cf. Index, 379), *ibid.*, 233; House Bill 5414, by Baker, January 20, 1890 (bill to organize the Indian Territory), *ibid.*, 709; House Bill 6786, by Perkins, February 11, *ibid.*, 1208.

THE FORMATION OF OKLAHOMA

committee was accepted by the House on April 21, and by the Senate on April 23.[33] After a delay incident to a mistake in describing boundaries, the bill became a law on May 2, 1890. The Territory of Oklahoma was thus finally established a little more than a year after the first authorized settlement within its limits.[34]

The new territory included seven counties. Six of these were in the Oklahoma district. Their county seats were named in the organic act, but their boundaries were left to be delimited by the governor as soon as he should be appointed. The seventh county was No Man's Land, which was opened to settlement by this act. The Indian reservations in the eastern part of the Cherokee outlet and in the Creek, the Seminole, and the Choctaw-Chickasaw cessions of 1866 were made a part of the territory, and were included within the jurisdiction of the territorial courts, although the rights of the existing tribal organizations were preserved. The unoccupied part of the Cherokee outlet, as has been said, was actually but not nominally included. At the same time the judicial district of the Indian Territory was confined to the reservations east of Oklahoma. The permanent existence of two organizations in the former Indian Territory was not contemplated, however, as it was provided that these reservations and the Cherokee outlet should be incorporated with Oklahoma by executive action as soon as the tribal occupants or owners should consent.[35]

---

33 *Ibid.*, 1371, 1425, 1502, 2220, 2336, 3618-3628, 3721. Cf. *H. Reports*, 51 Cong. 1 sess., I (2807), nos. 66, 205.
34 *Cong. Record*, 51 Cong. 1 sess., 3963, 3984, 4023, 4092.
35 *Statutes*, XXVI, 81.

SETTLEMENT OF OKLAHOMA TERRITORY

A separate law passed on May 14 dealing with the difficult problem of the town sites. The adjustment of disputes in each town was placed in the hands of a board of three trustees appointed by the Secretary of the Interior. The area that might be included in a plot was changed from three hundred and twenty to twelve hundred and eighty acres.[36]

The first governor of Oklahoma was George W. Steele of Indiana. He was appointed on May 15, 1890, and on May 22 he reached Guthrie, which had been made the capital. He proceeded at once to define the county boundaries and to establish the county governments. His next task under the law was to arrange for a census of the territory so that representation in the first legislature could be apportioned according to population. This census showed that the inhabitants of the six counties of the Oklahoma district numbered 57,435, and those of No Man's Land 2,982, a total of 60,417 in the territory. The population of Guthrie was found to be 5,884, and of Oklahoma City 5,086. Legislative districts were duly marked out, and the first election was called on August 5. The first legislature of the Territory of Oklahoma assembled at Guthrie on August 27.[37]

36 *Statutes*, XXVI, 109.
37 Report of the Governor of Oklahoma for 1891, *H. Ex. Docs.*, 52 Cong. 1 sess., XVI (2935), 449, 450. The population of the territory was distributed as follows: First county (Logan), 14,254, including Guthrie; second county (Oklahoma), 12,794, including Oklahoma City; third county (Cleveland), 7,011, including Norman, 764; fourth county (Canadian), 7703, including El Reno, 519; fifth county (Kingfisher), 8837, including Kingfisher, 1234; sixth county (Payne), 6836, including Stillwater, 625; seventh county (Beaver), 2982, including Beaver, not separately returned. The permanent county names were selected by popular vote at the first election.

THE FORMATION OF OKLAHOMA

The proper task of this body was the adoption of a code of laws for the territory. The Organic Act had authorized a session of one hundred and twenty days for this purpose. The governor in his first annual report said, "Until within a very few days of the time fixed for the session to close, comparatively little was accomplished." He added, "In the short time remaining, by unusual diligence and judicious selection a very fair code of laws was enacted."[38] The members of the first legislature seemed to have been more interested in the removal of the territorial capital and in the location of territorial institutions than in the passage of laws. The governor by his veto retained the capital at Guthrie; but he approved bills for the location of the territorial schools: namely, a university, a normal school, and an agricultural and mechanical college.[39] These are still in existence and are probably the most lasting results of the work of the first legislature.

The settlers were hardly in their new homes before Congress was called upon to give them aid. They did not enter Oklahoma in 1889 in time to seed their farms, and drought destroyed their growing crops in 1890. Many were practically destitute, and only the assistance given by the United States and by the newly organized counties and municipalities enabled them

---

38 *Ibid.*, 450.

39 Report of the Governor of Oklahoma for 1892, *H. Ex. Docs.*, 52 Cong. 2 sess., XIV (3089), 472, 475. The university was established at Norman; the normal school at Edmond; and the agricultural and mechanical college at Stillwater.

to live until 1891, which was a more propitious year.[40]

In spite of these conditions, every quarter-section of land was occupied in 1890, according to Governor Steele's report. Moreover, many quarters had more than one claimant.[41] In 1891 new territory was opened to settlement.

The Dawes act of 1887 had paved the way for the opening of the reservations in the Territory of Oklahoma. In accordance with the terms of this act, which was supplemented by special agreements with the tribes,[42] lands were allotted in severalty to two thousand seven hundred and eighteen Indians on the Iowa, Sac and Fox, and Pottawatomie-Shawnee reservations situated east of the Oklahoma district. After the Indians had received their allotments, nine hundred thousand acres remained in their reservations, and on September 22, 1891, this area was opened to settlement. The land was not given away. It was sold in tracts of one hundred and sixty acres each for a dollar and a quarter or a dollar and a half an acre, to

40 Report of the Governor of Oklahoma for 1891, *loc. cit.*, 450. The Atchison, Topeka, and Santa Fé, and the Chicago Rock Island, and Pacific railroads each furnished ten thousand dollars' worth of seed wheat to the settlers at actual cost, with free transportation, to be paid for after harvest.
41 *Ibid.*, 450.
42 These agreements were made by the so-called Cherokee commission which was authorized by the Springer amendment to the Indian appropriation act of 1889, the act which authorized the opening of Oklahoma. The agreement with the Iowas was made May 20, 1890; with the Sacs and Foxes, June 12; both were ratified by an act of February 13, 1891 (*Statutes*, XXVI, 749). The agreement with the Pottawatomies was made June 25, 1890; with the Shawnees, June 26; both were ratified by an act of March 3, 1891 (*Statutes*, XXVI, 1016). The Dawes act itself was amended on February 28, 1891, so that each member of the tribe regardless of age or sex received an equal quantity of land, fixed at eighty acres under the usual conditions (*Statutes*, XXVI, 794).

THE FORMATION OF OKLAHOMA

actual occupants only, who must also be qualified to enter land under the homestead law. Nevertheless, the rush was similar to the one of 1889. Practically every tract was occupied on the first day. Local governments were established before the settlers entered.[43]

The government was making preparations for the opening of the Cheyenne and Arapahoe reservations in the western part of the territory at the same time. It was not ready for occupants, however, until April 19, 1892. Three million acres remained to be sold after allotments had been given to three thousand three hundred Indians.[44] No rush attended this opening, as the land was not thought to be desirable, and most of it was far from a railroad. More than half of it was still unoccupied in October.[45]

Meanwhile the government had completed the

[43] Report of the Secretary of the Interior for 1891, *H. Ex. Docs.*, 52 Cong. 1 sess., XIV (2933), pp. iii, iv. The participants in this rush were estimated to number twenty thousand. Two town sites, Chandler and Tecumseh, were reserved by the government. The proclamation was issued September 18 (*Statutes*, XXVII, 989; *Messages and Papers of the Presidents*, IX, 156).

[44] Report of the Secretary of the Interior for 1891, *loc. cit.*, p. v. The agreement with the Cheyennes and Arapahoes was made by the commission in October, 1890, and ratified by an act of March 3, 1891 (*Statutes*, XXVI, 1021). The proclamation was issued April 12, 1892 (*Statutes*, XXVII, 1018; *Messages and Papers of the Presidents*, IX, 275). The land was sold to occupants under the usual regulations for one dollar and fifty cents an acre.

Incidentally, at this time Congress admitted the justice of the contention that Chickasaws and Choctaws, as well as Creeks and Seminoles, were entitled to additional compensation for the cession of 1866 if it should no longer be used exclusively for Indians. Congress appropriated nearly three million dollars for their claims to the portion of the Cheyenne and Arapahoe reservation lying south of the Canadian (act of March 3, 1891, *Statutes*, XXVI, 1025). Later the claims of the Chickasaws and Choctaws for additional compensation for the remainder of their cession of 1866, including Greer County, were left to the Court of Claims (act of June 28, 1898, *Statutes*, XXX, 513). Cf. act of March 2, 1895, *Statutes*, XXVIII, 898, and act of June 6, 1900, *Statutes*, XXXI, 680.

[45] Report of the Governor of Oklahoma for 1892, *loc. cit.*, 470, 474.

SETTLEMENT OF OKLAHOMA TERRITORY

negotiations with the Cherokees for the opening of the outlet. The commission authorized by the act which provided for the opening of the Oklahoma district failed to accomplish anything in 1889.[46] To insure the ultimate success of this commission, President Harrison on February 17, 1890, issued a proclamation warning cattlemen that they would no longer be permitted to occupy the outlet.[47] During the boomer agitation the authorities rather unwillingly had allowed the Cherokees to make leases.[48] In 1889 a syndicate of cattlemen had encouraged the Indians to reject the offers of the government.[49] This proclamation not only put a stop to the intrigues of the cattlemen, but it also made this western tract practically valueless to the Cherokees. They could not expand into the outlet, as other reservations separated it from the district in which they lived. Moreover, this action indicated that the government was willing to take steps to coerce them. Accordingly, the Cherokees yielded in January, 1892, and the outlet was relinquished to the United States.[50] Congress accepted the terms of the agreement by an act of March 3, 1893.[51]

46 Report of the Secretary of the Interior for 1889, *H. Ex. Docs.*, 51 Cong. 1 sess., XI (2724), p. xiii.

47 *Statutes*, XXVI, 1577; *Messages and Papers of the Presidents*, IX, 97.

48 For a summary of the actions of the government to 1889, see Noble to Fairchild, October 26, 1889, *H. Ex. Docs.*, 51 Cong. 1 sess., XI (2724), pp. cxlii-cli.

49 *Ibid.*, p. cxl. This syndicate was the Cherokee Strip Live Stock Association, already mentioned.

50 Agreement made December 19, 1891; approved by the Cherokees January 4, 1892 (*S. Ex. Docs.*, 52 Cong. 1 sess., V (2900), no. 56).

51 *Statutes*, XXVII, 640. Some minor changes were made in the agreement by Congress, which necessitated a new approval by the Cherokees. This was given on April 3, 1893, and a contract was signed on May 17 (report

THE FORMATION OF OKLAHOMA

The Cherokees gave up a tract of more than six million acres. For it they received eight and one-half million dollars. They also stipulated that seventy of their tribesmen should receive allotments in the cession. Finally, they secured a new promise that intruders should be removed from the country remaining to them.[52]

By the same act Congress ratified agreements made by the Cherokee commission with the other tribes. The Tonkawas in September, 1891, and the Pawnees in November, 1892, had consented to take allotments.[53] The reservations of these tribes were adjacent to the Cherokee outlet, and Congress authorized the president to open to settlement at the same time the surplus land of these tracts. He was further authorized to make additional regulations governing the manner in which persons might occupy the land after the opening.[54] Six million three hundred and sixty-one thousand acres, nearly ten thousand square miles, were ready for settlers after a thousand Indians had received allotments.[55]

---

of the Commissioner of Indian Affairs for 1893, *H. Ex. Docs.*, 53 Cong. 2 sess., XIV (3210), 33.

52 The total area of the land actually ceded was said to be 6,022,754.11 acres. The sum paid the Cherokees for this tract was $8,595,736.12, but a deduction was made for the stipulated allotments at one dollar and forty cents an acre. This amounted to less than eight thousand dollars, however. The Cherokees considered that the cession included all the former Cherokee lands west of the ninety-sixth meridian, as they insisted that they had not been fully paid for the Osage and other reservations hitherto ceded.

53 Agreement with the Tonkawas, October 21, 1891, *S. Ex. Docs.*, 52 Cong. 1 sess., I (2892), no. 13; with the Pawnees, November 23, 1892, *S. Ex. Docs.*, 52 Cong. 2 sess., I (3055), no. 16.

54 *Statutes*, XXVII, 642, 644.

55 Report of the Commissioner of Indian Affairs for 1893, *loc. cit.*, 33.

SETTLEMENT OF OKLAHOMA TERRITORY

The President issued his proclamation on August 19, 1893, declaring that the land would be opened to settlement at noon on September 16.[56] An attempt was made to use the power conferred on the executive department to prevent the recurrence of the disorders that had attended the first opening. In particular the settlers were given the protection of local government;[57] but this was not new, as it had been done at all openings after the first one. Preparations were also made to keep ineligible persons from taking part in the rush. On September 11 nine registration booths were established, five on the northern and four on the southern border. They were placed under the management of clerks detailed from the General Land Office, three to a booth. Each person who wished to purchase town lots or a homestead[58] was required to

---

The Indians were distributed as follows: Pawnees, 820, *ibid.*, Tonkawas, 70, report for 1892, *H. Ex. Docs.*, 52 Cong. 2 sess., XIII (3088), 79; Cherokees, not to exceed 70, report of the Secretary of the Interior for 1893, *H. Ex. Docs.*, 53 Cong. 2 sess., XIII (3209), p. xii.

56 *Statutes*, XXVIII, 1222; *Messages and Papers of the Presidents*, IX, 406.

57 The Secretary of the Interior was authorized to establish counties by the act of March 3, 1893 (*Statutes*, XXVII, 645). The outlet became a part of the Territory of Oklahoma as soon as the President had declared it open to settlement. "Whenever the interest of the Cherokee Indians in the land known as the Cherokee outlet shall have been extinguished, and the President shall make proclamation thereof, said outlet shall thereupon and without further legislation become a part of the Territory of Oklahoma" (organic act of Oklahoma, May 2, 1890, *Statutes*, XXVI, 82).

58 The land east of the meridian of ninety-seven and one-half degrees west longitude was sold for two dollars and fifty cents an acre; between ninety-seven and one-half and ninety-eight and one-half, for two dollars an acre; west of ninety-eight and one-half, for one dollar and fifty cents an acre (act of March 3, 1893, *Statutes*, XXVII, 642, 643, 644). The same act authorized the Secretary of the Interior to reserve town sites, one in each county. They were known as government town sites. Companies, however, could establish other towns under the general laws.

THE FORMATION OF OKLAHOMA

make a written declaration of his qualifications to occupy the land under the homestead law. He was given a certificate in return, and the officers were instructed to allow no one to enter without this certificate. The rush of applicants was extraordinary. More than one hundred thousand registered. The scenes of 1889 were reproduced on a much larger scale.[59]

Oklahoma first became a compact body of land as a result of this opening. Besides the strip projecting west of the hundredth meridian, No Man's Land, one-third of the Indian Territory was opened to settlement between 1889 and 1893. The portion of the present state of Oklahoma which lies east of the one hundredth meridian, in other words, the Indian Territory, as it was constituted for a long time, is a rectangle three hundred miles from east to west and two hundred miles from north to south. For convenience, it may be considered as made up of six plots each approximately one hundred miles square. At the close of 1893, two of these squares were open to white settlers, and four were still devoted to the use of the Indians. The northwestern and north-central squares were occupied by citizens of the United States. The northeastern, southeastern, and south-central squares were occupied by the Osages, the Five Civilized Tribes, and several small bands. The southwestern square contained the Wichita and the Kiowa-Comanche-Apache reservations and the tract of land claimed by Texas. In the

---

[59] Report of the Secretary of the Interior for 1893, *loc. cit.*, p. x. In all, one hundred and fifteen thousand persons secured certificates (report of the Commissioner of the General Land Office for 1894, *H. Ex. Docs.*, 53 Cong. 3 sess., XIV (3305), 101).

SETTLEMENT OF OKLAHOMA TERRITORY

eight years from 1893 to 1901 only two additions were made to the area that was open to settlement. One small reservation, that of the Kickapoos, was opened,[60] and the Supreme Court decided against the claims of Texas to the land between the forks of the Red River. During these eight years, within comparatively stable limits, the political development of Oklahoma as a mixed commonwealth really began.

The number of counties in the territory grew from seven in 1890 to twenty-three in 1896. Two new counties were formed from the reservations opened in 1891. They were designated as A and B. The Cheyenne and Arapahoe reservation was divided into six new counties, which were designated by the letters from C to H. The land opened in 1893 made seven new counties, and these were designated by the letters from K to Q. The voters of each country were allowed to select a permanent name for it.[61] The twenty-third county was formed out of the territory awarded to Oklahoma by the Supreme Court on March 16, 1896.[62] Congress in

---

60 See below, p. 207.

61 Report of the Governor of Oklahoma for 1892, *loc. cit.*, 474; for 1893, *H. Ex. Docs.*, 53 Cong. 2 sess., XV (3211), 453; for 1894, *H. Ex. Docs.*, 53 Cong. 3 sess., XVI (3307), 440; for 1895, *H. Ex. Docs.*, 54 Cong. 1 sess., XVI (3383), 515. Some of the land newly opened was attached on each occasion to existing counties. A became Lincoln; B, Pottawatomie; C, Blaine; D, Dewey; E, Day; F, Roger Mills; G, Custer; H, Washita; K, Kay; L, Grant, M, Woods; N, Woodward; O, Garfield; P. Noble; Q, Pawnee. The Wichita reservation, which will be considered below, was designated County I by the Secretary of the Interior at the time of the opening of the Cheyenne and Arapahoe reservation, and it appeared on maps as an unorganized county for a long time (report of the Governor of Oklahoma for 1899, *H. Docs.*, 56 Cong. 1 sess., XXI (3918), 742, map opp. p. 744).

62 United States *vs.* Texas, 162 U. S., 1. The court upheld the contention of the United States that the boundary fixed by the treaty of 1819 with Spain had followed the South Fork of the Red River to the true one-hun-

THE FORMATION OF OKLAHOMA

May enacted legislation erecting it into a county of Oklahoma.[63] It had been made a county under the name of Greer by the legislature of Texas in 1860.[64] The land had been occupied by settlers as a part of the domain of Texas, but Congress on January 18, 1897, passed an act declaring it open to settlement with provisions intended to secure the rights of the occupants.[65]

The population of Oklahoma increased rather uniformly in the decade between 1890 and 1900. It was sixty thousand in 1890. In 1892 the governor estimated that it was one hundred and thirty thousand, and in 1893 his successor placed it at one hundred and fifty thousand. These numbers were probably too large, as

---

dredth meridian. The decision was based on the fact that the South Fork was the larger and longer stream and that it kept the same general direction as the Red River below the junction of the forks. The counsel for the State of Texas contended that the North Fork was historically the more important. They also pointed out that Texas had occupied the disputed territory for nearly forty years and that the United States (probably inadvertently) had recognized this occupancy.

The inaccuracies of the Melish map, which was used by the framers of the treaty, gave rise to the controversy. On this map, published in 1818, the forks of the Red River were placed far to the west of the one-hundredth meridian.

The decision made this tract a part of Oklahoma without further legislation, as the southern and western borders of the territory were fixed at the boundary of the State of Texas by the organic act. The area of this addition was one million five hundred thousand acres. See also the report of the Texas Boundary Commission, 1887, *H. Ex. Docs.*, 50 Cong. 1 sess., XVIII (2550), no. 21.

63 Act of May 4, 1896, *Statutes*, XXIX, 113.

64 Sayles' *Early Laws of Texas*, Art. 2886, quoted in United States *vs.* Texas, 162 U. S., 67.

65 *Statutes*, XXIX, 490. The President had withdrawn Greer County from settlement on March 16, 1896 (*Statutes*, XXIX, 878; *Messages and Papers of the Presidents*, IX, 690). This gave Congress an opportunity to enact special legislation regarding it. It will be remembered that the Chickasaws and Choctaws also had claims for consideration, as this country had once belonged to them, if it had never belonged to Texas.

SETTLEMENT OF OKLAHOMA TERRITORY

the returns of the territorial census of February, 1894, showed a population of only two hundred and twelve thousand, and the settled area had recently been doubled by the opening of the Cherokee outlet and the Pawnee and Tonkawa reservations. The territorial census of 1896 showed that Oklahoma had two hundred and seventy-five thousand inhabitants, eight thousand five hundred of whom lived in Greer County, which was added to the territory in that year. In 1898 the population was three hundred and eleven thousand. In 1900 it was three hundred and ninety-seven thousand according to the territorial census, or three hundred and ninety-eight thousand according to the United States census.[66]

Some of the towns established at the openings after the first grew rapidly; but, because of better governmental provisions, their beginnings were hardly as turbulent as the beginnings of Oklahoma City or Guthrie. Enid in the Cherokee outlet had five thousand inhabitants shortly after its founding.[67]

The material progress of Oklahoma was bound up with the development of its railroads. They played a part in the settlement of the West similar to that of navigable rivers in the settlement of other parts of the

---

66 Report of the Governor of Oklahoma for 1891, *loc. cit.*, 449; for 1892, *loc. cit.*, 469; for 1893, *loc. cit.*, 453; for 1894, *loc. cit.*, 440; for 1896, *H. Docs.*, 54 Cong. 2 sess., XIV (3490), 422; for 1898, *H. Docs.*, 55 Cong. 3 sess., XVI (3758), 659; for 1900, *H. Docs.*, 56 Cong. 2 sess., XXX (4104), 580.

67 Report of the Secretary of the Interior for 1893, *loc. cit.*, p. xiii. Enid was one of the towns established by the government. It was in turmoil for a time because the Rock Island Railroad refused to stop its trains there. A station was established at North Enid, a company town site near, in which the railroad apparently was interested. Congress on August 8, 1894, passed an act designed especially to meet the situation (*Statutes*, XXVIII, 263).

{ 205 }

THE FORMATION OF OKLAHOMA

United States. A line of the Chicago, Rock Island, and Pacific was completed across Oklahoma and to the border of the Chickasaw district in 1890. This line was constructed nearly parallel to and from thirty to forty miles west of the line of the Atchison, Topeka, and Santa Fé, which had dominated the settlement of the Oklahoma district. In that year the Choctaw Coal and Railway Company completed a line from Oklahoma City westward to a junction with the Rock Island at El Reno, thus connecting the two other railroads of the territory. In 1895 this line was extended eastward from Oklahoma City into the Indian Territory to join sections of road already constructed.[68] This railroad, called for a time the Choctaw, Oklahoma, and Gulf, furnished means of communication with the Choctaw district and with Arkansas. It also connected with the Missouri, Kansas, and Texas at McAlester. The early construction of the Choctaw road was an important factor in the upbuilding of Oklahoma City.

The lines of the Atchison, Topeka, and Santa Fé and the Chicago, Rock Island, and Pacific, which served Oklahoma district, also served the eastern part of the Cherokee outlet. Another line of the Santa Fé crossed the western part of the outlet, passing out of it near its southwestern corner. These three roads played important parts in the opening of 1893.

In 1889 Oklahoma had eighty miles of railroad in operation, and in 1892 it had one hundred and seventy-two miles. In 1894 this number had become

---

[68] Report of the Governor of Oklahoma for 1892, *loc. cit.*, 471; for 1895, *loc. cit.*, 515; report of Leo Bennett, union agent, for 1890, *H. Ex. Docs.*, 51 Cong. 2 sess., XII (2841), 96.

SETTLEMENT OF OKLAHOMA TERRITORY

three hundred and eighty-two, as a result of the annexation of the Cherokee outlet to the territory. About fifty additional miles were constructed in 1895. The reports for 1896 and 1897 show little change in the mileage, but the growth in 1898, 1899, and 1900 was rapid. In the latter year seven hundred and eighty-two miles were in operation. Only four of the twenty-three counties were not reached directly. In 1901 nine hundred and twenty-five miles were in operation. Every county but one was reached directly, and the number of counties had become twenty-six.[69] In that year two new reservations were opened to settlement, and from the land contained in these reservations three new counties were formed.

About ten years before, the Cherokee commissioners had made three agreements for the dissolution of tribal reservations that had been without immediate results. One was made with the Indians of the Wichita reservation on June 4, 1891; one with the Kickapoos on September 9 of that year; and one with the Kiowa, Comanche, and Apache Indians on October 21, 1892.[70] The Kickapoo reservation was surrounded by land that had been opened to settlement in 1889 and 1891, and Congress by an act of March 3,

---

[69] Report of the Governor of Oklahoma for 1892, *loc. cit.*, 471; for 1894, *loc. cit.*, 441; for 1895, *loc. cit.*, 515; for 1896, *loc. cit.*, 423; for 1897, *H. Docs.*, 55 Cong. 2 sess., XIV (3642), 544; for 1898, *loc. cit.*, 685; for 1899, *H. Docs.*, 56 Cong. 1 sess., XXI (3918), 687-691; for 1900, *loc. cit.*, 620, map opp. p. 688; for 1901, *H. Docs.*, 57 Cong. 1 sess., XXVI (4293), 373, map opp. p. 446.

[70] Wichita reservation, *S. Ex. Docs.*, 52 Cong. 1 sess., I (2892), no. 14; Kickapoos, articles dated June 21, *Statutes*, XXVII, 557; Kiowas, etc., *S. Ex. Docs.*, 52 Cong. 2 sess., I (3055), no. 17.

THE FORMATION OF OKLAHOMA

1893, approved the agreement for its opening.[71] Two hundred and eighty-three Indians received allotments, and much of the remaining land was given to the territory as indemnity for sections of school land that had been appropriated to other uses. An area of less than two hundred thousand acres, more than half of which had been reserved, was opened by the President's proclamation in May, 1895. The land opened was sold under the usual regulations. No new counties were formed from this reservation, as the existing counties adjoining were extended to include it.[72] The agreement with the Indians of the Wichita reservation was approved in March, 1895, but this reservation was not opened until the contiguous Kiowa, Comanche, and Apache reservation was ready for settlement. The agreement with the latter Indians was not approved by Congress until June, 1900.[73]

Two million acres, about three thousand square miles, were ready to be opened in these reservations in July, 1901. About three thousand five hundred Indians

---

71 *Statutes*, XXVII, 562.

72 Report of the Secretary of the Interior for 1895, *H. Docs.*, 54 Cong. 1 sess., XIV (3381), p. viii; of the Commissioner of the General Land Office for 1895, *ibid.*, 137; of the Governor of Oklahoma for 1895, *loc. cit.*, 514, 524, 525. An act of March 2, 1895 (*Statutes*, XXVIII, 899), authorized a state or territory to select indemnity school lands from the surplus lands left in any reservation within its limits after the completion of allotments. Sections 16 and 36 had been reserved for the support of schools in all of Oklahoma, and at the later openings additional sections were reserved. Certain of these sections, however, had been allotted to the Indians. The loss on this account was made up in accordance with this act. The lands opened were sold for one dollar and fifty cents an acre. The President's proclamation was issued on May 18, and the reservation was opened on May 23 (*Statutes*, XXIX, 868; *Messages and Papers of the Presidents*, IX, 690).

73 Act of March 2, 1895, *Statutes*, XXVIII, 897; act of June 6, 1900, *Statutes*, XXXI, 679.

SETTLEMENT OF OKLAHOMA TERRITORY

had received allotments, and a large area had been reserved from settlement. The President had been authorized to prescribe additional regulations under which the land should be occupied. He approved a plan for disposing of the quarter-sections by lot to applicants who were qualified to enter land under the homestead law. Those who wished to participate in the drawing were required to register in person at one of the two land offices. Applicants were given choice of farms in the order in which their names were drawn. More than one hundred and fifty thousand persons registered, but the number of the successful was limited to thirteen thousand.[74]

The Secretary of the Interior had been authorized by law to divide the two reservations into counties. He delimited three new counties, and in each of them a county seat was established. The lots in these new towns were sold at auction. Lawton, the most prominent of the three, had four thousand five hundred inhabitants, according to a territorial census taken shortly after the opening.[75]

74 Report of the Secretary of the Interior for 1901, *H. Docs.*, 57 Cong. 1 sess., XXII (4289), pp. xxiv, cclviii (cf. act of March 3, 1901, *Statutes*, XXXI, 1094). The land offices were at El Reno, on the border of the new country, and at Lawton. Those who drew farms paid a dollar and a quarter an acre for their land, or two dollars and a half if they wanted a title in fourteen months. In accordance with the agreement of October, 1892, with the Kiowas, etc., and the act of June 6, 1900, which approved it, the Secretary of the Interior reserved four hundred and eighty thousand acres of grazing land for the Indians. This was selected in one large and three small tracts. The large tract, which contained four hundred thousand acres, came to be known as the "big pasture." These reservations, with a small wood reserve near them, which brought the total to over half a million acres, were sold to the highest bidder in tracts of one hundred and sixty acres in December, 1906 (act of June 5, 1906, *Statutes*, XXXIV, 213; report of the Governor of Oklahoma for 1907, *H. Docs.*, 60 Cong. 1 sess., XXVII (5296), 686).

75 Report of the Secretary of the Interior for 1901, *loc. cit.*, pp. ccxliv, cclxiv; of the Governor of Oklahoma for 1901, *loc. cit.*, 440. This sale of lots

THE FORMATION OF OKLAHOMA

At the close of 1901 half of the former Indian Territory had been opened to settlement. The western third and the northern part of the central third were almost completely occupied. According to the territorial census of 1902, the Territory of Oklahoma contained five hundred and forty thousand inhabitants, of whom ten thousand were Indians without tribal relations.[76] The remainder of the former Indian Territory consisted of two unequal parts: the unoccupied portion of the Territory of Oklahoma, including the Osage and the smaller reservations, Kaw, Ponca, and Otoe-Missouri,[77] and the diminished Indian Territory, including the country of the Five Civilized Tribes and their neighbors, the small tribes of the Neosho. In the meantime, however, settlers had occupied this area in advance of its formal opening.

---

was authorized by the act of March 3, 1901, which conferred many powers on the secretary of the interior. It was stipulated that the proceeds of the sale should be used for the benefit of the county. The new counties were named Kiowa, Comanche, and Caddo.

[76] Report of the Governor of Oklahoma for 1902, *H. Docs.*, 57 Cong. 2 sess., XXII (4461), 392, 452. One reason for the rapid growth after 1900 was the passage of the "free homes bill" on May 17, 1900 (*Statutes*, XXXI, 179). This measure not only provided that the unoccupied land in all the reservations opened before that date could be entered free, but also that unpaid balances should not be collected for land already entered.

[77] The total area of the four reservations in the northeastern corner of the Territory of Oklahoma was about twenty-seven hundred square miles (report of the Secretary of the Interior for 1901, *loc. cit.*, p. cxliv). Several small military, forest, and pasture reserves were included in the remaining thirty-six thousand square miles of the Territory of Oklahoma. The area of the Indian Territory as reduced was about thirty-one thousand square miles.

CHAPTER XI

THE SETTLEMENT OF THE INDIAN TERRITORY

THE settlement of the Indian Territory as diminished in 1890 went on contemporaneously with the boomer agitation and the occupation of the Territory of Oklahoma. Nevertheless, the two movements were unlike in many ways. Oklahoma was peopled by formally authorized rushes, while settlers filtered into the country of the Five Civilized Tribes without official invitation and before provision had been made for them. The government hesitated to abolish the Indian Territory, but it was hardly possible to keep a tract of available land with only two inhabitants to the square mile, when the adjoining state of Missouri had forty to the square mile. Accordingly, there was a steady drift across the border for many years, and the presence among the Indians of hundreds of thousands of persons who were outlanders under their own flag finally made it necessary to abolish the tribal organizations.

In 1880 twenty thousand Cherokees occupied a little less than eight thousand square miles of territory, sixteen thousand Choctaws occupied more than ten thousand square miles, six thousand Chickasaws occupied seven thousand square miles, fifteen thousand Creeks occupied five thousand square miles, and two thousand five hundred Seminoles occupied nearly six hundred

THE FORMATION OF OKLAHOMA

square miles. One thousand Indians of seven small bands occupied two hundred thousand acres in the extreme northeastern part of the territory. These sixty thousand Indians occupied the thirty-one thousand square miles to which the Indian Territory was to be confined ten years later.[1]

Immediately after the Civil War white persons who were not adopted tribal citizens began to drift into the eastern part of the Indian Territory.[2] In 1879 there were five thousand of these persons in the whole territory, besides twelve hundred other non-citizens made up of the employees of the railroads and their families.[3] In 1880 six thousand white persons were reported to be in the reservations of the Five Civilized Tribes. This number did not include the employees of the railroads, and it did not include certain laborers who had been authorized by the tribal officials to remain. Although the Indians called for the removal of the intruders, it is significant that some white persons who were not citizens were acceptable.[4] Land in the Indian Territory was made more valuable by the work of the

---

1 These numbers are taken from the report of John Q. Tufts, union agent, for 1880, *H. Ex. Docs.*, 46 Cong. 3 sess., IX (1959), 216, and from the report of D. B. Dyer, agent at the Neosho agency, for 1880, *ibid.*, 208. See also below, Appendix C and D. For a statement concerning the Seminole reservation see above, Chapter VI, footnote 7.

2 "A serious difficulty in the not distant future is before these tribes [i.e., the Five Civilized Tribes] arising from the large and steady influx of white people. Since the emancipation of their slaves, these Indians have sought exemption from labor by inviting emigration of . . . whites from the surrounding states, to whom they rent their lands for one-third of the crops raised. These whites once in the country are seldom known to leave" (from the report of the Commissioner of Indian Affairs for 1874, *H. Ex. Docs.*, 43 Cong. 2 sess., VI (1639), 381).

3 *S. Reports*, 45 Cong. 3 sess., III (1839), p. iii.

4 Report of Agent Tufts for 1880, *loc. cit.*, 216.

SETTLEMENT OF INDIAN TERRITORY

outlanders, and a movement had already begun that was to prove a factor in the dissolution of the Five Civilized Tribes.

The number of white persons in the eastern part of the Indian Territory increased rapidly in the decade between 1880 and 1890. In 1881 those with permits from the Indian authorities were said to number fifteen thousand. The government was trying to remove the thousands who were without permits, but it was hampered by the same conditions that kept it from checking Payne and his followers farther west.[5] In 1884 the number of outlanders living among the Indians of the Five Civilized Tribes was estimated to be thirty-five thousand, many of whom were intruders. In the words of Agent Tufts, these intruders when removed took "one or two breaths of state air" and returned to the territory.[6]

During the next four years the estimates were somewhat more conservative, as a new agent, Robert L. Owen, was in charge of the affairs of the Five Civilized Tribes. In 1885 he reported that there were seventeen thousand laborers in the five reservations under permit of the Indian authorities, three thousand employees of the government and the railroads, fifteen hundred travellers, and three or four thousand intruders, or in all twenty-five thousand white persons, including of course women and children. In his report for the next year he said that this number had grown

---

5 Report of Agent Tufts for 1881, *H. Ex. Docs.*, 47 Cong. 1 sess., X (2018), 161, 162. Cf. his report for 1882, *H. Ex. Docs.*, 47 Cong. 2 sess., XI (2100), 148.

6 *H. Ex. Docs.*, 48 Cong. 2 sess., XII (2287), 142, 143.

to thirty-two thousand, three thousand less than the number given by his predecessor two years before. He estimated that the intruders numbered five thousand and that the employees of the government and the railroads, together with the miners, numbered eight thousand. This was the first time that miners received separate mention in the estimates of the agents, although their presence in the Indian Territory had been noticed before. In 1888 Owen reported that thirty-eight thousand five hundred outlanders were living in the territory of the Five Civilized Tribes. The travellers were again said to number fifteen hundred and the intruders five thousand. The laborers with permits from the Indians were given as twenty-two thousand, and the other authorized employees with their families as ten thousand.[7]

The numbers in the report for 1889 are much larger. No doubt this may be due in part to the more liberal estimates of the new agent, Leo E. Bennett. According to him, there were forty-five thousand laborers and mechanics in the employ of the Indians, twenty-five thousand other employees, thirty-five thousand intruders, and three thousand travellers, out of a total population of one hundred and seventy-five thousand in the reservation of the Five Civilized Tribes. In 1890 the numbers were reported by him as forty-eight thousand, twenty-six thousand, sixty-four thousand, and two thousand, respectively, or one hundred and forty thousand white persons out of a total population of a little

7 Report for 1885, *H. Ex. Docs.*, 49 Cong. 1 sess., XII (2379), 329; for 1886, *H. Ex. Docs.*, 49 Cong. 2 sess., VIII (2467), 365; for 1888, *H. Ex. Docs.*, 50 Cong. 2 sess., XI (2637), 114.

SETTLEMENT OF INDIAN TERRITORY

more than two hundred and ten thousand. Bennett's estimate of the number of outlanders was probably somewhat too large, as the returns of the United States census of 1890 gave only one hundred and seventy-eight thousand as the total population of these reservations, and the two reports of the number of Indian citizens differed but little. Nevertheless, it is undoubtedly true that there was a remarkable influx of settlers into the territory of the Five Civilized Tribes in 1889 and 1890, the years of the occupation of the Oklahoma district.[8]

Two special factors, in addition to the success of the boomers in an adjoining area, contributed to this movement. One of these was the extension of the railroads; the other was the development of the mines.

Two railroads had entered the Indian Territory in the early seventies, as has already been stated. The Missouri, Kansas, and Texas, the first road to cross the territory from north to south, was constructed through Vinita, Muskogee, and McAlester in 1871 and 1872. The Atlantic and Pacific was extended from the southwestern corner of Missouri to Vinita in 1871.[9] After the completion of these railroads, no extensions were made for nearly a decade. In 1882 work began on the extension of the Atlantic and Pacific, now called the Saint Louis and San Francisco, westward from Vinita.[10] In

[8] Report for 1889, *H. Ex. Docs.*, 51 Cong. 1 sess., XII (2725), 202; for 1890, *H. Ex. Docs.*, 51 Cong. 2 sess., XII (2841), 89. For the population of the Indian Territory according to the census of 1890, see below, Appendix D, under that year.

[9] See above, Chapter VI, footnote 11.

[10] Report of the Commissioner of Indian Affairs for 1882, *H. Ex. Docs.*, 47 Cong. 2 sess., XI (2100), 19.

THE FORMATION OF OKLAHOMA

1887 and 1888 the mileage grew rapidly. A line of the Santa Fé system was completed through the Cherokee outlet, the Oklahoma district, and the Chickasaw district in 1887. In the same year a line of the Saint Louis and San Francisco was constructed from Fort Smith, Arkansas, across the Choctaw district to the Red River by way of the Kiamichi Valley. In 1888 the Kansas and Arkansas Valley Railroad completed a line from Fort Smith northeastward to Wagoner. In 1889 this road was extended to Coffeyville, Kansas, and the Saint Louis and San Francisco completed the extension westward from Vinita as far as Sapulpa. In 1889 and 1890 the Choctaw Coal and Railway Company constructed a line from McAlester eastward for eighty miles nearly to Fort Smith.[11] The new railroads not only gave employment to many persons, but they opened additional agricultural land to market.

The development of the mines was only less important than that of the railroads. Coal was first discovered at McAlester in 1872. In 1886 several mines were in operation. Large towns were growing up near them. McAlester, Krebs, and Lehigh were the most important. These towns were entirely without civil govern-

[11] Report of the union agent for 1887, *H. Ex. Docs.*, 50 Cong. 1 sess., XI (2542), 200; for 1888, *loc. cit.*, 127; for 1889, *loc. cit.*, 208; for 1890, *loc. cit.*, 96. The number of miles of railroad in the Indian Territory at the time of its division in 1890 was one thousand and forty-six (the eleventh census of the United States, *H. Misc. Docs.*, 52 Cong. 1 sess., L, vi (3016), 263). Two-thirds of this mileage had been completed in the preceding three years (compare map for 1890, *ibid.*, facing p. 242, with map for beginning of 1887, *H. Misc. Docs.*, 49 Cong. 1 sess., XXVI (2432), facing p. 852). The Cherokees sought to prevent the construction of railroads other than those authorized by the treaty of 1866, but an injunction was refused by the United States district court in February, 1888 (Cherokee Nation *vs.* Southern Kansas R. Co., *Federal Reporter*, XXXIII, 900).

SETTLEMENT OF INDIAN TERRITORY

ment. In 1888 Lehigh, on a spur of the Missouri, Kansas, and Texas, secured permission of the Indian agent to establish a provisional municipal government for itself.[12] It was evident that Congress must soon provide at least a partial reorganization of the Indian Territory.

The judicial system of the Indian Territory during this period was extremely unsatisfactory. While the court at Fort Smith had jurisdiction in any criminal case in which a citizen of the United States was accused, the difficulty of reaching this court was so great that prosecutions were avoided whenever it was possible. According to Agent Tufts, it was almost as great a hardship to be summoned to Fort Smith as a witness as to be taken there as an alleged criminal, since the fees and mileage did not cover the expense of the journey.[13] Moreover, no court had jurisdiction in civil cases in which white persons who were not tribal citizens were involved. For instance, it was found to be impossible to foreclose a mortgage on the section of the Atlantic and Pacific Railroad that was in the Cherokee reservation.[14] It was even asserted that many

12 Report of the union agent for 1886, *loc. cit.*, 379; for 1887, *loc. cit.*, 201; for 1888, loc. cit., 128. The population of the larger towns in 1890 was given as follows: Ardmore, 2100; Caddo, 2170; Krebs, 3000; Lehigh, 1600; McAlester, 3000; Muskogee, 1200; Purcell, 1060; Tahlequah, 1200; Vinita, 1200 (the eleventh census of the United States, Indians, *loc. cit.*, 260). Tahlequah was the only one of these places that was not on a railroad, but not all of the others were dominantly or even partly dependent on the mines.

13 Report of the union agent for 1881, *loc. cit.*, 161, 162 (cf. *Revised Statutes*, sections 2145, 2146).

14 Report of the union agent for 1881, *loc. cit.*, 161, 162; testimony of James Baker before Senate committee in 1878, *S. Reports*, 45 Cong. 3 sess., III (1839), 2.

THE FORMATION OF OKLAHOMA

of the intruders were lawless persons who had been attracted to the Indian Territory by its freedom from legal restraints.[15]

The act of January 6, 1883, which provided for the division of the territory among the western district of Arkansas, the district of Kansas, and the northern district of Texas, did not affect the reservations of the Five Civilized Tribes, for they were attached as before to the western district of Arkansas.[16] This act did not confer any additional jurisdiction on the courts, and conditions remained unchanged until 1889 in spite of numerous attempts to organize a judicial system.[17]

On March 1, 1889, an act was passed establishing a United States court at Muskogee for the Indian Territory. Jurisdiction was given to this court in civil cases in which citizens of the United States were inter-

15 Report of the Commissioner of Indian Affairs for 1881, *H. Ex. Docs.*, 47 Cong. 1 sess., X (2018), 48.

16 *Statutes*, XXII, 400. The reservations on the Neosho, however, were attached to the district of Kansas by this act.

17 George G. Vest, senator from Missouri, introduced a bill in each Congress from the Forty-sixth to the Fiftieth for the establishment of a United States court in the Indian Territory, and his bills were uniformly reported by the committee (Senate Bill 1418, *Cong. Record*, 46 Cong. 2 sess., 1298; Senate Bill 181, *Cong. Record*, 47 Cong. 1 sess., 22, 3966; Senate Bill 209, *Cong. Record*, 48 Cong. 1 sess., 18, 1142; Senate Bill 102, *Cong. Record*, 49 Cong. 1 sess., 128, 6480; Senate Bill 270, *Cong. Record*, 50 Cong. 1 sess., 24 858). None of these bills passed the Senate. Other bills with similar titles were introduced, but they were not reported or were reported adversely. In the Forty-ninth Congress a bill, H. R. 5545, by John H. Rogers of Arkansas, passed the House, proposing to confer civil jurisdiction on the United States district courts which already had criminal jurisdiction (*Cong. Record*, 49 Cong. 1 sess., 1346, 3795). The House passed a similar bill in the next Congress, House Bill 1204, by Rogers (*Cong. Record*, 50 Cong. 1 sess., 206, 683). The bill which finally passed the Fiftieth Congress was a fusion in conference committee of Vest's bill, Senate Bill 270, and a bill, House Bill 1874, by David B. Culberson of Texas, for the rearrangement of the judicial districts of Texas and the Indian Territory (*Cong. Record*, 50 Cong. 1 sess., 232, 2352, 2989, 2 sess., 1644, 1709, 1716, 1783, 2317, 2385, 2398, 2458, 2671).

SETTLEMENT OF INDIAN TERRITORY

ested, if the amount involved exceeded the sum of one hundred dollars. As the Indian Territory had no lawmaking body, Congress provided that certain laws of the state of Arkansas should be enforced. Appeals to the Supreme Court of the United States were authorized in important cases. Jurisdiction was also given to the new court over all offenses not punishable by death or by imprisonment at hard labor. The district courts of the western district of Arkansas, the district of Kansas, and the eastern district of Texas retained jurisdiction over the more serious offenses.[18]

Some provisions relating to the selection of juries[19] and the punishment of offenses were contained in this act, but the most important section of incidental legislation was the one which authorized the leasing of mines. Coal leases, like grazing leases, had been technically illegal hitherto, but by this law the mining industry was placed on a more secure basis.

The jurisdiction of the United States court in the Indian Territory was enlarged in the next year. Certain sections of the act providing for the establishment of the Territory of Oklahoma gave the court power to enforce the laws of the state of Arkansas which were applicable, except those in conflict with the laws of the United States governing territories. The Indian

---

18 *Statutes*, XXV, 783. The boundaries of the part attached to the district of Kansas were left unchanged, but the part attached to the eastern district of Texas included not only the part formerly attached to the northern district of Texas, but also the Chickasaw reservation and the southern and western portions of the Choctaw reservation, which by this act were detached from the western district of Arkansas.

19 All "male residents of the Indian Territory, over twenty-one years of age, and understanding the English language," were declared eligible to serve as jurors.

THE FORMATION OF OKLAHOMA

Territory, confined by the organization of Oklahoma to the reservations of the Five Civilized Tribes and the small reservations on the Neosho, was thus provided with a fairly complete code of laws. The tribal courts, however, were allowed to retain exclusive jurisdiction in all cases, civil and criminal, in which only members of the tribes were concerned. The power of the United States court to punish offenses was also enlarged by this act, but the jurisdiction of the courts of the district of Kansas, the western district of Arkansas, and the eastern district of Texas was continued in certain capital cases in the parts of the territory attached to their respective districts.[20]

Other steps were taken at this time that helped to give the Indian Territory a complete judicial system. The judge of the court was given the power of a governor to extradite persons charged with crime and to issue requisitions for the return of such persons. Three divisions were established in the territory, and at least two terms of court in a year were provided for each division. Finally, nine United States commissioners were authorized by this law. They were given the powers of justices of the peace under the law of Arkansas.[21]

[20] Act of May 2, 1890, *Statutes* XXVI, 93. The tribal courts enforced only tribal laws.

[21] The first division consisted of the country occupied by the Creeks, the Cherokees, and the small tribes living northeast of them; the second division, of the country occupied by the Choctaws; and the third division, of the country occupied by the Chickasaws and the Seminoles. The court towns were Muskogee, South McAlester, and Ardmore. Numerous provisions were enacted to make the law of Arkansas applicable. For example, when sheriff and county were mentioned in the state law, marshal and division were to be read in the territory.

SETTLEMENT OF INDIAN TERRITORY

The people of the Indian Territory who were not Indian citizens were given by this act a judicial system similar to that of the organized territories, but they remained without provisions for local government. Many persons were still far from a court, as each of the new court divisions was larger than the state of Massachusetts The Indian agent declared that at least forty United States commissioners were needed instead of nine.[22] Now that Congress had begun to reorganize the Indian Territory, it was hardly possible for it to stop with halfway measures.

The movement of settlers into the country of the Five Civilized Tribes seems to have been checked during 1891 and 1892. In the latter year Agent Bennett reported that the total population of the five reservations was two hundred thousand. This was only twenty thousand more than it had been two years before, according to the census of 1890, or indeed ten thousand less than it had been at that time according to Bennett's estimate. The officials of the government, as well as the Indian authorities, were making serious efforts to remove intruders and to keep undesirable persons out of the territory. Moreover, the construction of new railroads practically stopped in 1891. It is not remarkable that the growth of the population was less rapid in 1891 and 1892 than in the preceding years.[23]

---

22 Report of Leo Bennett, union agent, for 1891, *H. Ex. Docs.*, 52 Cong. 1 sess., XV (2934), 241.

23 Report of the union agent for 1891, *loc. cit.*, 241, 251; for 1892, *H. Ex. Docs.*, 52 Cong. 2 sess., XIII (3088), 247. Bennett said in his report for 1891, p. 241, that his previous estimates of the number of intruders had been based on information given him by the tribal authorities. This was obviously intended to account for the large numbers in his report for 1890.

THE FORMATION OF OKLAHOMA

The conditions among the Indians themselves called for the attention of Congress, however. Under the system of the tribal ownership of land with the free use of it by individuals, less than one-fourth of the Indians occupied nearly all that was desirable. Energetic, aggressive tribesmen, usually adopted whites or persons of mixed descent, had possession of farms of hundreds or even thousands of acres. The settlement of the Indian Territory by outlanders provided the holders of these farms with a supply of labor, and the railroads afforded them access to markets for their products. The Indian of pure blood usually lived as far as possible from a town and cultivated a plot of a few acres. His live stock perhaps consisted of a single pony. These conditions provided a strong argument for the allotment of lands in severalty.[24]

The governments of the several tribes were not very successful. The Indians were hardly to blame for this, as persons wholly or partly of white or negro descent controlled the elections. The shortcomings of the two important tribes were especially well known. The treasury of the Cherokees was practically empty. In 1891 their warrants were sold for sixty cents on the dollar. In 1892 the Choctaws seemed on the verge of civil war as a result of a disputed election. The interests of the Indian citizens, as well as those of the out-

[24] Report of Leo Bennett, union agent, for 1891, *loc. cit.*, 241; for 1892, *loc. cit.*, 251. Agent Owen in his report for 1886 (*loc. cit.*, p. 375) said that there was one farm of eight thousand acres in the Washita Valley. See also the report of the Commissioner of Indian Affairs for 1886 (*loc. cit.*, 81-86), and the first report of the Commission to the Five Civilized Tribes, November 20, 1894 (*H. Ex. Docs.*, 53 Cong. 3 sess., XIV (3305), pp. lxvii, lxviii). Chairman Dawes declared that one white person, through rights gained by marriage, occupied in 1894 fifty thousand acres.

{ 222 }

landers, were said to demand a reorganization of the Indian Territory.[25]

As early as 1886 a definite assertion that the Five Civilized Tribes would be required soon to accept allotment in severalty and a state government was made by Commissioner J. D. C. Atkins in his report for that year.[26] Nevertheless, they were exempted from the operation of the allotment act passed a few months later. In the act providing for the establishment of the Territory of Oklahoma, the way was left open, as has been said, for the union of one or all of the tribes with that territory. On January 6, 1892, Representative Clifton R. Breckinridge of Arkansas introduced a resolution providing that the Committee on Indian Affairs should inquire into the attitude of the people of the Indian Territory toward the admission of it as a state.[27] This resolution was reported favorably by the committee on July 16. The most important statement in the report was "The obvious policy of the United States is to bring all of the territory within its limits, with the exception of the District of Columbia, to statehood."[28]

25 Report of Leo Bennett for 1891, *loc. cit.*, 240, 241; for 1892, *loc. cit.*, 260-263.
26 Report of the Commissioner of Indian Affairs for 1886, *loc. cit.*, 87.
27 *H. Misc. Docs.*, 52 Cong. 1 sess., I (2959), no. 325.
28 *H. Reports*, 52 Cong. 1 sess., VII (3048), no. 1927. The report was presented by Hosea H. Rockwell of New York. Two bills were introduced in the first session of the Fifty-second Congress for the admission of the Indian Territory: Senate Bill 2594, for the adjustment, etc., with a view to the creation of a state, by James H. Berry of Arkansas, March 15, 1892 (*Cong. Record*, 52 Cong. 1 sess., 2079); House Bill 5994, for the immediate admission, by Samuel W. Peel of Arkansas, February 15 (*ibid.*, 1164). Neither bill received consideration. Numerous bills were introduced dealing with particular matters in the Indian Territory (*Cong. Record*, 52 Cong. 1 sess., Index, 330).

THE FORMATION OF OKLAHOMA

The first legislation preparatory to the dissolution of the Five Civilized Tribes was enacted before the adjournment of this Congress, the Fifty-second. On December 6, 1892, Senator Vest introduced a joint resolution authorizing the appointment of a commission to treat with these Indians to induce them to take homesteads. This resolution was considered on several occasions during the month. On January 23, 1893, Senator James H. Berry of Arkansas proposed to attach a provision for this commission as an amendment to a House bill to ratify the agreement for the purchase of the Cherokee outlet. This amendment was adopted by the Senate, and the bill was passed as amended. It did not become a separate law, however, as the houses failed to reach an agreement. On March 2 the Senate incorporated this whole measure, including a provision for a commission to the Five Civilized Tribes, in the Indian appropriation bill, which with the Senate amendment passed finally on the next day.[29]

This act provided for the appointment of three commissioners who were authorized to enter into negotiations with the Five Civilized Tribes for the extinguishment of the tribal title to their lands. The commission was further authorized to secure the consent of the

[29] *Cong. Record*, 52 Cong. 2 sess., 17, 26, 77, 97, 267, 312, 785, 792, 1194, 1377, 2382, 2393, 2522, 2537, 2543, 2585, 2597, 2610 (cf. *H. Reports*, 52 Cong. 2 sess., III (3142), no. 2455). Senator Dawes presented the report on March 2 in which the committee recommended the insertion of the provision for the commission in the Indian appropriation bill. Two new bills were introduced in this session for the admission of the Indian Territory: Senate Bill 3656, for the immediate admission of Oklahoma and the Indian Territory, by Bishop W. Perkins of Kansas, December 22, 1892 (*Cong. Record*, 52 Cong. 2 sess., 290); House Bill 10169, to adjust, etc., with a view of making a state, by W. A. B. Branch of North Carolina, January 13, 1893 (*ibid.*, 551). Other bills were also introduced dealing with the Indian Territory.

SETTLEMENT OF INDIAN TERRITORY

Indians to such an adjustment of their affairs as would prepare the Indian Territory for admission into the Union. Another section of the act gave the consent of the United States to the immediate allotment of land to any individual members of the Five Civilized Tribes. No power, however, was given to the commission at this time except to negotiate and report.[30]

The chairman and principal member of the commission appointed by President Cleveland was Henry L. Dawes of Massachusetts, who had been for thirty-four years a member of Congress and during a part of this time chairman of the Senate Committee on Indian Affairs. Because of the prominence of Chairman Dawes, the body was usually referred to as the Dawes Commission.[31]

The newly appointed members labored earnestly but unsuccessfully during 1894. They held their first meeting in Washington in December, 1893. In January, 1894, they proceeded to the Indian Territory, and they at once sent to the chief or governor of each tribe an official notice of their appointment, together with a statement of their objects in the territory. Conferences were held with the officials of the several tribes, and later an intertribal council was summoned, to which came delegates from each tribe except the Seminoles. These delegates voted not to enter into negotiations with the commission. They were encouraged to take this action, it was alleged, by messages

30 *Statutes*, XXVII, 645.
31 Dawes had been sixteen years a member of the House of Representatives, and eighteen years a member of the Senate. The allotment act of 1887 usually bears his name.

from Washington containing assurances that the members of the government, and of Congress in particular, would not take any steps toward the reorganization of the Indian Territory without the consent of the Indians. The decision of the council was approved by the tribes separately. The commissioners declared in their first annual report that a change must be made in the status of the Five Civilized Tribes; but they admitted that the tribal governments, as then constituted, would not agree to this.[32]

Meanwhile, the number of non-citizens was growing at the rate of fifty thousand a year. In 1893 there were one hundred and fifty thousand of them in the Indian Territory, in addition to seventy thousand tribesmen. In 1894 the number of outlanders had reached two hundred thousand according to the estimate of Agent Dew M. Wisdom, or two hundred and fifty thousand according to the estimate of the Dawes Commission. In 1895 it was two hundred and fifty thousand according to one estimate, or three hundred thousand according to the other. The outlanders had become four times as numerous as the Indian citizens.[33]

The new influx of settlers was doubtless due in part

---

32 Report of the Commission to the Five Civilized Tribes, November 20, 1894, *H. Ex. Docs.*, 53 Cong. 3 sess., XIV (3305), pp. lix, lxx. See also the report of Dew M. Wisdom, union agent, for 1894, *H. Ex. Docs.*, 53 Cong. 3 sess., XV (3306), 141; and the report of the Commissioner of Indian Affairs for 1894, *ibid.*, 27. The report of the Dawes Commission was preceded by a report with similar findings made by Henry M. Teller of Colorado for a select committee of the Senate, May, 1894 (*S. Reports*, 53 Cong. 2 sess., V (3183), no. 377).

33 Report of the Commission to the Five Civilized Tribes for 1894, *loc. cit.*, p. lxviii; for 1895, *H. Docs.*, 54 Cong. 1 sess., XIV (3381), p. xc; report of Wisdom for 1893, *H. Ex. Docs.*, 53 Cong. 2 sess., XIV (3210), 150; for 1894, *loc. cit.*, 141; for 1895, *H. Docs.*, 54 Cong. 1 sess., XV (3382), 162.

SETTLEMENT OF INDIAN TERRITORY

to the promise of an immediate reorganization of the Indian Territory implied in the establishment of the Commission to the Five Civilized Tribes. The constantly increasing number of non-citizens made it necessary to fulfil this promise.

The status of the outlander had become a serious and urgent problem. The white person or the negro who paid his occupation tax was not an intruder according to the tribal laws, and the expulsion of all non-citizens would have destroyed the existing industrial system. The Indians would hardly have consented to this. At first, few settlers had invested money in the territory; but before 1895 substantial towns, containing from one to five thousand inhabitants each, had been built on the land belonging to the Indians. Millions of dollars had been expended by those who had no other title than that of tenants at will.[34]

The Indian citizens formed a caste that had a monopoly, not only of the land, but of the schools and the local governments so far as they existed. The good order prevailing in the towns, which did not have authority even to appoint a constable, was considered

---

[34] Report of the Commission to the Five Civilized Tribes for 1894, *loc. cit.*, pp. lxviii, lxxxviii, lxxxix; for 1895, *loc. cit.*, p. xc. The intruders, that is, those who refused to pay the monthly tax or to conform to the tribal laws, were numerous and troublesome at times; and the government seemed powerless to control them. The intruders in the Cherokee territory claimed to be Indian citizens, but their claims were rejected by the tribe. Intruders who did not make any excuse for their presence were especially numerous in the Chickasaw district. See the report of Wisdom for 1893, *loc. cit.*, 143. On the attitude of the Indians toward outlanders who paid the occupation tax, see the report submitted by Teller in May, 1894, *S. Reports*, 53 Cong. 2 sess., V (3183), no. 377, p. 7: "We did not hear from any Indian the suggestion that the white people there, with the consent of the Indian, should be removed."

THE FORMATION OF OKLAHOMA

remarkable by the commissioners, but an uneasy and impatient feeling was becoming apparent. The most pressing need of the non-citizens was a better education system. Their children were growing up practically without training. The tribal schools were for Indians only, and the private schools were neither very numerous nor very successful.[35]

In the rural communities order was not preserved as in the towns. Murder and robbery were all too common. Under the system of personal, rather than territorial jurisdiction, it was hard to punish offenders. Such conditions were not favorable to the promotion of civilization among the Indians.[36]

The distribution of the land among the tribal citizens was becoming less and less equitable. One million acres of the three millions occupied by the Creeks were in the hands of sixty-one persons, according to a widely heralded statement, and conditions were equally bad elsewhere.[37] The monopoly of the land by a few adopted white persons or Indians of mixed descent, in the opinion of the commissioners, freed the United States from the treaties guaranteeing the perpetuity of the tribal titles.

---

35 Report of the Commission to the Five Civilized Tribes for 1894, *loc. cit.*, p. lxix; for 1895, *loc. cit.*, pp. lxxxix, xc. Cf. Teller report, *loc. cit.*, 11.

36 Report of the Commission to the Five Civilized Tribes for 1894, *loc. cit.*, p. lxviii. According to this report, fifty-three murders occurred in the territory of one of the tribes within eight weeks, "and not a single person [was] brought to trial."

37 Address of W. H. Walker, editor of the Purcell *Register*, before a press association at Salt Lake City, August 27, 1895, quoted and approved in the report of Wisdom for 1895, *loc. cit.*, 159. Compare with this a statement in the Teller report, *loc. cit.*, p. 12: "The monopoly is so great that in the most wealthy and progressive tribe [the Cherokees?] your committee were told that one hundred persons had appropriated fully one-half of the best land."

SETTLEMENT OF INDIAN TERRITORY

The commissioners in their second annual report, made in November, 1895, recommended that the United States should take charge of affairs in the five reservations. They had been unsuccessful in their efforts to negotiate, and it was apparent that nothing could be accomplished in that way. The recommendation was specific. "It is," the commissioners declared, "the imperative duty of Congress to assume at once political control of the Indian Territory." They reported that the tribal governments in all their branches were "wholly corrupt, irresponsible, and unworthy to be trusted." Finally, they asserted that the promises in the treaties were not binding under the changed conditions.[38]

These recommendations placed the matter squarely before Congress. Bills for the reorganization of the Indian Territory were introduced early in the session of the next Congress, the Fifty-fourth, but they received little attention for some time.[39] The House Committee on Indian Affairs in February, 1896, drew up the Indian appropriation bill without an item for the support of the Dawes Commission. The committee evidently intended to prepare a separate measure dealing with the Five Civilized Tribes. The appropriation bill passed the House without this item, but the

[38] Report of the Commission to the Five Civilized Tribes for 1895, *loc. cit.*, esp. pp. xcv, xcvi. The number of commissioners had been increased to five by the sundry civil appropriation act of March 2, 1895 (*Statutes*, XXVIII, 939).

[39] Among the bills were three for the establishment of the Territory of Indianola: Senate Bill 584, by James H. Berry of Arkansas, December 9, 1895 (*Cong. Record*, Cong. 1 sess., 60); House Bill 819, by John S. Little of Arkansas, December 9 (*ibid.*, 97); Senate Bill 1719, by Vest (by request), January 23, 1896 (*ibid.*, 896).

THE FORMATION OF OKLAHOMA

Senate at the last moment added it.[40] In the conference committee the managers for the House refused to agree to this unless the commission should be empowered to do something more than carry on useless negotiations. Accordingly, an amendment was added directing the Dawes Commission to make out the rolls of Indian citizens preparatory to allotment. In order that the purpose of this should be fully understood, the committee added this statement: "It is hereby declared to be the duty of the United States to establish a government in the Indian Territory which will rectify the many inequalities and discriminations now existing in said territory and afford needful protection to the lives and property of all citizens and residents thereof." The House accepted this report on May 26, but the Senate agreed only after a debate that extended until June 4.[41] The bill was passed finally on June 9, and it became a law on June 10. The Dawes Commission was thus enabled to continue its work under different conditions.[42]

In the next two years rapid progress was made in

[40] *Ibid.*, 1887, 1989, 4316. This action was taken by the Senate on April 23 after an amendment had been ruled out of order to continue the commission with power to make out the rolls of Indian citizens and proceed with allotment (*ibid.*, 4263, 4312).

[41] *Ibid.*, 5736, 5771, 6085. The vote in the Senate was twenty-seven to twenty, forty-two not voting. The power to make out the lists of tribal citizens included the power to pass on the rights of claimants to citizenship. The tribes had exercised this function hitherto. Appeals from the commission to the courts were authorized. Representative James S. Sherman of New York, afterwards vice-president of the United States, seems to have been responsible in a large measure for the action taken. The House on June 6 passed a separate bill, introduced by Sherman, for the Committee on Indian Affairs, House Bill 7907, which included similar legislation (*ibid.*, 5969; 6197; *H. Reports*, 54 Cong. 1 sess., IV (3460), no. 1102).

[42] *Cong. Record*, 54 Cong. 1 sess., 6327, 6357, 6441; *Statutes*, XXIX, 339, 340.

SETTLEMENT OF INDIAN TERRITORY

the dissolution of the Five Civilized Tribes. During 1897 the commission made agreements with four of the tribes regarding the details of allotment. The agreement with the Creeks, however, was not approved by the tribe. The Cherokees refused to negotiate. In June of that year an act was passed which meant the end of the tribal courts. Jurisdiction was given to the United States courts in all civil and criminal cases originating after the close of the year. On June 28, 1898, further important legislation was enacted. The tribal courts were abolished, and all cases were transferred to the United States courts. Tribal laws were done away with, and the Indians were brought under the laws of the United States. The Dawes Commission was authorized to proceed with the allotment of lands as soon as the rolls of citizens should be completed. Oil, coal, asphalt, and mineral lands were reserved from allotment and set aside to be leased for the benefit of the tribes. The town sites were also reserved, and provisions were made for the sale of town lots under rules intended to protect the rights both of Indians and of owners of improvements.[43]

This act also provided for the incorporation of towns in the territory of the Five Civilized Tribes. For this

[43] Agreement with the Chickasaws and Choctaws (the Atoka agreement), April 23, 1897, ratified June 28, 1898, *Statutes*, XXX, 505; with the Seminoles, December 16, 1897, ratified July 1, 1898, *Statutes*, XXX, 567; report of the Commission to the Five Civilized Tribes for 1898, *H. Docs.*, 55 Cong. 3 sess., XV (3757), 1052, 1054; for 1899, *H. Docs.*, 56 Cong. 1 sess., XIX (3916), 9; act of June 7, 1897, *Statutes*, XXX, 83; act of June 28, 1898, *Statutes*, XXX, 495-518. The latter act was known as the Curtis act, as it had been introduced by Charles Curtis, senator from Kansas, afterwards Vice-President of the United States. The number of commissioners was reduced to four by the Indian appropriation act of July 1, 1898 (*Statutes*, XXX, 591).

purpose the clerks of the United States courts were made recording officials. Both Indian citizens and citizens of the United States were declared to be voters in municipal elections. This was a distinct step toward self-government in the Indian Territory and toward the political amalgamation of its inhabitants.

The number of courts in the territory had been increased to care for the additional business. Three judicial districts, with a separate judge for each, were established in 1895. The three judges were constituted a court of appeals. At the same time the jurisdiction in the Indian Territory of the United States district courts of the surrounding states was finally abolished.[44] In 1897 the appointment of a fourth judge was authorized, and in 1902 a fourth judicial district was established.[45]

Meantime, the members of the small bands living northeast of the Cherokees had become allottees and prospective citizens of the United States. It was only because of their location that their history is in any way connected with that of the Five Civilized Tribes. The allotment act of 1887 applied to all of these bands except the Peorias and Miamis, and an act of 1889 extended its provisions to them.[46] Allotments were com-

44 Act of March 1, 1895, *Statutes*, XXVIII, 693-698. The jurisdiction of the United States district courts was to cease after September 30, 1896. The southern district consisted of the Chickasaw country, the central district of the Choctaw country, and the northern district of the remainder of the Indian Territory.

45 Act of June 7, 1897, *Statutes*, XXX, 84; act of May 27, 1902, *Statutes*, XXXII, 275. The western district established in 1902 consisted of the Creek and the Seminole reservations with some additional territory.

46 Act of March 2, 1889, *Statutes*, XXV, 1013. They were to receive two hundred acres each, however. The Confederated Peorias and Miamis had been practically one tribe since March 3, 1873 (*Statutes*, XVII, 633). The act of 1889 made a division of the land between them, and henceforth the reservations of this agency were sometimes spoken of as eight.

SETTLEMENT OF INDIAN TERRITORY

pleted in all the reservations in 1892, except in that of the Quapaws, and their allotments were made in 1893. The surplus lands, however, were not sold at the time.[47]

The Indians of this agency, known after 1871 as the Quapaw agency, numbered thirteen hundred and twenty-seven in 1892, and the white persons on their lands were estimated to number fifteen hundred. The sale of lots in the town of Miami had been authorized by an act passed in 1891. The town was said to contain one thousand inhabitants in 1896, and the total number of outlanders within the limits of the agency was placed at five thousand. The Indians were only slightly more numerous than they had been four years before. They were rapidly losing all feelings of tribal unity.[48]

The tribes in the Indian Territory were nearly dissolved before the end of the nineteenth century. The governments of the Five Civilized Tribes were still in existence, but they were little more than consulting agents in the management of the business of the tribes. No court could enforce tribal laws, and the Indians were as completely under the Government of the United States as were the citizens of the United States. According to the census of 1900, the population of the Indian Territory was nearly four hundred thou-

---

47 Report of the agent for the Quapaws for 1892, *H. Ex. Docs.*, 52 Cong. 2 sess., XIII (3088), 243; for 1893, *H. Ex. Docs.*, 53 Cong. 2 sess., XIV (3210), 141. The Quapaws, too, insisted on retaining two hundred acres each, and a special act was passed to ratify this on March 2, 1895 (*Statutes*, XXVIII, 907).

48 Report of the agent for the Quapaws for 1892, *loc. cit.*, 244; for 1896, *H. Docs.*, 54 Cong. 2 sess., XIII (3489), 144, 149, 150; act of March 3, 1891, *Statutes*, XXVI, 1010.

THE FORMATION OF OKLAHOMA

sand. In 1902 it contained one hundred and forty-seven incorporated towns, twenty-one of which had more than one thousand inhabitants each. Two thousand four hundred miles of railroad in operation or under construction provided means of communication with all parts of the territory. The barriers to intercourse were entirely removed.[49]

An act of March 3, 1901, declared that all the Indians in the Indian Territory were citizens of the United States. A great deal was still to be done to close up the affairs of the Five Civilized Tribes, but they had ceased to exist except as financial corporations.[50] The

---

[49] Report of the Commission to the Five Civilized Tribes for 1902, *H. Docs.*, 57 Cong. 2 sess., XX (4459), 47, 48. The following towns had more than one thousand inhabitants, according to the census of 1900: Ardmore, 5681; Chickasha, 3209; Coalgate, 2614; Davis, 1346; Duncan, 1164; Durant, 2969; Hartshorne, 2352; Lehigh, 1500; Marlow, 1016; Miami, 1527; Muskogee, 4254; Pauls Valley, 1467; Poteau, 1182; Purcell, 2277; South McAlester, 3479; Sulphur Springs, 1198; Tahlequah, 1482; Tulsa, 1390; Vinita, 2339; Wagoner, 2372; Wynnewood, 1907.

[50] Act of March 3, 1901, *Statutes*, XXXI, 1447. A supplementary agreement was made with the Seminoles concerning the details of allotment on October 7, 1899, ratified by Congress on June 2, 1900 (*Statutes*, XXXI, 250), approved by the Seminoles previously. An agreement was made with the Creeks on March 8, 1900, ratified by Congress on March 1, 1901 (*Statutes*, XXXI, 761), approved by the Creeks on May 25, 1901. A supplementary agreement was made in 1902, ratified by Congress on June 30, 1902 (*Statutes*, XXXII, 500), approved by the Creeks on July 26, 1902. An agreement supplementary to the Atoka agreement was made with the Choctaws and Chickasaws on March 21, 1902, ratified by Congress on July 1, 1902 (*Statutes*, XXXII, 641), approved by| the Chickasaws and Choctaws on September 25, 1902. A previous agreement had been made on February 7, 1901, but it was not ratified by Congress. An agreement was negotiated with the Cherokees on April 9, 1900, ratified by Congress on March 1, 1901 (*Statutes*, XXXI, 848), rejected by the Cherokees on April 29, 1901. An agreement made sometime in 1902 was ratified by Congress on July 1, 1902 (*Statutes*, XXXII, 716), and was approved by the Cherokees on August 7, 1902. See report of the Commission to the Five Civilized Tribes for 1900, *H. Docs.*, 56 Cong. 2 sess., XXVI (4100), p. clxvi; of the Secretary of the Interior for 1901, *H. Docs.*, 57 Cong. 1 sess., XXII (4289), p. xxxviii; for 1902, *H. Docs.*, 57 Cong. 2 sess., XVIII (4457), 41. The Cherokees meantime had tested the constitutionality of the Curtis act, but they were beaten (The Cherokee

SETTLEMENT OF INDIAN TERRITORY

Indian Territory contained nearly half a million inhabitants, and the Territory of Oklahoma as many more. A million citizens of the United States were in need of state government in an area which twelve years before had been unorganized Indian country.

Nation *vs.* Ethan A. Hitchcock, secretary of the interior, December 1, 1902, 187 U. S. 294). The Commission to the Five Civilized Tribes continued until July 1, 1905. For a statistical summary of the work done by this commission see Appendix I.

CHAPTER XII

THE ADMISSION OF OKLAHOMA

THE act of 1898 providing for the dissolution of the Five Civilized Tribes made necessary the speedy formation of one or more states from the area that had been the Indian Territory between 1854 and 1890. The formation of two separate commonwealths was never probable, if indeed it was ever possible; but many persons both in what is now Oklahoma and in other parts of the United States were committed to such an arrangement. The delay incident to the reorganization of the Five Civilized Tribes gave opportunity for a full discussion of the question, and the struggle between those who wanted one state and those who wanted two seemed at the time to overshadow everything else.

The agitation for statehood began soon after the establishment of the Territory of Oklahoma. It is possible to say that it began even earlier. The settlers had hardly crossed the border before they began to ask for the forms of government to which they had been accustomed, and a bill was introduced in Congress in December, 1889, for the admission of a part of the Indian Territory as the state of Columbia.[1] This bill, however, did not receive consideration. In 1891 the people of Oklahoma began to ask seriously that it should be admitted. In December of that year there

---

[1] House Bill 224, for the admission of a part of the Indian Territory as the state of Columbia, by William M. Springer of Illinois, December 18 (*Cong. Record*, 51 Cong. 1 sess., 233; cf. Index, 379).

ADMISSION OF OKLAHOMA

was held at Oklahoma City a convention which sent a memorial to Congress asking for statehood. In January, 1892, David A. Harvey, the first territorial delegate to Congress, introduced a bill in the House of Representatives for the same purpose. Abraham J. Seay, the second governor of the territory, in his report for 1892 asserted that Oklahoma would be entitled to admission into the Union in a very short time.[2]

The plan for two states was already receiving attention. It will be remembered that two bills were introduced in Congress by members from Arkansas as early as the spring of 1892 which provided for the formation of a separate state from the country occupied by the Five Civilized Tribes. Several bills of different sorts for the reorganization of the former Indian Territory were proposed between December, 1892, and the beginning of 1895. On December 20, 1893, the House Committee on Territories, whose leading members were Southern men, presented a report favorable to a bill introduced by its chairman, Joseph Wheeler of Alabama, for the admission of the Territory of Oklahoma. Facts were presented in this report to show that Oklahoma alone had sufficient resources for a state. It was apparent that many Southern congressmen preferred that two new states should be formed from this section of the Southwest to offset in part the new states that had been formed recently in the Northwest.[3]

[2] Memorial of statehood convention presented and bill, House Bill 4629, introduced by Harvey, January 25 (*Cong. Record*, 52 Cong. 1 sess., 522); report of the Governor of Oklahoma for 1892, *H. Ex. Docs.*, 52 Cong. 2 sess., XIV (3089), 477.

[3] For the bills introduced between 1892 and 1895, see *Cong. Record*,

THE FORMATION OF OKLAHOMA

A division of sentiment at once became evident in the territories. William C. Renfrow, the third governor of Oklahoma, in his first annual report in October, 1893, took a stand for the admission of the two territories, as one state—joint statehood, or single statehood, as it soon became known.[4] In January, 1894, the members of the Democratic central committee of the Indian Territory protested against union with Oklahoma.[5] They preferred separate statehood, or double statehood, as it was also called. Both plans had supporters in the two territories during the next ten or twelve years.

Between 1895 and 1901 little attention was given to the proposals for the admission of Oklahoma. As a result of the election of 1894, the Republicans secured control of both houses of Congress. They postponed the consideration of statehood for Oklahoma until affairs in the Indian Territory could be adjusted in preparation for a reunion of the two territories. The North and the East generally disapproved of more Western, or especially Southwestern, states than was necessary. Several bills dealing with Oklahoma were introduced in Congress during this period, but not one of them received serious consideration.[6]

---

52 Cong. 2 sess., Index, 94, 120; 53 Cong. 1 sess., Index, 167; 2 sess., Index, 298; 3 sess., Index, 133. For the bill introduced by Wheeler, December 18, House Bill 4857, see *H. Reports*, 53 Cong. 2 sess., I (3269), no. 242.

4 Report of the Governor of Oklahoma for 1893, *H. Ex. Docs.*, 53 Cong. 2 sess., XV (3211), 461. See also report for 1894, *H. Ex. Docs.*, 53 Cong. 3 sess., XVI (3307), 449. Three statehood conventions met in Oklahoma and the Indian Territory in 1893; one at El Reno on August 8, one at Purcell on September 30, one at Kingfisher on October 28. Sentiment at these conventions favored one state out of the two territories.

5 *Cong. Record*, 53 Cong. 2 sess., 1797. Their memorial was presented in the House on February 1.

6 *Cong. Record*, 54 Cong. 1 sess., Index, 297, 410; 2 sess., Index, 120,

ADMISSION OF OKLAHOMA

Meanwhile, the two territories were developing under different conditions. Oklahoma was occupied by small landowners. The Indian Territory was a community of landlords and lease-holders, either of farms and ranches or of coal, gas, oil, and asphalt rights. The government at Washington was trying to introduce the usual system of land tenure in the Indian Territory, but with each year of delay the irregular and accidental boundary between it and Oklahoma became more important.

Moreover, Congress needlessly permitted the territories to develop as separate political units. Their administrative systems were entirely different, since one was an organized territory, and the other unorganized. Their codes of laws also were different, since the code of Arkansas was used in the Indian Territory instead of the code of Oklahoma. The union of the two could have been accomplished with less friction in 1898 than in 1906, and the authority of the United States would have been a powerful force in preparing the enlarged territory for statehood.[7]

158; 55 Cong. 1 sess., Index, 136, 188; 2 sess., Index, 299, 397; 3 sess., Index, 147, 191; 56 Cong. 1 sess., Index, 376, 524; 2 sess., Index, 151, 208. The only bill that was reported during this period was House Bill 3209, introduced by Delegate Dennis Flynn of Oklahoma, January 3, 1896 (*Cong. Record*, 54 Cong. 1 sess., 476). This bill, as reported on May 23, provided for the admission of the Territory of Oklahoma at once with provision for the annexation of the Indian Territory by reservations, as they were prepared for statehood (*H. Reports*, 54 Cong. 1 sess., VIII (3464), no. 1988). This plan was known as "piecemeal absorption."

[7] Max Farrand, in *The Legislation of Congress for the Government of the Organized Territories of the United States*, p. 54, points out that a period of territorial government under the control of Congress has been an important factor in the establishment of orderly administration in a new state. He cites California as an example of a state which, entering the Union without previous experience as a territory, encountered great difficulties in its beginnings.

THE FORMATION OF OKLAHOMA

A bill was introduced in both houses of Congress in 1898 for the union of the Indian Territory and Oklahoma prior to their admission as a state.[8] This plan was not considered as it should have been. The differences between the two sections were numerous and important, but a territorial government could have been devised to meet the situation. Those who did not wish the union to take place at all, joined with those who did not wish to act until it should become absolutely necessary, were able to keep the territories separate for the time.

Most of the people of the Territory of Oklahoma preferred to wait for admission until the two territories could be formed into one state. Cassius M. Barnes, the fourth governor of Oklahoma, appointed in 1897, said in his report for 1899: ". . . I agree with the larger and more conservative part of our people that it is better to wait a reasonable time and eventually, by a union of the two territories, establish one grand state. . . ." In 1900, however, a party division began to appear. The Democratic territorial convention declared for the union of the territories. The Republican convention declared for the admission of Oklahoma with such boundaries as Congress wished to give it. Governor Barnes in his report for that year called for the immediate admission of the Territory of Oklahoma, but he did not say whether he wished it to be admitted

---

[8] House Bill 5872, by Delegate James Y. Callahan of Oklahoma, January 6, 1898, *Cong. Record*, 55 Cong. 2 sess., 414; Senate Bill 133, by William V. Allen of Nebraska (by request), January 12, *ibid.*, 557. Callahan also proposed a new bill to organize the reservations attached to the Quapaw agency as a county of Oklahoma (House Bill 2774, April 10, 1897, *Cong. Record*, 55 Cong. 1 sess., 678).

ADMISSION OF OKLAHOMA

separately or in conjunction with the Indian Territory.[9]

The people of the Indian Territory gave separate statehood somewhat more favorable consideration, although they were interested chiefly in the work of the Dawes Commission. They knew that their territory would not be ready for admission for a few years, and the proposal that it should be annexed to Oklahoma, one reservation at a time, was particularly distasteful to them. Many thought that a union of the territories would be unfair to the Indian Territory, since the capital and the leading public institutions probably would be located in the fully organized portion of the state. They believed, too, that the people of that portion would control the important offices at first because of their political experience.[10]

Public opinion in the country at large regarding the admission of new states was of more significance than the attitude of the people of Oklahoma and the Indian Territory. The conventions of both the great parties in

9 Report for 1899, *H. Docs.*, 56 Cong. 1 sess., XXI (3918), 743; for 1900, *H. Docs.*, 56 Cong. 2 sess., XXX (4104), 686. Compare the report for 1897, *H. Docs.*, 55 Cong. 2 sess., XIV (3642), 561: "It is generally conceded that the best interests of the whole people will best be subserved by the union of the Indian Territory and Oklahoma into one state. . . ." In March, 1899, Governor Barnes vetoed a resolution of the territorial legislature authorizing a convention to form a constitution. This was a plan to secure the consideration of Congress for immediate statehood for Oklahoma alone. The veto message is reprinted in *Cong. Record*, 59 Cong. 1 sess., 2605.

10 "The double statehood idea is most popular in the Indian Territory, where it is argued that Oklahoma, with its experience and organization in politics and its public buildings, would probably secure the capital as well as control of the offices of the new state" (Charles Moreau Harger, "The Next Commonwealth: Oklahoma," *Outlook*, February 2, 1901, LXVII, 280). See also report of Dew M. Wisdom, union agent, for 1898, *H. Docs.*, 55 Cong. 3 sess., XV (3757), 156 with quotation from the Muskogee *Phoenix*, August 11, 1898.

THE FORMATION OF OKLAHOMA

1900 declared unequivocally for statehood for Arizona, New Mexico, and Oklahoma, but the form of statehood for Oklahoma was not specified. It was expected that the Congress elected in 1900 would take up the matter at once when it met in December, 1901.[11]

Two of the seven bills[12] introduced in the House of Representatives during this session for the better government of Oklahoma and the Indian Territory were reported by the committee. One for the organization of the Indian Territory under the name of Jefferson, introduced by John A. Moon of Tennessee, the leading member of the minority on this committee, was reported favorably by its author on March 14, 1902;[13] the other for the admission of Oklahoma, Arizona, and New Mexico, introduced by William S. Knox of Massachusetts, the chairman of the committee, was also

[11] "We favor home rule for and the early admission to statehood of the territories of New Mexico, Arizona, and Oklahoma" (Republican platform, 1900). "We denounce the failure of the Republican party to carry out its pledges to grant statehood to the territories of Arizona, New Mexico, and Oklahoma, and we promise the people of these territories immediate statehood" (Democratic platform, 1900).

[12] House Bill 152, for the admission of Oklahoma, by Dennis Flynn of Oklahoma, December 2, 1901, *Cong. Record*, 57 Cong. 1 sess., 54; House Bill 279, to establish the Territory of Jefferson, by John A. Moon of Tennessee, December 2, *ibid.*, 56; House Bill 4570, for the admission of Oklahoma and the Indian Territory as one state, by Thomas C. McRae of Arkansas, December 10, *ibid.*, 248; House Bill 9675, for same, by John H. Stephens of Texas, January 21, 1902, *ibid.*, 851; House Bill 11802, for the admission of Oklahoma, by Flynn, February 25, *ibid.*, 2180; House Bill 12268, Territory of Jefferson, by Moon, March 7, *ibid.*, 2521; House Bill 12543, by William S. Knox of Massachusetts, March 14, *ibid.*, 2814. Two bills for the admission of Oklahoma were introduced in the Senate at this session: Senate Bill 186, Oklahoma alone, by Charles W. Fairbanks of Indiana, December 4, 1901 (*ibid.*, 123); Senate Bill 3368, both territories as one state, by Thomas M. Patterson of Colorado, January 30, 1902 (*ibid.*, 1108).

[13] *H. Reports*, 57 Cong. 1 sess., IV (4402), no. 956. Bills for the organization of the Indian Territory as Indianola or Jefferson had been introduced before, but none had ever been reported.

ADMISSION OF OKLAHOMA

reported favorably by its author on April 1.[14] The Knox bill provided that Oklahoma should be admitted alone, but that the new state must give its consent irrevocably to the annexation of the Indian Territory, wholly, or in part, if Congress should determine upon such a plan. The Moon bill provided for the government of the Indian Territory in the meantime.

These reports were clearly the result of a compromise that was intended to defer the settlement of the matter. Those who favored single statehood for the two territories believed that Congress finally would annex the Indian Territory to Oklahoma. Those who wanted each territory to form a separate state believed that the union of the two would be impossible if Oklahoma should be admitted alone.[15] The Moon bill received no further consideration, but the bill for the admission of Oklahoma, Arizona, and New Mexico passed the House on May 9, in spite of the opposition of members who thought that the people of the Indian Territory either should be allowed to participate in the organization of the new commonwealth or should be separated from it permanently.[16]

The opponents of the statehood bill in the Senate at once adopted a policy of delay. While party lines had not been drawn in the House, the Democrats of

14 *H. Reports*, 57 Cong. 1 sess., V (4403), no. 1309.
15 The constitutional phases of this question were debated in the House on May 8, 1902 (*Cong. Record*, 57 Cong. 1 sess., 5197). For a decision on the power of the United States to bind a state in the enabling act, see Coyle *vs.* Oklahoma, decided May 29, 1911 (221 U. S., 559).
16 *Cong. Record*, 57 Cong. 1 sess., 5136, 5178, 5186, 5196, 5198, 5224, 5230. The bill passed without a yea-and-nay vote. Thomas C. McRae of Arkansas was the principal opponent of the measure as passed.

THE FORMATION OF OKLAHOMA

the Senate seem to have united in support of the bill, and the Republicans seem to have opposed it. Matthew S. Quay of Pennsylvania, a member of the Committee on Territories, was the most prominent Republican who was out of harmony with his party. The committee, controlled by the Republicans without the aid of Quay, refused to report the bill for consideration by the Senate at this session; but Quay forced the chairman, Albert J. Beveridge of Indiana, to agree to make a report at the beginning of the next session in December, 1902. The committee was composed of eleven members. Quay and the four Democrats presented minority reports favorable to the House bill on December 10 and December 15, respectively, but the majority report made on December 10 was adverse to it.[17] A substitute bill for the admission of Oklahoma and the Indian Territory as one state was included in a preliminary report of the committee made on December 3, but it was withdrawn for revision when the final report was presented.[18] Quay tried many times to bring the House bill to a vote, but on March 3, 1903, the session came to an end without action.[19]

The contest over the statehood bill gave the people of Oklahoma and the Indian Territory an opportunity to present their views. Both factions in the Senate ap-

[17] *Cong. Record*, 57 Cong. 1 sess., 7356, 7357; 2 sess., 180, 187, 297. The majority of the committee presented a preliminary report on December 3 (*ibid.*, 25). See also *S. Reports*, 57 Cong. 2 sess., I (4410), no. 2206.

[18] *Cong. Record*, 57 Cong. 2 sess., 25, 194. This bill is printed in *ibid.*, 185.

[19] See *Cong. Record*, 57 Cong. 2 sess., Index, under H. R. 12543. The leading Republicans of the Senate evidently were not certain that the bill would be defeated if it came to a vote, and they did not desire to take any unnecessary risk.

ADMISSION OF OKLAHOMA

pealed to them for support. A subcommittee of the Committee on Territories in November and December, 1902, gave a series of public hearings.[20]

Two important elements were found to be opposed to the immediate admission of the territories as one state. The governments of the Five Civilized Tribes declared in favor of the separate admission of the Indian Territory. On November 28, 1902, Indian officials held a meeting at Eufaula, where they adopted a statement regarding their position. The tribes also protested separately against union with Oklahoma.[21] Many of the active Republicans of the Territory of Oklahoma were as much opposed to union with the Indian Territory. They made their appeal on purely partisan grounds. Oklahoma alone would be a close state politically, so ran their appeal, but in time they hoped that it would be safely Republican. If this should prove true, it ought to be kept separate from the Indian Territory, which would be overwhelmingly Democratic. If this should not prove true, Congress could join it to the Indian Territory so that only one new Democratic state might be admitted. Congress, however, ought to give the Republicans a chance to carry Oklahoma before doing this.[22] Thus the wishes of the

20 *S. Docs.*, 57 Cong. 2 sess., V (4420), no. 36.
21 *Cong. Record*, 57 Cong. 2 sess., 567; *S. Docs.*, 59 Cong. 1 sess., IV (4912), no. 143, pp. 27, 30, 34. A similar convention was held at Eufaula May 21, 1903 (*ibid.*, p. 29).
22 Chairman of the Republican Territorial Committee and others to the Republican members of Congress, July 8, 1903 (*S. Docs.*, 59 Cong. 1 sess., IV (4912), no. 143, pp. 36-42). The final paragraph of this communication contains the substance of the whole: "In conclusion we beg to suggest as a proper disposition of the subject that Congress now admit Oklahoma, reserving the right to attach the Indian Territory in the future. This would give

THE FORMATION OF OKLAHOMA

Indians and party expediency were the chief arguments against single statehood.

In the Territory of Oklahoma a sectional division became manifest. This appeared in the attitude of the four leading towns of the territory. It was evidently due in part to the local benefits expected to come from the particular form of statehood favored. Enid and Guthrie openly declared for the House bill and the immediate admission of Oklahoma. Shawnee and Oklahoma City were committed to a union of the territories.[23]

The form in which the question of statehood was presented to the people of the Indian Territory did not allow them a free choice of answers. To many it seemed that union with Oklahoma would be inevitable in the end. Accordingly, they preferred to become a part of the new state at the beginning. The non-citizens apparently favored immediate single statehood rather uniformly. Those of the Chickasaw district in particular desired union at once. These in the eastern and central parts were noncommittal. An opportunity to choose freely between the immediate admission of the territory

---

Oklahoma an opportunity to demonstrate whether she can be relied on as a Republican state or not. If she should prove to be a Democratic state, the Indian Territory could then be merged into her and one Democratic state be made. If, on the other hand, she should demonstrate her loyalty to the Republican party, as we know she would, we have no fear that Congress would ever desire to obliterate her identity by casting her into the arms of a Democratic majority in the Indian Territory."

23 Resolutions of the Enid Commercial Club, December 10, 1902, *Cong. Record*, 57 Cong. 2 sess., 356; resolutions of the Guthrie Commercial Club, December 8, 1902, *ibid.*, 123; resolutions of the Oklahoma City Commercial Club, February 4, 1902, *Cong. Record*, 57 Cong. 1 sess., 5140. For the attitude of Shawnee, see the letter of the Republican Territorial Committee, *loc. cit.*, p. 41.

ADMISSION OF OKLAHOMA

with Oklahoma and the immediate admission of it as a separate state might have brought out somewhat different replies.[24]

The people of the two territories on the whole clearly expected and probably favored joint statehood. In anticipation of this, religious, fraternal, and commercial organizations had already ignored the line between the territories in many cases. It was argued that one state government would be less expensive than two, and that Oklahoma and the Indian Territory together would make a state only approximately as large as Kansas, or Missouri, or Nebraska, or one of the Dakotas. Separately, they seemed very small in proximity to the state of Texas, eight times as large as either of them. To many persons it seemed most important that the joint state should contain within its limits agricultural and mineral resources to form a well-balanced industrial unit, in which commerce could be regulated by the state.[25]

It soon became clear that the leaders in Congress

24 Sentiment at Ada, Ardmore, Bristow, Chickasha, Claremore, Muskogee, Purcell, Sulphur, and Vinita seems to have favored immediate single statehood. Sentiment at Holdenville seems to have favored the House bill. See *Cong. Record*, 57 Cong. 2 sess., 175, 187, 1110, 1297, 1719, and hearings before the subcommittee of the Committee on Territories, *S. Docs.*, 57 Cong. 2 sess., V (4420), no. 36, pp. 193, 197, 199, 200, 203, 204, 216.

25 *Ibid.*, esp. p. 205. Compare also the resolutions of statehood conventions at Oklahoma City, December 3, 1902, January 6, 1903 (*Cong. Record*, 57 Cong. 2 sess., 45, 565): "Single statehood confirms and cements a social fellowship already established by interterritorial organizations of the Methodist Episcopal Church South, the Methodist Episcopal Church, the Episcopal Church, the Presbyterian Church, the Catholic Church, the Federation of Women's Clubs, and the Masonic and other fraternities. . . [and] a business fellowship already established by interterritorial organizations of the cottonseed oil manufacturers, the lumber dealers, the ice manufacturers, the grain dealers, the flour manufacturers, and other business organizations."

THE FORMATION OF OKLAHOMA

had determined upon a union of the territories. In November, 1903, Congress met in a brief special session. A bill was introduced in each house for the immediate admission of Oklahoma alone, but this was the last serious effort to admit Oklahoma without the immediate inclusion of the Indian Territory.[26] In the regular session a number of new statehood bills were introduced, and in April, 1904, the House Committee on Territories by its chairman, Edward L. Hamilton of Michigan, prepared and reported favorably a bill for the admission of two new states: one made up of Oklahoma and the Indian Territory, and one of Arizona and New Mexico.[27] This bill was hurriedly considered by the House and passed on April 19.[28] In the Senate the bill was not taken up until the next session of Congress, which began in December, 1904.[29] On February 7, 1905, the Senate rejected the sections of the House bill which provided for the union of Arizona and New

26 Senate Bill 1693, by Quay, November 23, 1903, *Cong. Record*, 58 Cong. 1 sess., 419; House Bill 4078, by Bird S. McGuire of Oklahoma, November 18, *ibid.*, 349. Two years later, however, it was proposed by the friends of separate statehood for the Indian Territory to admit Oklahoma as a permanently separate state. A bill was introduced in the House at this session for joint statehood, House Bill 24, by John H. Stephens of Texas, November 9 (*ibid.*, 151).

27 Senate Bill 3625, by Quay, for joint statehood for Oklahoma and the Indian Territory, January 17, 1904, *Cong. Record*, 58 Cong. 2 sess., 861; House Bill 10010, by James M. Robinson of Indiana, for joint statehood, January 14, *ibid.*, 785; House Bill 13524, by Moon, for the admission of the Indian Territory as the State of Jefferson, March 5, *ibid.*, 2902; House Bill 14671, by Hamilton, for the admission of Oklahoma and the Indian Territory as one state and of Arizona and New Mexico as one state, April 1,*ibid.*, 4131; House Bill 14749, by Hamilton, same title, April 4, *ibid.*, 4281, reported on April 8, *H. Reports*, 58 Cong. 2 sess., VII (4583), no. 2335.

28 *Cong. Record*, 58 Cong. 2 sess., 5153. The vote stood 147 to 104, present 21, not voting 109.

29 The bill was not reported by the Senate committee until December 16, 1904 (*S. Reports*, 58 Cong. 3 sess., I (4755), no. 2747).

ADMISSION OF OKLAHOMA

Mexico. It accepted the provisions for the admission of Oklahoma and the Indian Territory as the state of Oklahoma. The House refused to concur in the Senate amendments, and a conference committee failed to agree.[30] The fact that the fortunes of Oklahoma were bound up with those of Arizona and New Mexico kept it from becoming a state at this time.

A new agitation for the admission of the Indian Territory as a separate state was an important development in 1905. Hitherto the immediate admission of the Territory of Oklahoma had been discussed seriously, but after the beginning of 1904 this plan was abandoned. The Republican territorial convention of that year declared for the immediate admission of the two territories as one state, as provided in the House bill.[31] The Republicans were consistent, literally at least, for their platform in previous years had called for the immediate admission of Oklahoma with such boundaries as Congress wished to give it. During 1904 it became clear that Congress wished to join the territories, and the Republicans of Oklahoma acquiesced. After the supporters of the separate admission of Oklahoma had given up, the leading Indian citizens of the Indian Territory headed a movement for the formation of a state from the districts recently governed by the Five Civilized Tribes.

The Indian Territory was undoubtedly ready for a better organization. The Dawes Commission disbanded

---
30 *Cong. Record*, 58 Cong. 3 sess., 2001-2005, 2062, 2789, 3824, 3870.
31 Remarks of Bird S. McGuire, delegate from Oklahoma, April 19, 1904 (*Cong. Record*, 58 Cong. 3 sess., 5122).

THE FORMATION OF OKLAHOMA

on June 30, 1905, and its work of allotment was so nearly completed that the Department of the Interior could carry it to a successful conclusion. The town sites were surveyed and appraised, and the sale of them was nearing completion.[32] As early as February, 1903, Congress had been compelled to provide for rudimentary counties, known as recording districts.[33] Under the existing laws all tribal institutions, including their executive and legislative departments, their schools, and their public charities, must come to an end on March 4, 1906.[34] The establishment of a state or a territorial government in the country of the Five Civilized Tribes was clearly imminent.

Good reasons were given for the separate admission of the Indian Territory. In area and in population it was on a par with the state of Maine. Its industrial development and its natural resources were in some respects greater than those of Oklahoma. It contained three hundred incorporated towns, and more than

---

[32] Final report of the Commission to the Five Civilized Tribes, June 30, 1905, *H. Docs.*, 59 Cong. 1 sess., XIX (4959), 635, 640; report of the Indian inspector for the Indian Territory for 1905, *ibid.*, 716-725.

[33] Act of February 19, 1903, *Statutes*, XXXII, 841. Twenty-five recording districts were established at this time. By an act of March 7, 1904 (*Statutes*, XXXIII, 60), a twenty-sixth district was established; and by an act of June 21, 1906 (*Statutes*, XXXIV, 342), four more districts were authorized.

[34] Provisions were made for the discontinuance of the government of the Chickasaws and Choctaws, of the Creeks, and of the Cherokees, to take effect on March 4, 1906, in the respective agreements with those tribes of 1897, 1900, and 1902; see above, Chapter XI, footnotes 43 and 50. The same provision was extended to the Seminole government by an act of March 3, 1903 (*Statutes*, XXXII, 1008). See also the report of the Commissioner of Indian Affairs for 1905, *H. Docs.*, 59 Cong. 1 sess., XIX (4959), 109. By a joint resolution of March 2, 1906 (*Statutes*, XXXIV, 822), Congress extended the tribal existence and the tribal governments until their property should be distributed. This provision was re-enacted on April 26, 1906 (*Statutes*, XXXIV, 148).

three thousand miles of railroad were in operation within its borders. The production of coal from its mines for the year ending June 30, 1905, amounted to three million tons. The development of its great oil and gas fields was just beginning. Its deposits of asphalt, granite, marble, lead, zinc, iron, and building stone were hardly touched. Much of its land was in the hands of Indian allottees, and it would not be subject to taxation for many years; but the assessable wealth of the territory, aside from land, was more than two hundred million dollars, and was said to be sufficient to support a state government.[35]

The union with Oklahoma would bring together two unlike divisions. Oklahoma had developed a system of roads and public schools. These were yet to be provided in the rural parts of the Indian Territory. The Indians of Oklahoma were few in number, and their holdings were comparatively unimportant. The affairs of the Five Civilized Tribes would require special state legislation, and their political strength would be relatively twice as great in a separate commonwealth as in the joint state of Oklahoma. The Indians were able to point to a section in the Atoka agreement of 1897 which supported their claim for separate statehood. It is not surprising that they made a vigorous though

[35] Memorial for the proposed state of Sequoyah, 1905, *S. Docs.*, 59 Cong. 1 sess., IV (4912), no. 143, pp. 1-27; final report of the Commission to the Five Civilized Tribes, June 30, 1905, *H. Docs.*, 59 Cong. 1 sess., XIX (4959), 614; report of the mine inspector for the Indian Territory for 1905, *ibid.*, 645; report of the Indian inspector for the Indian Territory for 1905, *ibid.*, 711-720. The incorporated towns contained two hundred and fifty thousand inhabitants.

THE FORMATION OF OKLAHOMA

unsuccessful effort to convince Congress of the justice of their cause.[36]

The executives of four of the five tribes in July, 1905, joined in a call for a constitutional convention to meet at Muskogee on August 21. All residents of the Indian Territory were invited to participate in the selection of delegates. The meeting of this convention was of ultimate importance chiefly because it brought about the first political co-operation on a large scale between the Indian citizens and the outlanders. No doubt some took part in the movement who were not in favor of separate statehood. They believed that the opportunity to join with the Indians in a request for better government should not be lost. The name adopted for the proposed state was Sequoyah, selected in honor of the "Cherokee Cadmus," and the Indians were given important parts in the deliberations of the convention. A constitution was adopted on September 8, and provisions were made for submitting it to a vote of the people on November 7.

The constitution was ratified at this election by a vote of fifty-six thousand to nine thousand. The conditions under which the vote was taken were such that it did not afford a test of the popular attitude toward separate statehood. Those who voted against the ratification of the constitution were not allowed to take part in the choice of the proposed officials or to help select

36 Memorial for the proposed state of Sequoyah, *loc. cit.*, 7, 15, 23. The Atoka agreement spoke of the preparation of the lands of the five tribes "for admission as a state of the Union." It was included in the act of June 28, 1898, *Statutes*, XXX, 505. For the relative importance of the different tribes in 1907, see below, Appendix D.

ADMISSION OF OKLAHOMA

county seats in the forty-eight counties delimited by the convention. Most persons opposed to separate statehood did not go to the polls, and not more than half of the qualified voters took part in the election. Some opposed to separate statehood may have voted for the ratification of the constitution in order that they might be permitted to cast their votes on the other questions.[37]

The plan for a state of Sequoyah did not receive a hearing in Congress. A bill for the admission of it was introduced in each house—in the House of Representatives on December 4, 1905, and in the Senate on January 24, 1906.[38] Nothing further, however, was heard of the proposal. The union of Oklahoma and the Indian Territory had already been agreed upon at Washington.

The admission of the four territories as two states had received consideration at once in this Congress. President Roosevelt in his message of December 4, 1905, recommended joint statehood, and in the first four days of the session five bills were introduced for the admission of Oklahoma and the Indian Territory

---

[37] Memorial for the proposed state of Sequoyah, *loc. cit.*, 1, 24, 25, 85. Two (undated) calls were made. The chief executive of the Chickasaws did not sign either call. The constitution as adopted was given in the memorial on pages 47 to 87. The vote on the ratification as announced stood 56,279 to 9,073. The Indian Territory at the time must have contained as many as one hundred and thirty thousand voters, as the population in 1907, as will appear, was seven hundred thousand.

[38] House Bill 79, by Arthur P. Murphy of Missouri, *Cong. Record*, 59 Cong. 1 sess., 47; Senate Bill 3680, by |Porter McCumber of North Dakota, *ibid.*, 1527. At the same time Murphy introduced a bill for the admission of the Territory of Oklahoma as a separate state in order to dispose of it (House Bill 97, *ibid.*, 47).

THE FORMATION OF OKLAHOMA

as one state.³⁹ Two of these bills, one by Senator Beveridge and one by Representative Hamilton, the chairmen of the respective committees on territories, provided also for the admission of Arizona and New Mexico as one state. On January 23, 1906, the House committee reported favorably a modified joint-statehood bill that had been introduced the day before by Chairman Hamilton. This bill passed the House two days later. On January 29 it was reported by the Senate committee with minor amendments, and it was debated on several occasions. On March 9 the Senate by a decisive vote adopted a proviso that the admission of Arizona and New Mexico as one state should be effective only if it should be ratified by a majority of the voters of each territory. Later on the same day, the Senate agreed to strike out all reference to Arizona and New Mexico and passed the bill amended to apply only to Oklahoma and the Indian Territory. Both houses had voted a second time to admit the enlarged Oklahoma, but Arizona and New Mexico still blocked its admission.⁴⁰

39 Altogether, seven bills were introduced in this session for the admission of Oklahoma and the Indian Territory as one state: Senate Bill 1158, by Beveridge, an omnibus bill, December 7, 1905 (*ibid.*, 222); House Bill 1, by McGuire, December 4 (*ibid.*, 45); House Bill 183, by Frank Clark of Florida, December 4 (*ibid.*, 49); House Bill 441, by John H. Stephens of Texas, December 4 (*ibid.*, 54); House Bill 3186, House Bill 10719, House Bill 12707, by Hamilton, omnibus bills, December 5, 1905, January 6, 22, 1906 (*ibid.*, 116, 778, 1407). House Bill 9300, introduced by Robert M. Wallace of Arkansas, December 19, 1905, proposed the annexation of the Chickasaw and Choctaw districts to Arkansas (*ibid.*, 614).

40 *H. Reports*, 59 Cong. 1 sess., I (4906), no. 496; *S. Reports*, 59 Cong. 1 sess., I (4904), no. 427; *Cong. Record*, 59 Cong. 1 sess., 1433, 1587, 1667, 3591-3597. The amendment for the submission of statehood to the vote of Arizona and New Mexico separately, proposed by Joseph B. Foraker, senator from Ohio, was adopted by a vote of forty-two to twenty-nine, not voting

ADMISSION OF OKLAHOMA

The conference committee did not make a report until June 2. This report accepted the House bill practically unchanged. When it became apparent that the Senate would not agree to this, the report was withdrawn. On the same day, June 12, a new report was presented. It provided for the admission of Oklahoma and the Indian Territory as one state, and of Arizona and New Mexico as another; but the union and admission of the two latter territories could take place only with their consent given separately, as the Senate bill had proposed for a short time on March 9. The Senate accepted this report on June 13, the House on June 14. The bill received the approval of the President on June 16. The formation and adoption of a constitution was all that remained between Oklahoma and statehood.[41]

The enabling act as passed authorized a constitutional convention of one hundred and twelve members — fifty-five for the Indian Territory, fifty-five for Oklahoma, and two for the Osage reservation, the only part of the Territory of Oklahoma in 1906 that had not been placed under county government.[42] This act

---

eighteen. The sections of the bill relating to Arizona and New Mexico were stricken out by a vote of thirty-seven to thirty-five, not voting seventeen.

41 *Ibid.*, 7736, 8309, 8403, 8529; *S. Docs.*, 59 Cong. 1 sess., VIII (4916), nos. 478, 487, or *H. Reports*, III (4908), nos. 4660, 4925; act of June 16, 1906, *Statutes*, XXXIV, 267.

42 The governor, the chief justice, and the secretary of the Territory of Oklahoma were constituted a board to divide Oklahoma into fifty-five districts for the election of delegates to the convention. The commissioner to the Five Civilized Tribes and two judges to be designated by the President were authorized to delimit the districts in the Indian Territory.

An act of April 21, 1904 (*Statutes*, XXXIII, 217), had provided for the division of the Ponca, Otoe-Missouri, and Kaw reservations among the three adjoining counties. The divisions of the Kaw reservation among the members

THE FORMATION OF OKLAHOMA

also prescribed that the constitution to be formed should prohibit the sale of intoxicants in the Indian Territory, as it then existed, and in the Osage reservation, which, it was specified, was to become a separate county in the new state.

The task before the constitutional convention was an extremely difficult one. The proposed state had four times as many inhabitants as any other state had at the time of admission. No other convention was under the necessity of forming a commonwealth out of two distinct political units. The difficulties were greater because of the unorganized conditions in the Indian Territory. Other similar conventions dealt only with an organized territory or with part of a former state, except the convention of California; and the unorganized portion of Oklahoma had eight times as many inhabitants as California had when it was admitted into the Union.[43]

Under the conditions the convention adopted much legislation that was properly statutory and not constitutional. The demand for so-called progressive legislation, strong in all the Western states, had to be met.

---

of the tribe had already been authorized by an act of July 1, 1902 (*Statutes*, XXXIII, 636); and the allotment under the general law of other reservations was authorized by the act assigning them to counties. The land was all allotted to the Indians. See the article by Fred L. Wenner, in the report of the Governor of Oklahoma for 1906, *H. Docs.*, 59 Cong. 2 sess., XVI (5119), 301.

[43] The population of Oklahoma by the special census of 1907 was 1,414,177. Of these 722,441 were in the Territory of Oklahoma, and the remainder were in the Indian Territory. See the report of the Secretary of the Interior for 1907, *H. Docs.*, 60 Cong. 1 sess., XXVI (5295), 49, and the report of the Governor of Oklahoma for 1907, *H. Docs.*, 60 Cong. 1 sess., XXVII (5296), 668. For a comparison of the population of states at the time of admission into the Union, see table in *H. Reports*, 53 Cong. 2 sess., I (3269), no. 242.

ADMISSION OF OKLAHOMA

Moreover, Oklahoma has more Indian citizens than any other state, but it also has many negroes, with the resulting negro problem. The question of prohibition for the entire state was likewise a troublesome one, but it was submitted to a popular vote separately. One purely local matter caused much bitterness at the time. New counties were marked out in the hitherto unorganized portion of the state without reference to the boundaries of the existing districts, and in some cases new counties were established in the former Territory of Oklahoma.[44]

The members of the convention were elected on November 6, 1906, and the first meeting of the body was held on November 20. It adjourned on March 15, 1907, but it was in session again from April 16 to April 22 and from July 10 to July 16. On September 17 the constitution as submitted was ratified by a vote of one hundred and eighty thousand to seventy-three thousand.[45]

On November 16, 1907, President Roosevelt issued a proclamation declaring that Oklahoma was a state.[46] Thus one hundred and four years after its acquisition by the United States as a part of the Louisiana Pur-

[44] The constitution of Oklahoma as adopted is printed in *S. Docs.*, 60 Cong. 1 sess., VII (5240), no. 187. The journal of the Constitutional Convention has been deposited with the Oklahoma Historical Society by the president of the convention, William H. Murray. Copies of the journal have been made by Professor Royden James Dangerfield of the University of Oklahoma. These copies are on file in the library of the department of government of the university.

[45] The vote stood 180,333 to 73,059. Prohibition for the entire state was accepted by a vote of 130,361 to 112,258. See the report of the Secretary of the Interior for 1907, *loc. cit.*, 49.

[46] *Statutes*, XXXV, 2160.

THE FORMATION OF OKLAHOMA

chase, it was finally admitted into the Union. No distinctively Indian commonwealth has been established, but one-third of the Indians of the United States participated as citizens in the organization of Oklahoma, the home of the red man, which has become in a modified sense the Indian state.

APPENDICES

APPENDIX A

THE EASTERN BOUNDARY OF OKLAHOMA

As stated in the text, pages 5, 8, 10, the eastern boundary of Oklahoma depends theoretically on two points: the southwestern corner of Missouri and a point of the Arkansas River one hundred paces east of the old military post of Fort Smith. Actually the surveys were inaccurate, and the line between Oklahoma and Arkansas does not conform to the specifications. By an act of March 3, 1875 (*Statutes*, XVIII, 476) the line as originally surveyed was declared the permanent eastern boundary of the Indian Territory. The boundary north of the Arkansas River, as surveyed, "instead of following a direct line between its fixed extremities, curves slightly to the westward." The boundary south of the Arkansas, as surveyed, diverges "to the west from a due south course." At the Red River it is over three miles out of its proper course. About one hundred and forty thousand acres were lost to Oklahoma as a result of these errors, one hundred and thirty-seven thousand five hundred acres south of the Arkansas and two thousand five hundred acres north of it. See communications of the Commissioner of the General Land Office, April 8, May 15, 1878, in *S. Reports*, 45 Cong. 3 sess., II (1838), no. 714, pp. 3, 4; cf. letter of the Commissioner of Indian Affairs, June 29, 1867, *H. Ex. Docs.*, 40 Cong. 2 sess., XI (1337), no. 133, p. 3.

The site of old Fort Smith (cf. the treaty of June 22, 1855, with the Chickasaws and Choctaws, *Statutes*, XI, 611, reprinted in Kappler, II, 706), was selected by Major S. H. Long in 1817 and called by him Belle Point. It occupied the high ground just east of the junction of the Poteau and the Arkansas. It was named in honor of General Thomas A. Smith, who then commanded the ninth military department. See James, *Account of an Expedition... under the Command of Major Stephen H. Long,* III, 35 (reprinted in Thwaites, *Early Western Travels*, XVI, 187).

By an act of February 10, 1905 (*Statutes*, XXXIII, 714), the state of Arkansas was authorized to extend its limits to include the narrow strip of land on which this post had stood. The cession was bounded on the north by the Arkansas, on the west by the Poteau, and on the south by Mill Creek.

THE FORMATION OF OKLAHOMA

For a more detailed discussion of certain phases of this matter, see the article on "The Western Boundary of Arkansas," by John Hugh Reynolds, in Arkansas Historical Association, *Publications*, II, 210-236.

APPENDIX B

THE GREAT AMERICAN DESERT

Between 1840 and 1854 prospective settlers were interested in the Pacific Coast rather than the larger Indian Territory. One reason for this was the belief that the land between the ninety-sixth meridian and the Rocky Mountains was worthless. This belief was due in part to the report of S. H. Long, who about 1820 spoke of this country as a desert. "The traveller who shall at any time have traversed its desolate sands, will, we think, join us in the wish that this region may forever remain the unmolested haunt of the native hunter, the bison, and the jackal" (James, *Account of an Expedition. . . under the Command of Major Stephen H. Long*, III, 24, reprinted in Thwaites, *Early Western Travels*, XVI, 174). As late as 1856, Alfred Cumming, the superintendent of Indian Affairs at Saint Louis, reported that no part of the territories of Kansas and Nebraska, "with the exception of a narrow belt," was suitable for agriculture. The transported Indians occupied this narrow belt. The superintendent thought, however, that other parts of the country might "perhaps eventually prove valuable for grazing districts." See *S. Ex. Docs.*, 34 Cong. 3 sess., II (875), 617.

Long before this, however, a constantly increasing number of men were confident that the land near the rivers, at least, would prove valuable. Whitney, Benton, Douglas, and Hall alike believed that the Pacific railroad would make available a considerable area of productive territory.

APPENDICES

APPENDIX C

AREA OF RESERVATIONS IN THE INDIAN TERRITORY

BEFORE 1866

	Acres		Acres
Quapaw	75,167	Creek	6,998,808
Seneca-Shawnee	63,767	Seminole	1,682,883
Seneca	73,364	Choctaw-Chickasaw	19,032,174
Cherokee	13,172,235		

IN 1878

Quapaw	56,685	Cherokee	5,931,351
Peoria, etc.	50,301	*Creek	3,215,495
Ottawa*	14,860	*Seminole	200,000
Modoc	4,040	*Choctaw	6,688,000
Shawnee	13,948	Chickasaw	4,650,935
Wyandotte	21,406	Unoccupied Cherokee lands, "Cherokee outlet"	6,344,562
Seneca	51,958		
Osage	1,466,167		
Kansas	100,141	Creek and Seminole cessions of 1866, unoccupied, "Oklahoma district"	2,329,029
Pawnee	283,026		
Sac and Fox	479,667		
Pottawatomie-Shawnee	575,877		
Kiowa and Comanche	2,968,893	Choctaw-Chickasaw cession of 1866, unoccupied portion claimed by Texas	1,511,579
Wichita	743,610		
Cheyenne and Arapahoe	4,297,771		

* Not surveyed in 1878. No surveys had been made in 1866. Taken from a letter of the Commissioner of Indian Affairs, February 16, 1878, *S. Ex. Docs.*, 45 Cong. 2 sess., I (1780), no. 32.

THE FORMATION OF OKLAHOMA

APPENDIX D

INDIAN POPULATION AT DIFFERENT PERIODS OF THE AREA NOW INCLUDED IN OKLAHOMA

In 1844

Cherokees........	25,911	Quapaws.........	400
Chickasaws.......	4,111	Seminoles........	3,136
Choctaws........	12,410	Senecas..........	125
Creeks..........	24,594	Seneca - Shawnee band...........	211

Report of the Commissioner of Indian Affairs for 1844, *H. Ex. Docs.*, 28 Cong. 2 sess., I (463), no. 2, p. 315.

In 1855

Cherokees........	17,530	Quapaws.........	314
Chickasaws.......	4,787	Seminoles........	2,500
Choctaws........	16,000	Senecas..........	180
Creeks..........	25,000	Seneca - Shawnee band...........	271

Report of the Commissioner of Indian Affairs for 1855, *S. Ex. Docs.*, 34 Cong. 1 and 2 sess., I (810), 575, 576.

In 1866

Cherokees........	14,000	Seminoles........	2,000
Chickasaws.......	4,500	Senecas..........	130
Choctaws........	12,500	Seneca - Shawnee band...........	210
Creeks..........	14,000		
Quapaws........	350	Mixed tribes of the Wichita agency...	1,800

Report of the Commissioner of Indian Affairs for 1866, *H. Ex. Docs.*, 39 Cong. 2 sess., II (1284), 351.

In 1879

Cherokees........	19,000	Choctaws........	16,000
Including Mixed...	6,000	Including Mixed....	6,000

APPENDICES

Negroes.. 3,500		Whites.... 1,300	
Whites... 700		Not including	
Chickasaws.......	5,800	freedmen.......	2,600
Including		Creeks..........	14,260
Mixed... 2,500		Including	
Whites... 365		Mixed.... 1,200	
Not including		Negroes... 2,500	
freedmen. 4,000		Whites......136	
Quapaws........	38	Thirty-mile-square	
Most of them were		reservation......	910
with the Osages		Absentee Shaw-	
Seminoles........	2,443	nees...... 660	
Senecas..........	235	Citizen Pot-	
Shawnees (Eastern)	80	tawatomies 250	
Modocs.........	99	Cheyenne and Ara-	
Ottawas.........	140	pahoe reservation	5,496
Peoria reservation	184	Cheyennes. 3,593	
Peorias, etc. 122		Arapahoes. 1,903	
Miamis.... 62		Wichita reservation	1,271
Wyandottes......	260	Wichitas... 209	
Osage and Kansas		Wacoes.... 49	
reservations.....	2,645	Towaconies 155	
Osages.... 2,135		Kechies.... 75	
Kaws..... 360		Caddoes... 543	
Quapaws.. 150		Delawares.. 81	
Nez Percés.......	370	Comanches of	
Pawnees.........	1,251	Wichita... 159	
Poncas..........	530	Kiowa, Comanche,	
Sac and Fox res-		and Apache res-	
ervation........	873	ervation.........	2,896
Sacs and		Kiowas.... 1,138	
Foxes.... 423		Comanches 1,393	
Others, chief-		Apaches... 315	
ly Mexican			
Kickapoos. 450			

The numbers, except of the Pawnees and of the Five Civilized Tribes, are taken from the reports made in 1879 to the Commissioner of Indian Affairs, *H. Ex. Docs.*, 46 Cong. 2 sess., IX (1910), 163-183. The census of the Pawnees is for 1881 (no returns for

THE FORMATION OF OKLAHOMA

1879 and 1880), and is from the agent's report for 1882, *H. Ex. Docs.*, 47 Cong. 2 sess., XI (2100), 137. The numbers of the Five Civilized Tribes are from the report of the Senate investigating committee (Patterson report), made February 11, 1879, *S. Reports*, 45 Cong. 3 sess., III (1839), p. iii. The Otoes and Missouris, who were removed to the Indian Territory in 1881, numbered 282 in 1883 (report of the agent for 1883, *H. Ex. Docs.*, 48 Cong. 1 sess., XI (2191), 133), and the agent for the Sacs and Foxes had four hundred new arrivals in 1880 (report for 1880, *H. Ex. Docs.*, 46 Cong. 3 sess., IX (1959), 212).

In 1890

The population of the Five Civilized Tribes was 178,097, including Indians, 50,055; negroes, 18,636; and other, 109,406. The Indians of the Quapaw agency numbered 1,224, and a few whites among them and on military reservations brought the total population of the diminished Indian Territory up to 180,182. The Indians of the Territory of Oklahoma numbered 13,167 (from the eleventh census of the United States, Indians, *H. Misc. Docs.*, 52 Cong. 1 sess., L, vi (3016), 242, 254, 528).

Indian Population of Oklahoma in 1907

The Five Civilized Tribes

	Total	Mixed	Inter-married	Freedmen	Full-blood
Cherokee	41,798	6,601	29,986	286	4,925
Chickasaw	10,989	1,538	4,146	635	4,670
Choctaw	26,615	8,319	10,717	1,585	5,994
Creek	18,702	6,812	5,083	......	6,807
Seminole	3,124	1,399	739	......	986
	101,228	24,669	50,671	2,506	23,382

Other Indians

Quapaw	290	Iowa	86
Seneca	390	Sac and Fox	522
Shawnee (Eastern)	107	Mexican Kickapoo	290
Modoc	51	Absentee Shawnee	590
Ottawa	211	Citizen Pottawatomie	1,702

APPENDICES

Peoria............	207	Cheyenne.........	1,901
Miami...........	130	Arapaho..........	886
Wyandotte.......	379	Wichita, etc.......	441
Osage...........	2,156	Caddo...........	555
Kaw............	196	Kiowa...........	1,235
Oto and Missouri.	390	Comanche........	1,440
Pawnee..........	644	Apache..........	159
Ponca...........	578		
Tonkawa........	49	Total..........	15,603

The above is taken from the report of the Secretary of the Interior for 1907, *H. Docs.*, 60 Cong. 1 sess., XXVI (5295), 21, 49.

APPENDIX E

PRINCIPAL BILLS RELATING TO INDIAN TERRITORY INTRODUCED BETWEEN 1865 AND 1879

BETWEEN 1865 AND 1870

Bills to organize the Indian Territory: Senate Bill 28, by James H. Lane of Kansas, December 12, 1865, *Senate Journal*, 39 Cong. 1 sess., 23; House Bill 43, by Asahel W. Hubbard of Iowa, December 18, *House Journal*, 39 Cong. 1 sess., 32; House Bill 583, by Shelby M. Cullom of Illinois, May 14, 1866, *ibid.*, 691; House Bill 647 (Territory of Lincoln), by William Lawrence of Ohio, June 4, *ibid.*, 787, 936 (cf. Parker's *Calendar*, 149); House Bill 928, by John H. Rice of Maine, January 7, 1867, *House Journal*, 39 Cong. 2 sess., 116; House Bill 1181 (committee substitute for House Bill 928), by Rice, February 18, *ibid.*, 416; Senate Bill 81, by Samuel C. Pomeroy of Kansas, March 18, *Senate Journal*, 40 Cong. 1 sess., 57 (cf. Parker, *loc. cit.*), reported adversely, February 1, 1869, *Senate Journal*, 40 Cong. 3 sess., 173; House Bill 86 (Territory of Lincoln), by Lawrence, March 25, 1867, *House Journal*, 40 Cong. 1 sess., 15, 107; House Bill 367, by Robert T. Van Horn of Missouri, January 6, 1868, *House Journal*, 40 Cong. 2 sess., 150 (cf. Parker, *loc. cit.*); House Bill 1208 (committee substitute for House Bill 367), by Van Horn, June 9, *ibid.*,

THE FORMATION OF OKLAHOMA

828 (cf. Parker, *loc. cit.*); Senate Bill 685, by Pomeroy, December 14, *Senate Journal*, 40 Cong. 3 sess., 40; House Bill 1795, by Thomas D. Eliot of Massachusetts, January 25, 1869, *House Journal*, 40 Cong. 3 sess., 205; House Bill 299, by Van Horn, March 29, *House Journal*, 41 Cong. 1 sess., 130 (cf. Parker, *loc. cit.*), reported January 24, 1870, *House Journal*, 41 Cong. 2 sess., 193; House Bill 422 (tribal territories), by George W. Julian of Indiana, April 9, 1869, *House Journal*, 41 Cong. 1 sess., 238 (cf. Parker, *loc. cit.*); House Bill 1001 (Territory of Lincoln), by Cullom, January 28, 1870, *House Journal*, 41 Cong. 2 sess., 223 (cf. Parker, *loc. cit.*); House Bill 1777, by Sidney Clarke of Kansas, April 13, *House Journal*, 41 Cong. 2 sess., 614.

Bill to organize a United States court: House Bill 929, by Rice of Maine, January 7, 1867, *House Journal*, 39 Cong. 2 sess., 116 (cf. Parker, *loc. cit.*). Bill to carry into effect treaties of 1866: House Bill 1873, by Clark, April 25, 1870, *House Journal*, 41 Cong. 2 sess., 672.

Bill to establish the Territory of Oklahoma: Senate Bill 679, by Benjamin F. Rice of Arkansas, March 17, 1870, *Senate Journal*, 41 Cong. 2 sess., 382 (cf. Parker, *loc. cit.*), reported April 27, *S. Reports*, 41 Cong. 2 sess. (1409), no. 131.

FROM DECEMBER, 1870, TO MARCH, 1873

Bills to establish the Territory of Oklahoma: Senate Bill 1186, by Daniel T. Jewett of Missouri, January 10, 1871, *Senate Journal*, 41 Cong. 3 sess., 106 (cf. Parker, *loc. cit.*); House Bill 299, reported with amendments from the Committee on Indian Affairs by Van Horn, January 19, *Cong. Globe*, 41 Cong. 3 sess., 600; House Bill 3043 (substitute of committees on Territories and Indian Affairs for House Bill 299), by Van Horn, February 25, *House Journal*, 41 Cong. 3 sess., 344 (cf. Parker, *loc. cit.*); Senate Bill 17, by Rice of Arkansas, March 7, *Senate Journal*, 42 Cong. 1 sess., 10; House Bill 113, by Harrison E. Havens of Missouri, March 13, *House Journal*, 42 Cong. 1 sess., 113 (cf. Parker, *loc. cit.*); House Bill 561, by Erastus Wells of Missouri, December 11, *House Journal*, 42 Cong. 2 sess., 52 (cf. Parker, *loc. cit.*); House Bill 1376, by Isaac C. Parker of Missouri, February 5, 1872, *ibid.*, 268 (cf. Parker, *loc. cit.*); Senate Bill 653, by Francis P. Blair of Missouri, February 16, *Senate Journal*, 42 Cong. 2 sess., 250; House Bill 2635

APPENDICES

(substitute for House Bill 1376), by Parker for Committee on Territories, May 1, *H. Reports*, 42 Cong. 2 sess. I (1528), no. 61; House Bill 3086, by Parker, December 9, *House Journal*, 42 Cong. 3 sess., 49 (cf. Parker, *loc. cit.*); Senate Bill 1244, by Pomeroy, December 13, *Senate Journal*, 42 Cong. 3 sess., 64; House Bill 3578, by Daniel W. Voorhees of Indiana, January 20, 1873, *House Journal*, 42 Cong. 3 sess., 208 (cf. Parker, *loc. cit.*); Senate Bill 1513, by Rice of Arkansas, February 3, *Senate Journal*, 42 Cong. 3 sess., 264, reported by James Harlan for the Committee on Indian Affairs, February 20, *S. Reports*, 42 Cong. 3 sess., III (1550), no. 471.

Bills to ratify the Okmulgee constitution: Senate Bill 1237, by Harlan, January 20, 1871, *Senate Journal*, 41 Cong. 3 sess., 147 (cf. Parker, *loc. cit.*), reported by Harlan for the Committee on Indian Affairs, January 25, *ibid.*, 164; Senate Bill 80, by Harlan, March 9, *Senate Journal*, 42 Cong. 1 sess., 15.

Bills to organize a system of courts: Senate Bill 628, by Rice of Arkansas, February 12, 1872, *Senate Journal*, 42 Cong. 2 sess., 228, reported with amendments by the committee on judiciary, May 1, *ibid.*, 645 (bill printed as amended in *Cong. Globe*, 42 Cong. 2 sess., 3416); House Bill 1476, by Horatio C. Burchard of Illinois, February 12, *House Journal*, 42 Cong. 2 sess., 326 (cf. Parker, *loc. cit.*); Senate Bill 830, by Pomeroy, March 18, *Senate Journal*, 42 Cong. 2 sess., 390; Senate Bill 951, by Pomeroy, April 10, *ibid.*, 527; Senate Bill 979, by Powell Clayton of Arkansas, April 16, *ibid.*, 553; Senate Bill 1197, by Pomeroy, December 2, *Senate Journal*, 42 Cong. 3 sess., 6.

Bills to repeal the conditional land grants: House Bill 1132, by John P. C. Shanks of Indiana, January 22, 1872, *House Journal*, 42 Cong. 2 sess., 196 (cf. Parker, *loc. cit.*); Senate Bill 853, by Lot M. Morrill of Maine, March 22, *Senate Journal*, 42 Cong. 2 sess., 414.

Bill to authorize a delegate in Congress for the Indian Territory: Senate Bill 1082, by Harlan, December 6, 1870, *Senate Journal*, 41 Cong. 3 sess. 25 (cf. Parker, *loc. cit.*), reported December 9 by Harlan, *ibid.*, 35.

From December, 1873, to the Close of 1878

Bills to establish a Territory of Oklahoma: Senate Bill 27, by

THE FORMATION OF OKLAHOMA

John J. Ingalls of Kansas, December 2, 1873, *Cong. Record*, 43 Cong. 1 sess., 12; House Bill 151, by Parker, December 4, *ibid.*, 66; House Bill 164, by William J. Hynes of Arkansas, December 4, *ibid.*, 67; Senate Bill 570, by Stephen W. Dorsey of Arkansas, March 5, 1874, *ibid.*, 1977; House Bill 4164; by Stephen A. Cobb of Kansas, January 6, 1875, *Cong. Record*, 43 Cong. 2 sess., 277; House Bill 4264, by Havens, January 11, *ibid.*, 376; Senate Bill 1129, by Carl Schurz of Missouri, January 14, *ibid.*, 447; Senate Bill 213, by Dorsey, January 10, 1876, *Cong. Record*, 44 Cong. 1 sess., 310; House Bill 943, by Benjamin J. Franklin of Missouri, January 12, *ibid.*, 378; Senate Bill 661, by Henry L. Dawes of Massachusetts, by request, March 27, *ibid.*, 1968; House Bill 3285, by Henry L. Pierce of Massachusetts, May 1, *ibid.*, 2859; House Bill 3922, by William P. Caldwell of Tennessee for the committee on territories, July 18, *ibid.*, 4701; Senate Bill 1174, by Lewis V. Bogy of Missouri, by request, January 22, 1877, *Cong. Record*, 44 Cong. 2 sess., 795; House Bill 1596, by Franklin, November 22, *Cong. Record*, 45 Cong. 1 sess., 608; House Bill 1709, by Jordan E. Cravens of Arkansas, November 27, *ibid.*, 725; Senate Bill 529, by Dorsey, January 16, 1878, *Cong. Record*, 45 Cong. 2 sess., 353; Senate Bill 747, by Dorsey, February 14, *ibid.*, 1014, 1015; Senate Bill 759, by George E. Spencer of Alabama, February 18, *ibid.*, 1129.

Numerous bills to establish the judicial district of Oklahoma, as well as other bills dealing with the Indian Territory, were introduced between December, 1873, and the close of 1878.

APPENDIX F

TWO SAMPLE PETITIONS FOR THE OPENING OF OKLAHOMA

PETITION FROM THE BOOMERS

To the Honorable the Senate and House of Representatives in Congress assembled:

We, the people of Oklahoma, assembled in public meeting, at the town of Stillwater, in Oklahoma, do most earnestly and respectfully request the immediate attention of Congress to the following facts:

APPENDICES

Oklahoma was bought by the United States from the Creek and Seminole Indians eighteen years ago. It has been paid for in full. The title rests solely and exclusively in the United States. There are no limitations of any kind whatever. No Indian or tribe of Indians, owns, controls, or claims to control, one foot of these lands.

No one disputes any of these statements, yet notwithstanding these plain and undeniable facts, and notwithstanding the further fact that all the western part of our country has been settled and improved, exactly as we have settled and improved this county, in advance of official invitation, we have repeatedly been driven from our homes by military force, our houses burned, our property destroyed, and our bodies dragged hundreds of miles into out-of-the-way places, and held for weeks, beyond the reach of civil processes, and then dismissed without trial or explanation.

When we have cited laws to these men wearing Federal uniforms, and asked them for justice, they have cursed us and told us they cared nothing for laws, they had the power and would use it.

We thoroughly and with one accord believe that our right to make homes for ourselves and our families upon these lands would not have been questioned had it not been for the fact that rich cattle syndicates were here ahead of us.

These men are few in number, but strong in the use of unlimited capital.

They do not pretend to have even a lease of these lands from any source whatever, yet they hold and enclose them with wire fences, and the Federal Army is used as their private police.

We are now in Oklahoma again.

We are here with our axes and our plows. Hundreds and thousands of our friends are on their way to join us from all states of the West.

We are here to stay. We deny the right of any man, or mob of men, whether in uniform or plain clothes, to molest us.

We do most earnestly request that Congress will henceforth guarantee to us our plain and undeniable rights under the laws and Constitution of our country; and as a means to secure and maintain these rights, we request that Congress may immediately order the withdrawal of the Federal troops from our midst, and

THE FORMATION OF OKLAHOMA

at as early a day as possible organize Oklahoma as a territory of the United States, and provide for the appointment of a governor and the election of other necessary officers.

(Presented in the Senate, January 7, 1885; *Cong. Record*, 48 Cong. 2 sess., 505).

PETITION FROM HOWARD, KANSAS

Howard, Kansas, January 10, 1885.

At a meeting of the citizens of Howard and vicinity, held at the courthouse, the following proceedings were had and the following resolutions were adopted:

The meeting was called to order by L. Scott, and on his motion B. L. Brush was elected chairman. John W. Marshall was elected secretary. Some very able speeches were delivered by B. L. Brush, L. Scott, J. F. Lewis, W. D. Parker, H. S. Douthitt, J. M. White, D. W. Dunnett, S. B. Oberlender, and others on the question of opening Oklahoma and the rights of the people to settle therein.

The following resolutions were adopted as an expression of the sense and desire of the meeting:

Whereas, The armed forces of the United States have been directed against peaceable citizens that have entered on public lands in the Indian Territory, known as Oklahoma: Therefore,

Be it resolved, That we denounce as an outrage the treatment of loyal American citizens, who are striving to make homes for themselves and their families on lands belonging to the people of the United States; and we further denounce it as the grossest injustice to the people of those states that border on the Indian Territory.

Resolved, That we are opposed to the policy of the Government in using the army to drive out or interfere with actual settlers upon any of the public domain, as being foreign to the genius of our institutions.

Resolved, That we demand that the armed force of the United States be immediately withdrawn from Oklahoma, and that all American citizens, that so desire, be allowed peaceably to enter these lands, under no restrictions whatever, other than those that would be found in any other part of the public domain.

Resolved, As this selfsame, bold spirit, that is now advancing to the front, has ever existed since the Pilgrim Fathers set their

APPENDICES

feet on Plymouth Rock, and will ever exist so long as we remain citizens of this grand Republic, that we, the citizens of Howard and vicinity, pledge ourselves to firmly support this grand element —the vanguard of civilization.

Resolved, That the leasing of any public lands to cattlemen is in direct violation of the laws of the United States and rights of the people, and we demand that all such leases be immediately cancelled.

Resolved, That we denounce the inaction of our Representatives and Senators concerning said lands, and that we demand of them to use all means in their power to secure the proper recognition of the rights of the people in this matter from the Government of the United States, and for the faithful performance of this duty we hold them responsible at the ballot-box.

Resolved, That we are opposed to the settlement of any more bands of wild Indians in the Indian Territory.

Resolved, That our Representative, B. W. Perkins, be requested to present to Congress the sentiments of our people upon this question, and to use all honorable means in his power to secure the necessary legislation at this session of Congress.

Resolved, That a copy of these resolutions be sent to each of our Representatives in Congress, to the head of the Department of the Interior, to the chairman of the Senate Committee on Indian Affairs, and to the President of the United States.

It is the sense of this meeting that the *Democrat* and *Courant* publish these resolutions, and that the remaining [Elk] county papers copy the same.

Much enthusiasm existed during the adoption of the above resolutions.

On motion of W. D. Parker to appoint a committee on organization W. D. Parker, Robert Shelby, S. B. Oberlender, Thomas Greenwood, and B. L. Brush were appointed as such committee, to report at the next meeting of the people.

Adjourned to meet at the court-house on Saturday, January 17, at 7 o'clock P.M.

B. L. BRUSH, Chairman,
JOHN W. MARSHALL, Secretary.

(Presented in the House of Representatives on January 20, 1885; *Cong. Record*, 48 Cong. 2 sess., 868.)

THE FORMATION OF OKLAHOMA

APPENDIX G

PRECEDENTS FOR THE BOOMER INVASIONS

The claim that all the western part of the United States had been settled in advance of official invitation had considerable basis in fact. Two quotations from speeches made in the United States Senate will serve to demonstrate this.

The first of these speeches was made by Augustus C. Dodge, senator from Iowa, February 25, 1854 (*Cong. Globe*, 33 Cong. 1 sess., Appendix, 381):

". . .Why, sir, the whole Western country has been settled and occupied by pioneers, who did so in defiance of your marshals, district attorneys, and Indian agents. Every one knows that there are laws which prohibit, in the most positive terms, settlements upon the public domain in the Indian country. The Senator from Wisconsin, on my right [Henry Dodge, the father of the speaker] has been a violator of that law throughout the greater portion of his life. He has had these laws, with the proclamations of United States officers, read to himself and neighbors, when upon the Indian country in Wisconsin, more than a quarter of a century ago, commanding him and them to abandon the settlements they had made. He disregarded the mandates of these officers, threw up a stockade fort, provided himself and neighbors with several hundred guns, and announced that if the officers and soldiers of the regular Army desired to expel him they could come and try it."

Since this was not a part of the country set apart for the Indians from the eastern states, the government apparently did not try very hard to drive out the Dodges and their friends. As soon as a part of the larger Indian Territory had been organized, the country assigned to Indians from the East was subject to the same sort of invasion. This is indicated by a speech of James H. Lane, senator from Kansas, May 13, 1862 (*Cong. Globe*, 37 Cong. 2 sess., 2097):

"We have twenty-three sections of [Indian] land on the Kansas River. . . .A great many settlers have come from New England

APPENDICES

...and...settled on those twenty-three sections. The Government sent troops to drive those men off twice that I know of, burned their houses, destroyed their crops, and yet the same men are there today, and will remain there until they get titles to their land. . . .

"There were twenty-three sections of land that belonged to a parcel of Indians who were absentees, and our people thought it was wrong, wrong to God, to permit that fine land to remain there uncultivated. They were governed by the higher law. It is a byword in Kansas that where the people determine to go, there is not power enough on earth to keep them from going. . . ."

APPENDIX H

CREEK AND SEMINOLE AGREEMENTS OF 1889

The Creek cession of 1866 comprised 3,402,428.88 acres. Of this, 732,673.99 acres had been sold to the Seminoles, Sacs and Foxes, and Pawnees; 1,277,050.19 acres had been assigned to the Cheyennes, Arapahoes, Iowas, Kickapoos, and Pottawatomies; 1,392,704.70 acres remained unassigned in 1889. This tract constituted the part of the Oklahoma district which lay north of the North Fork of the Canadian. The Creeks received ninety-five cents an acre as additional compensation for the unassigned land, seventy-five cents an acre for the land assigned to other Indians, and no additional compensation for the land that had been sold to other Indians. It was necessary, however, to include this in the new cession, since the government in carrying out the allotment of it according to the terms of the Dawes act would be embarrassed by the restrictions in the cession of 1866. The total additional compensation for the entire cession was placed at $2,280,857.10, and the agreement mentioned only this total without explaining how it had been computed. Of this sum, two million dollars was retained in the United States treasury, and the annual interest was set aside for the support of Creek schools. The details of the agreement are given in *S. Ex. Docs.*, 50 Cong. 2 sess., III (2612), no. 98.

The Seminole cession of 1866 contained 2,037,414.62 acres.

THE FORMATION OF OKLAHOMA

Of this, 1,542,327.75 acres had been assigned before 1889 to Cheyennes, Arapahoes, Pottawatomies, and Shawnees. The remainder, 495,086.87 acres, comprised the part of the Oklahoma district that lay south of the North Fork of the Canadian. None of this cession had been sold to other Indians. The Seminoles had received fifteen cents an acre less than the Creeks in 1866, and their additional compensation in 1889 was made larger by that amount. The estimate of the number of acres in the cession of 1866 was too large, and the Seminoles were paid more at that time than the treaty called for. Therefore a corresponding deduction seems to have been made in 1889. The total compensation was fixed in the agreement at $1,912,942.02. Of this sum, $1,500,000 was placed in the United States treasury to the credit of the Seminoles, and the remainder was paid to them at the time. Some details are given in *S. Ex. Docs.*, 50 Cong. 2 sess., III (2612), no. 122; but see *Cong. Record*, 50 Cong. 2 sess., 2367, and also *S. Ex. Docs.*, 51 Cong. 1 sess., IX (2686), no. 78, pp. 20-22.

The clauses in the treaties of 1866 that made these cessions necessary read as follows:

"In compliance with the desire of the United States to locate other Indians and freedmen thereon, the Creeks hereby cede and convey to the United States, to be sold to and used as homes for such other civilized Indians as the United States may choose to settle thereon, the west half of their entire domain. . . .

"In compliance with the desire of the United States to locate other Indians and freedmen thereon, the Seminoles cede and convey to the United States their entire domain. . . ."

APPENDICES

APPENDIX I

THE WORK OF THE DAWES COMMISSION

SUMMARY OF APPLICANTS

	Applicants	Enrolled	Dismissed	Undetermined
Choctaw and Chickasaw	66,217	35,638	27,719	2,860
Cherokee	46,464	35,394	4,639	6,431
Creek	20,110	15,513	1,157	3,450
Seminole	3,171	2,750	7	414
	135,962	89,295	33,522	13,155

SUMMARY OF ALLOTMENTS

	Acres	Reserved	Allotted	Subject to allotment
Choctaw and Chickasaw	11,660,952	507,607	6,413,876	4,739,468
Cherokee	4,420,077	20,000	3,542,842	857,234
Creek	3,079,094	19,632	2,453,042	606,419
Seminole	365,851	2,272	344,586	18,992
	19,525,976	549,513	12,754,347	6,222,115

The above summaries are from the final report of the Dawes Commission, June 30, 1905, *H. Docs.*, 59 Cong. 1 sess., XIX (4959), 579-640.

PLAN OF ALLOTMENT

The Cherokees received 110 acres each, and of this a homestead of forty acres was made inalienable for twenty-one years or for the lifetime of the allottee (act of July 1, 1902, *Statutes*, XXXII, 717).

The Chickasaws and Choctaws received 320 acres each, with a homestead of 160 acres inalienable as above, and the freedmen of these tribes received forty acres each as a homestead, also

THE FORMATION OF OKLAHOMA

inalienable as above (act of July 1, 1902, *Statutes* XXXII, 642).

The Creeks received 160 acres each, with a homestead of forty acres inalienable as above (act of March 1, 1901, *Statutes*, XXXI, 862; act of June 30, 1902, *Statutes* XXXII, 503).

The land of the Seminoles was divided among them in accordance with the agreement of December 16, 1897, ratified by act of July 1, 1898 (*Statutes*, XXX 567-569). A homestead of forty acres was made inalienable as above (act of March 3, 1903, *Statutes* XXXII, 1008).

Restrictions on the alienation of lands other than homesteads could be removed only with the approval of the Secretary of the Interior.

BIBLIOGRAPHY

BIBLIOGRAPHY

UNITED STATES RECORDS

Reports of officials are not listed separately, as they are cited in the volumes of the Congressional Documents. The number between the parenthesis is the serial number of the volume of the Congressional Documents. The number of the document is given only when the volume contains more than one document.

Congressional Documents

American State Papers, Miscellaneous, I, *Indian Affairs,* II, Washington, 1834.

House Documents, 54 Cong. 1 sess., XIV (3381), XV (3382), XVI (3383); 54 Cong. 2 sess., XIII (3489), XIV (3490); 55 Cong. 2 sess., XIV (3642); 55 Cong. 3 sess., XV (3757), XVI (3758); 56 Cong. 1 sess., XIX (3916), XXI (3918); 56 Cong. 2 sess., XXVI (4100), XXX (4104); 57 Cong. 1 sess., XXII (4289), XXIII (4290), XXVI (4293); 57 Cong. 2 sess., XVIII (4457), XXII (4461); 59 Cong. 1 sess., XIX (4959); 59 Cong. 2 sess., XVI (5119); 60 Cong. 1 sess., XXVI (5295), XXVII (5296).

House Executive Documents, 26 Cong. 2 sess., I (382), no. 2; 28 Cong. 2 sess., I (463), no. 2; 30 Cong. 2 sess., I (537); 33 Cong. 1 sess., I, i (710), XVIII, ii (737); 33 Cong. 2 sess., I, i (777); 37 Cong. 3 sess., II (1157); 38 Cong. 1 sess., III (1182); 38 Cong. 2 sess., V (1220); 39 Cong. 1 sess., II (1248); 39 Cong. 2 sess., II (1284); 40 Cong. 2 sess., XI (1337), no. 133; 40 Cong. 3 sess., II (1366); 41 Cong. 2 sess., III (1414); 41 Cong. 3 sess., IV, i (1449); 42 Cong. 2 sess., III, i (1505); 42 Cong. 3 sess., III, i (1560); 43 Cong. 1 sess., IV, i (1601); 43 Cong. 2 sess., VI (1639); 44 Cong. 1 sess., II, i (1674); IV, i (1680); 44 Cong. 2 sess., II, i (1742), IV, i (1749); 45 Cong. 2 sess., VIII (1800); 45 Cong. 3 sess., IX (1850); 46 Cong. 2 sess., II (1903), IX (1910); 46 Cong. 3 sess., II (1952), IX (1959); 47 Cong. 1 sess., II (2010), X (2018), XXII (2030), no. 145; 47 Cong. 2 sess., II (2091), XI (2100); 48 Cong. 1 sess., II (2182), XI (2191), XIII (2193), no. 17; 48 Cong. 2 sess., II (2277), XI (2286), XII (2287); 49 Cong. 1 sess., II (2369), XI (2378), XII (2379); 49 Cong. 2 sess., II (2461), VIII (2467); 50 Cong.

THE FORMATION OF OKLAHOMA

1 sess., II (2533), X (2541), XI (2542), XVIII (2550), no. 21, XXIX (2561), no. 292; 50 Cong. 2 sess., XI (2637), XII (2638); 51 Cong. 1 sess., II (2715), XI (2724), XII (2725); 51 Cong. 2 sess., XII (2841); 52 Cong. 1 sess., XIV (2933), XV (2934), XVI (2935); 52 Cong. 2 sess., XIII (3088), XIV (3089); 53 Cong. 2 sess., XIII (3209), XIV (3210), XV (3211); 53 Cong. 3 sess., XIV (3305), XV (3306), XVI (3307).

House Journal, 39 Cong. 1 sess., (1243); 39 Cong. 2 sess., (1280); 40 Cong. 1 sess., (1310); 40 Cong. 2 sess., (1321); 40 Cong. 3 sess., (1363); 41 Cong. 1 sess., (1400); 41 Cong. 2 sess., (1410); 41 Cong. 3 sess., (1444); 42 Cong. 1 sess., (1469); 42 Cong. 2 sess., (1501); 42 Cong. 3 sess., (1551).

House Miscellaneous Documents, 30 Cong. 2 sess., (544), nos. 35, 38, 39; 35 Cong. 2 sess., I (1016), no. 21; 37 Cong. 2 sess., (1141), no. 75; 39 Cong. 2 sess., (1302), no. 37; 42 Cong. 2 sess., III (1526), no. 166; 42 Cong. 3 sess., II (1572), no. 42; 43 Cong. 1 sess., II (1618), nos. 85, 88; 49 Cong. 1 sess., XXVI (2432); 52 Cong. 1 sess., I (2959), no. 325, L, vi (3016).

House Reports, 30 Cong. 1 sess., III (526), no. 736; 32 Cong. 1 sess., (656), no. 101; 42 Cong. 2 sess., I (1528), no. 61, IV (1543), no. 89; 43 Cong. 2 sess., IV (1659), no. 151; 44 Cong. 1 sess., I (1708), no. 299; 45 Cong. 3 sess., II(1867), no. 188; 46 Cong. 1 and 2 sess., I (1934), no. 13 (1 sess.), no. 29 (2 sess.), 2 sess., II (1935), no. 474, III (1936), no. 755, V (1938), no. 1576; 48 Cong. 2 sess., I (2328), no. 2247; 49 Cong. 1 sess., IV (2438), no. 1076, VI (2440), no. 1684; 50 Cong. 1 sess., II (2599), no. 263, III (2600), no. 839, VIII (2605), no. 2857; 51 Cong. 1 sess., I (2807), nos. 4, 66, 205; 52 Cong. 1 sess., VII (3048), no. 1927; 52 Cong. 2 sess., III (3142), no. 2455; 53 Cong. 2 sess., I (3269), no. 242; 54 Cong. 1 sess., IV (3460), no. 1102, VIII (3464), no. 1988; 57 Cong. 1 sess., IV (4402), no. 956, V (4403), no. 1309; 58 Cong. 2 sess., VII (4583), no. 2335; 59 Cong. 1 sess., (4906), no. 496, III (4908), nos. 4660, 4925.

Senate Documents, 57 Cong. 2 sess., V (4420), no. 36; 59 Cong. 1 sess., IV (4912), no. 143, VIII (4916), nos. 478, 487; 60 Cong. 1 sess., VII (5240), no. 187.

Senate Executive Documents, 32 Cong. 1 sess., III (613); 33 Cong. 2 sess., I (746), XIII, i (758); 34 Cong. 1 and 2 sess., I (810);

BIBLIOGRAPHY

34 Cong. 3 sess., II (875); 35 Cong. 1 sess., II (919); 35 Cong. 2 sess., I (974); 36 Cong. 1 sess., I (1023); 36 Cong. 2 sess., I (1078); 37 Cong. 2 sess., I (1117); 41 Cong. 3 sess., I (1440), no. 26; 42 Cong. 2 sess., II (1479), no. 51; 45 Cong. 2 sess., I (1780), no. 32; 46 Cong. 1 sess., I (1869), nos. 20, 26, 29; 46 Cong. 2 sess., I (1882), no. 10; 47 Cong. 1 sess., V (1990), no. 111; 48 Cong. 1 sess., IV (2165), nos. 51, 54; 48 Cong. 2 sess., I, [i] (2261), no. 17, II [i] (2263), nos. 50, 54; 49 Cong. 1 sess., I (2333), no. 14; 50 Cong. 1 sess., I (2504), no. 41, X (2513), no. 166; 50 Cong. 2 sess., III (2612), nos. 98, 122; 51 Cong. 1 sess., V (2682), no. 33, IX (2686), nos. 72, 78, XXXI (2746), no. 209; 52 Cong. 1 sess., I (2892), nos. 13, 14, V (2900), no. 56; 52 Cong. 2 sess., I (3055), nos. 16, 17.

Senate Journal, 39 Cong. 1 sess., (1236); 40 Cong. 1 sess., (1307); 40 Cong. 3 sess., (1359); 41 Cong. 2 sess., (1404); 41 Cong. 3 sess., (1439); 42 Cong. 1 sess., (1465); 42 Cong. 2 sess., (1477); 42 Cong. 3 sess. (1544).

Senate Miscellaneous Documents, 32 Cong. 2 sess., (670), no. 5; 41 Cong. 2 sess., (1408), no. 83; 42 Cong. 2 sess., I (1481), no. 49; 43 Cong. 2 sess., I (1630), nos. 34, 66, 71, 72; 47 Cong. 1 sess., IV (1996), no. 117; 51 Cong. 1 sess., II (2698), no. 74.

Senate Reports, 32 Cong. 1 sess., II (631), no. 344; 33 Cong. 1 sess., I (706), no. 15, II, [i] (707), no. 379; 41 Cong. 2 sess., (1409), nos. 113, 131; 42 Cong. 3 sess., III (1550), no. 471; 45 Cong. 3 sess., II (1838), no. 714, III (1839); 46 Cong. 2 sess., VI (1898), no. 665; 48 Cong. 1 sess., I (2173), no. 64; 49 Cong. 1 sess., VIII (2362), IX (2363); 50 Cong. 1 sess., II (2520), no. 353; 53 Cong. 2 sess., V (3183), no. 377; 57 Cong. 2 sess., I (4410), no. 2206; 58 Cong. 3 sess., I (4755), no. 2747; 59 Cong. 1 sess., I (4904), no. 427.

CONGRESSIONAL RECORDS

Annals of the Congress of the United States. 42 vols. Washington, 1834-1856.

[*Congressional Debates*]. *Register of Debates in Congress.* 29 vols. Washington, 1825-1837.

Congressional Globe, containing the debates and Proceedings. 108 vols. Washington, 1834-1873.

THE FORMATION OF OKLAHOMA

Congressional Record, containing the Proceedings and Debates. Vols. I-XL in many parts (to 1906). Washington, 1873-.

LAWS OF THE UNITED STATES

Revised Statutes. 2d ed. Washington, 1878.
Statutes at Large of the United States of America. Vols. I-XXXV (to 1907). Boston and Washington, 1850-

REPORTS OF JUDICIAL PROCEEDINGS

Federal Reporter. Saint Paul, 1880-.
[United States Reports.] Cases. . . in the Supreme Court. Various places and dates.

SPECIAL RECORDS AND REPORTS

Census of the United States, Twelfth, Population. 2 vols. Washington, 1901.
Census of the United States, Thirteenth, Population by Counties and Minor Civil Divisions, 1910, 1900, 1890. Washington, 1912.
Cherokee Question, The. Compiled by Office of Indian Affairs. Washington, 1866.
Confederate States of America, Journal of the Congress of. 7 vols. Washington, 1904-1905. Senate Documents, 58 Cong. 2 sess., XXV-XXXI (4610-4616).
Indian Affairs: Laws and Treaties. 2d ed. 2 vols. Washington, 1904. Senate Documents, 58 Cong. 2 sess., XXXVIII, XXXIX (4623, 4624). Charles J. Kappler, compiler.
Messages and Papers of the Presidents, 1789-1897, Compilation of. 10 vols. Washington, 1899. Also in *House Miscellaneous Documents*, 53 Cong. 2 sess., XXXVIII (3265, parts 1-10. James D. Richardson, ed.
Report of the Board of Indian Commissioners for 1876. Washington, 1877.
Treaties, Conventions, International Acts, Protocols, and Agreements between the United States and other Powers, 1776-1902. 2 vols. Washington, 1910. Senate Documents, 61 Cong. 2 sess., XLVII, XLVIII (5646, 5647). William M. Malloy, compiler.
War of the Rebellion: a Compilation of the Official Records of the Union

BIBLIOGRAPHY

and *Confederate Armies.* 130 vols. Washington, 1880-1901. Also in *Congressional Documents.*

OTHER PRIMARY MATERIAL

BARBER, JOHN WARNER.
Our Whole Country. 2 vols. New York, 1863. In collaboration with Henry Howe.
CRAWFORD, SAMUEL J.
Kansas in the Sixties. Chicago, 1911.
FARNHAM, THOMAS J.
Travels in the Great Western Prairies. 2 vols. London, 1843. Reprinted in *Early Western Travels,* XXVIII, XXIX. Reuben Gold Thwaites, ed. Cleveland, 1906.
GIHON, JOHN H.
Geary and Kansas. Philadelphia, 1857.
GREGG, JOSIAH.
Commerce of the Prairies. 2 vols. New York and London, 1844. Philadelphia, 1845. Reprinted in *Early Western Travels,* XIX, XX. Reuben Gold Thwaites, ed. Cleveland, 1905.
HARGER, CHARLES MOREAU.
"The Next Commonwealth: Oklahoma," in *Outlook,* LXVII, 273-281. New York, 1901.
JAMES, EDWIN.
Account of an Expedition from Pittsburgh to the Rocky Mountains, performed in the Years 1819 and '20 under the Command of Major Stephen H. Long. 2 vols. Philadelphia, 1823. 3 vols. London, 1823. Reprinted in *Early Western Travels,* XIV-XVII. Reuben Gold Thwaites, ed. Cleveland, 1905.
JEFFERSON, THOMAS.
The Writings of. 10 vols. New York, 1892-1899. Paul Leicester Ford, ed.
JENNESS, THEODORA R.
"The Indian Territory," in *Atlantic Monthly,* XLIII, 444-452. Boston, 1879.
KELLY, H. B.
"No Man's Land," in Kansas State Historical Society, *Collections,* IV, 324-331. Topeka, 1890.
MAXIMILIAN, ALEXANDER PHILIPP, PRINCE OF WIED-NEUWIED.
Travels in the Interior of North America. Translated from the Ger-

man by H. Evans Lloyd. London, 1843. Reprinted with additions in *Early Western Travels*, XXII-XXIV. Reuben Gold Thwaites, ed. Cleveland, 1906.

MORSE, JEDEDIAH.
A Report to the Secretary of War of the United States, on Indian Affairs, comprising a Narrative of a Tour performed in the Summer of 1820. New Haven, 1822.

Nation, XXXIV, XLVIII. New York, 1882, 1889.

Niles' Register, LIV, LXVII. Baltimore, 1838, 1844.

NUTTALL, THOMAS.
Journal of Travels into the Arkansas Territory during the Year 1819. Philadelphia, 1821. Reprinted in *Early Western Travels*. XIII. Reuben Gold Thwaites, ed. Cleveland, 1905.

WALKER, FRANCIS A.
The Indian Question. Boston, 1878.

WICKS, HAMILTON S.
"The Opening of Oklahoma," in *Cosmopolitan*, VII, 460-470. New York, 1899.

WILLIAMS, A. M.
"A Grand Council at Okmulgee," in *Lippincott's*, XXIV, 371-375. Philadelphia, 1879.

WYETH, JOHN B.
Oregon. Cambridge, 1833. Reprinted in *Early Western Travels*, XXI. Reuben Gold Thwaites, ed. Cleveland, 1905.

SECONDARY AUTHORITIES

ABBOTT, LUTHER J.
History and Civics of Oklahoma. Boston, 1910.

ABEL, ANNIE HELOISE.
"History of Events resulting in Indian Consolidation West of the Mississippi River," in American Historical Association, *Annual Report, 1906*, I, 233-450. Washington, 1908.

"Indian Reservations in Kansas," in Kansas State Historical Society, *Collections*, VIII, 72-109. Topeka, 1904.

"Proposals for an Indian State, 1778-1878," in American Historical Association, *Annual Report, 1907*, I, 87-104. Washington, 1908.

BUCK, SOLON J.
"The Settlement of Oklahoma," in Wisconsin Academy of

BIBLIOGRAPHY

Science, Arts, and Letters, *Transactions*, XV, 325-380. Madison, 1907.

BURGESS, JOHN WILLIAM.
The Middle Period. New York, 1897.

DONALDSON, Thomas.
The Public Domain. 3d ed. Washington, 1884. *House Miscellaneous Documents*, 47 Cong. 2 sess., XIX (2158).

FARRAND, MAX.
The Legislation of Congress for the Government of the Organized Territories of the United States, 1789-1895. Newark, 1896.

GANETT, HENRY.
"Boundaries of the United States and of the Several States and Territories. . .," in United States Geological Survey, *Bulletin 226*. 3 ed. Washington, 1904. Also in *House Documents*, 58 Cong. 2 sess., LX (4686), no. 678.

HODDER, FRANK HEYWOOD.
"Genesis of the Kansas-Nebraska Act," in State Historical Society of Wisconsin, *Proceedings, 1912*, 69-86. Madison, 1913.

HODGE, FREDERICK WEBB, ed.
Handbook of American Indians North of Mexico, in Smithsonian Institution, Bureau of American Ethnology, Bulletin 30. 2 vols. Washington, 1907-1910. Also in *House Documents*, 59 Cong. 1 sess., LXI, LXII (5001, 5002).

JOHNSON, ALLEN.
Stephen A. Douglas. New York, 1908.

MCLAUGHLIN, ANDREW CUNNINGHAM.
Lewis Cass. Boston, 1891.

MCMASTER, JOHN BACH.
History of the People of the United States from the Revolution to the Civil War. 8 vols. New York, 1883-1913.

MARSHALL, THOMAS MAITLAND.
A History of the Western Boundary of the Louisiana Purchase, 1819-1841, in University of California, *Publications in History*, II. Berkeley, 1914.

MOONEY, JAMES.
Myths of the Cherokees, in Smithsonian Institution, Bureau of American Ethnology, *Nineteenth Annual Report*, pt. i. Washington, 1900. Also in *House Documents*, 56 Cong. 2 sess., CXVIII (4192).

THE FORMATION OF OKLAHOMA

PARKER, DAVID W.
 Calendar of Papers in Washington Archives relating to the Territories of the United States (to 1873), in Carnegie Institution, Publication no. 148. Washington, 1911.

RAY, PERLEY ORMAN.
 Repeal of the Missouri Compromise. Cleveland, 1909.

REYNOLDS, JOHN HUGH.
 "The Western Boundary of Arkansas," in Arkansas Historical Association, Publications, II, 211-236. Little Rock. 1908.

RHODES, JAMES FORD.
 History of the United States from the Compromise of 1850. 7 vols. New York, 1896-1906.

ROYCE, CHARLES C.
 Cherokee Nation of Indians, in Smithsonian Institution, Bureau of American Ethnology, Fifth Annual Report, 129-378. Washington, 1887. Also in House Miscellaneous Documents, 49 Cong. 2 sess., X (2497).
 Indian Land Cessions of the United States, in Smithsonian Institution, Bureau of American Ethnology, Eighteenth Annual Report, pt. ii. Washington, 1899. Also in House Documents, 56 Cong. 1 sess., XCVIII (4015).

TURNER, FREDERICK JACKSON.
 Rise of the New West. New York, 1906.

UTLEY, JOSEPH S.
 "Graves of Eminent Men," in Arkansas Historical Association, Publications, II, 254-295. Little Rock, 1908.

SUPPLEMENTARY LIST FOR SECOND EDITION

Following is a list of the more important recent books dealing with the period covered in this volume. The reader should consult also the last footnote in Chapter V of this edition.

ALFORD, THOMAS WILDCAT.
 Civilization. Norman, 1936.

BASS, ALTHEA.
 Cherokee Messenger. Norman, 1936.

DALE, EDWARD EVERETT.
 The Range Cattle Industry. Norman, 1930.
 Readings in Oklahoma History. Evanston, 1930. With Jesse Lee Rader.

BIBLIOGRAPHY

DEBO, ANGIE.
The Rise and Fall of the Choctaw Republic. Norman, 1934.

EATON, RACHEL CAROLINE.
John Ross and the Cherokee Indians. Chicago, 1921.

FOREMAN, GRANT.
Advancing the Frontier. Norman, 1933.
Indians and Pioneers: The Story of the American Southwest before 1830. New Haven, 1930. Second edition, Norman, 1938.
The Five Civilized Tribes. Norman, 1934.
Marcy and the Gold Seekers. Norman, 1939.
Pioneer Days in the Early Southwest. Cleveland, 1926.
A Traveler in Indian Territory, The Journal of Ethan Allen Hitchcock. Cedar Rapids, 1930.

GLASSCOCK, C. B.
Then Came Oil. Indianapolis, 1938.

"BUNKY" (GEFFS, IRVING).
The First Eight Months of Oklahoma City. Oklahoma City, 1890. Reprinted, Oklahoma City, 1939.

JAMES, MARQUIS.
The Raven, A Biography of Sam Houston. Indianapolis, 1929.

JOHNSON, ROY M. (Compiler.)
Oklahoma History South of the Canadian. 3 vols. Chicago, 1925.

LEWIS, ANNA.
Along the Arkansas. Dallas, 1932.

LYON, E. WILSON.
Louisiana in French Diplomacy, 1759-1804. Norman, 1934.

MARCY, CAPTAIN R.B., and MCCLELLAN, CAPTAIN G.B.
Adventure on Red River: Report on the Exploration of the Headwaters of the Red River. Norman, 1938.

PELZER, LOUIS.
Marches of the Dragoons in the Mississippi Valley. Iowa City, 1917.

RICHARDSON, RUPERT NORVAL.
The Comanche Barrier to the South Plains Settlement. Glendale, 1933.

RIDINGS, SAM P.
The Chisholm Trail. Guthrie, 1936.

STEWART, DORA ANN.
The Government and Development of Oklahoma Territory. Oklahoma City, 1933.

THE FORMATION OF OKLAHOMA

THOBURN, JOSEPH B. and WRIGHT, MURIEL.
    Oklahoma, A History of the State and Its People. 4 vols. New York, 1929.

WARDELL, MORRIS L.
    A Political History of the Cherokee Nation, 1838-1907. Norman, 1938.
    "Southwest's History Written in Oklahoma's Boundary Story," in *Chronicles of Oklahoma*, V, 287-296. Oklahoma City, 1927.

INDEX

INDEX

Absentee Shawnees, settle in Oklahoma, 107; allotments, 108, 170; opening of reservation, 197; area of, shared in 1878 with Pottawatomies, 263; number in Oklahoma in 1879 and 1907, 265, 266

Acts of: May 28, 1830, authorizing larger Indian Territory, 13
June 30, 1834, reorganizing department of Indian Affairs, 25
June 30, 1834, revising intercourse act, and providing partial judicial organization of Indian country, 26, 138
March 3, 1853, authorizing negotiations for opening of Nebraska, 42
March 3, 1853, authorizing surveys for Pacific railroad, 44
July 5, 1862, authorizing President to annul treaties with southern tribes, 83, 88, 92
March 3, 1863, authorizing removal of Kansas Indians to Oklahoma, 84
March 3, 1871, adopting new policy of treating with Indians, 111
January 6, 1883, attaching part of Indian Territory to district of Kansas and northern district of Texas, 139, 218
See Dawes Act; Kansas-Nebraska act; names of authors of; names of tribes

Aldrich, Cyrus, bill for Territory of Lanniwa, 82, 83

Allotment in severalty, proposed before Civil War, 59, 62, 65; adopted for certain tribes, 62; plan of Thompson, 66, 101, incorporated in treaties 1866 to 1869, 100, 161; bills for, 1880 to 1886, 161, 170. *See* Dawes act. *See also* Arapahoes; Cheyennes; Dawes Commission; Five Civilized Tribes; Kiowas; Modocs; Ottawas; Peorias; Pottawatomies; Quapaws.

Apaches of Arizona, 109. *See* Kiowas

Arapahoes, allotment proposed in 1867, 101; reservation of 1867, 109; of 1869, 109; proposed reservations of 1872, 1873, 110; cattle leases declared void, 160; opening of reservation, 198; area of reservation in 1878, 263; number in Oklahoma in 1879 and 1907, 265, 267

Arizona, removal of Indians to Indian Territory forbidden, 112; admission of Oklahoma complicated by inclusion of statehood bill with, 242, 243, 248, 249, 254, 255

Arkansas, Territory of, established, 4; proposed western boundary of 1823, 7, 31; altered in 1824, 7; in 1828, 10; state mentioned, 15; name Arkansas or West Arkansas applied to Oklahoma, 26; attitude of people toward opening of larger Indian Territory, 42; petition of legislature for south central route to Pacific, 66; attitude of people toward further concentration of Indians in Indian Territory, 112; code of, enforced in Indian Territory, 219, 239; bill for annexation of part of Indian Territory, 254; extension of western boundary authorized, 261

Arthur, President, recommendation of law for prosecution of trespass-

{ 293 }

ers on Indian lands, 141; proclamation warning intruders, 159
Atchison, David R., attitude on Nebraska bill of 1853, 48
Atchison, Topeka, and Santa Fe Railroad. See Santa Fe railroad.
Atkins, J. D. C., commissioner of Indian Affairs, opinion on concentration of Indian allotments, 161, 178; on dissolution of Five Civilized Tribes, 223
Atlantic and Pacific Railroad, builds short line in Indian Territory, 100, 115, 215; bankrupt, 100, 217; taken over by Saint Louis and San Francisco, 115, 215
Atoka agreement, 231, 252

Baker, James, on bankruptcy of Atlantic and Pacific Railroad, 100
Barnes, Cassius M., fourth governor of Territory of Oklahoma, on form of statehood, 240, 241.
Barnes, George T., opinion on concentration of Indian allotments, 178
Bell, James M., heads colony in Cherokee outlet, 125
Bell, John, attitude toward opening of large Indian Territory, 42, 46
Bell, L. B., Cherokee official, 122
Bennett, Leo, estimates of population of Indian Territory, 214, 215, 221
Benton, Thomas H., and railroad to Pacific, 36, 37, 262
Berry, James H., bill for preparation of Indian Territory for statehood, 223; favors commission to Five Civilized Tribes, 224
Beveridge, Albert J., favors admission of Oklahoma and Indian Territory as one state, 244, 254
Big pasture, opening, 209

Black Hills reservation, invasion by miners, 121; opening, 121; effect on invasion of Indian Territory, 121
Blair, Henry W., bill for settlement of freedmen in Indian Territory, 149
Blunt, James G., Union commander in Kansas, 77, 78, 79
Boomers, agitation begins, 118; invasion checked, 123; under Payne, 127-135; under Couch, 136, 143, 158-160, 177, 178; origin of name, 135; character, 143; court proceedings against, 130, 135, 138-143; peculiarities of court decisions, 141, 142; laws against, recommended, 140, 141
Borland, Solon, attitude toward opening of larger Indian Territory, 42; mentioned, 55
Boudinot, Elias, leader of treaty faction of the Cherokees, killed, 62
Boudinot, Elias C., in council at Fort Smith, 90; agitation for opening of Indian Territory, 118-120; mentioned, 121, 125, 128
Bowen, Thomas M., bill to remove Indians of Colorado to Indian Territory, 164
Breckenridge, Clifton R., resolution on statehood for Indian Territory, 223
Brown, John F., Seminole leader, 181

Caddos. See Wichitas
Calhoun, John C., plan of Indian removal in 1825, 13; endeavor to close Northwest to settlement, 47; denounces the Missouri Compromise, 47
California, influence of need for railroad to, on opening of north-

INDEX

ern part of larger Indian Territory, 34; comparisons with Oklahoma, 239, 256

Callahan, James Y., bills relating to Oklahoma, 240

Camp Holmes, treaty of 1835 made at, 22

Camp Napoleon, council of 1865 at, 81, 87

Camp Russell, boomers arrested at, 132

Cannon, Joseph G., opposed to further concentration of Indians, 166

Carpenter, C. C., first leader of boomers, 122, 127

Cass, Lewis, on popular sovereignty, 50

Chahta (variant of Choctaw), organization of Territory of proposed, 58

Chandler, government town site, 198

Chase, Owen G., delegate from "Cimarron Territory," 173

Chelokee (variant of Cherokee), proposed, 58, 60

Cherokees, early migration west of the Mississippi, 5; movement of Western Cherokees, 6; treaty of 1828, 10; reservation delimited in 1833, 19; treaty of 1835, 21; conditions among, in 1854, 62; desire to remain neutral in the Civil War, 70, 71; treaty with the Confederates, 73; factions, 77; struggles between, 79; in council at Fort Smith, 90; loyalty attacked at close of war, 92; treaty of 1866, 99; oppose railroads, 216; faults of their government, 222; agreements with Dawes Commission, 231, 234; declared citizens of the United States, 234; area of reservation in 1866 and 1878, 263; number in Oklahoma in 1822, 6, in 1844, 1855, 1866, 1879, and 1907, 264-267, 277. *See* Chelokee; Dawes Commission; Five Civilized Tribes; Indian Territory; Neosho

Cherokee commission, authorized, 183; its work, 197, 199, 207

Cherokee neutral land, origin, 9; acquired by Cherokees, 21; opening desired, 81; ceded to United States, 98

Cherokee outlet, origin, 6, 11; in treaty of 1833, 20; in treaty of 1866, 99; status according to judicial decisions, 140; negotiations for purchase authorized, 137, 154-156, 183; in Oklahoma Territory, 193, 201; purchased and opened to settlement, 199-202; area in 1878, 263, in 1893, 200

Cherokee strip, origin, 98; name sometimes applied to Cherokee outlet, 98

Cherokee Strip Live Stock Association, 144, 199

Cherokee Tobacco case, 119, 120

Cheyennes and Arapahoes, allotment proposed in 1867, 101; reservation of 1867, 109, of 1869, 109; proposed reservations of 1872, 1873, 110; cattle leases declared void, 160; opening of reservation, 198; area of reservation in 1878, 263; number in Oklahoma in 1879 and 1907, 265, 267

Chicago, Rock Island, and Pacific Railroad. *See* Rock Island railroad

Chickasaws, early migration west of Mississippi, 5; acquire rights with the Choctaws, 22; separate from Choctaws, 63, 64; treaty provision for railroads, 66; resolution of legislature in May, 1861, 70; treaty with Confederates, 72; dur-

{ 295 }

ing Civil War, 80, 94; in council at Fort Smith, 90; cede land in 1866, 98; additional compensation for cession, 198; agreements with Dawes Commission, 231, 234; declared citizens, 234; area of reservation in 1866 and 1878, 263; number in Oklahoma in 1844, 1855, 1866, 1879, and 1907, 264-266, 277. *See* Dawes Commission; Five Civilized Tribes; Indian Territory; Neosho

Choctaws, early migration west of Mississippi, 5; cession of 1820, 7; treaty of 1825, 8, of 1830, 7, 17; Chickasaws admitted to their territory, 22; separation from Chickasaws, 64; treaty provisions for railroads, 66; resolutions of legislature in February, 1861, 69; proclamation of chief in June, 1861, 70; treaty with Confederates, 72; during Civil War, 80, 94; in council at Fort Smith, 90; land ceded to United States in 1866, 98; United States in 1866, 98; additional compensation for cession, 198; danger of civil war in 1892, 184; agreements with Dawes Commission, 231, 234; declared citizens, 234; area of reservation in 1866 and 1878, 263; number in Oklahoma in 1844, 1855, 1866, 1879, and 1907, 264-266, 230. *See* Chahta; Dawes Commission; Five Civilized Tribes; Indian Territory; Neosho

Choctaw, Oklahoma, and Gulf Railroad, 206, 216

Cimarron meridian, established, 171

Cimarron Territory proposed, 172; petition of council for organization of Oklahoma Territory, 178

Cleveland, President, recommends law to check boomers, 141; proclamation warning boomers, 159; recommends an Indian commission, 162; approves bill for opening of Oklahoma district, 182; proclamation opening Cherokee outlet, 201; selects Dawes Commission, 225

Coal, in Indian Territory, 214, 216, 251; leases authorized, 219

Coffin, W. G., superintendent of Indian Affairs in Indian Territory during Civil War, 72; recommendations, 82; on hostility of southern Indians during Civil War, 91

Colorado Indians, removal to Indian Territory proposed, 111, 164

Columbia, statehood bill, 236

Comanches, acquisition of hunting rights in Oklahoma, 22; treaty with Confederates, 72; allotment, 1867, 101, 170; reservation, 108, opening, 208, area in 1878, 263; number in Oklahoma in 1879, and 1907, 265, 267

Confederate States, seizure of Indian Territory, 69-74

Cooley, D. N., president of council at Fort Smith, 88-90

Cooper, Douglas H., agent for Chickasaws and Choctaws before Civil War, 65; influence exercised for Confederates, 71

Couch, W. L., joins boomers, 142; succeeds Payne as leader, 136; invasion of Oklahoma, 136, 153; starved out, 137, 1580 arrested on criminal charge, 158; charges dismissed, 159; trip to Washington, 159; second invasion, 160; mentioned, 132, 133, 134, 140, 143,

INDEX

144, 146, 177; mayor of Oklahoma City, 190

Council Grove, boomer camps, 160

Coyle vs. Oklahoma, 243

Craven, Jordan E., report on removal of Indians to Indian Territory, 112

Creeks, first migration to Oklahoma, treaties of 1825 and 1826, 9; later migration and union with Seminoles, 18, 19; reservation delimited, 19, 20; condition in 1854, 51; separation from Seminoles, 65; treaty with Confederates, 72; attitude toward Civil War, 75; sufferings of Union Creeks, 76, 80; unratified treaty during Civil War, 85; in council at Fort Smith, 91; cede land to United States in 1866, 97, 275; release United States from restriction on use of cession of 1866, 179, 180, 275; conditions in 1895, 228; agreements with Dawes Commission, 231, 234; declared citizens, 234; area of reservation in 1866 and 1878, 263; number in Oklahoma in 1844, 1855, 1866, 1879, and 1907, 264-266, 277. See Dawes Commission; Five Civilized Tribes; Indian Territory; Neosho

Crook, George H., in Black Hills invasion, 121

Cumming, Alfred, opinion on value of Nebraska and Kansas, 262

Curtis, Charles, act dealing with Five Civilized Tribes, 231

Davis, Jefferson, report favoring southern route to Pacific, 44; authorized to send agent to treat with southern Indians, 69

Dawes, Henry L., chairman Senate committee on Indian Affairs, 146; bill for allotment in severalty, 169; "sooner" amendment, 180; commission favored to the Five Civilized Tribes, 224; appointed chairman of commission, 225

Dawes act, passed, 169; effect on territory of Oklahoma, 197; amended, 197

Dawes Commission, authorized, 224, appointed, 225; work of, 225-235, 249, 250, 277, 278

Deep Fork colony, 132

Delawares, outlet, 20; reservation in Kansas, 23; among Cherokees, 99; on Wichita reservation, 110; number on Wichita reservation in 1879, 265

Democrats, attitude toward statehood for Oklahoma and the Indian Territory, congressmen, 237, 241, local men, 238, 240

Dickinson, Daniel S., on popular sovereignty, 49

Dixon, Archibald, repeal of Missouri Compromise favored, 52

Doaksville, Choctaw capital, 22; village in 1844, 28; proposed capital of Chahta Territory, 58

Dodge, Augustus C., bill for organization of Nebraska, 45; on spread of slavery, 50; on intruders in Indian country, 274

Dole, William P., recommendations, 81, 85

Doolittle, James S., remarks on Harlan bill, 87

Dorn, Andrew J., treaty with Quapaws, etc., 72, 73

Doty, James Duane, approval of plan for removal of northern Indians, 35

Double statehood, agitated, 237, 238; favored by many in the Indian

{ 297 }

Territory, 238, 241, 245, 246, 247, 250-253; by Democrats in Congress, 237, 243, 244, by Republicans in Oklahoma, 240, 245, 246. *See* Sequoyah

Douglas, Stephen A., Nebraska bills, 33, 34, 38, 41; landgrant legislation of 1850, 37; support of Richardson bill, 41; on location of Indian Territory, 45; willing to open Oklahoma, 46; dilemma in 1854, 48, 49; accused of forcing the Nebraska question, 48; not originator of popular sovereignty, 49, 50; opinion on its effect, 50; mistakes, 51; favorable report on Dodge bill, 52; mentioned, 262

Dyer, D. B., agent for the Quapaws, etc., 212; first Mayor of Guthrie, 190

Eastern Shawnees, separation from Seneca-Shawnee band, 106; cession of part of diminished reservation to Modocs, 112; allotments authorized, 170, completed, 233; area of reservation in 1878, 263; number in 1879 and 1907, 264-266

Edmond, location for normal school, 196

Elk vs. Wilkins, 170

El Reno, population in 1890, 195; drawing, 209; convention, 238

Emory, William H., withdrawal of United States troops from Indian Territory, 68

Enid, government town site, 205; attitude toward statehood, 246

Eufaula conventions, 244

Everett, Edward, opposition to opening of larger Indian Territory, 46, 49

Five Civilized Tribes, first use of name, 18; established in Oklahoma by 1837, 22; position during Civil War, 68, 83, 91-95; Conditions among, 1890 to 1900, 222, 228; not included in Dawes act, 169, 223; attempts to bring about allotment in severalty, 100, 224, 225; Dawes Commission, 225, 227-235; corrupt governments in 1895, 229; dissolution, 229-235; allotments, 231, 250, 277; corporations, 234. *See* Cherokees; Chickasaws; Choctaws; Creeks, Seminoles

Flynn, Dennis, free homes act, 210; bills for "piecemeal absorption," 239-242

Foraker, Joseph B., amendment to statehood bill, 254, 255

Fort Smith, site fixes eastern boundary of Oklahoma, 10, 261; town captured by Union army, 79; council in 1865, 81, 87-91; court at, 87, 129, 139, 140, 217; selection of site, name, 261

Fox Indians. *See* Sacs and Foxes

Freedmen, declared Indian citizens by treaty stipulation, 99; 150; number in 1879 and 1907, 114, 264-266; proposal to place in Oklahoma district, 150, 151

Freedmen's Oklahoma Association, 148, 149

Frost, R. Graham, bill to organize Territory of Oklahoma, 124; substitute reported, 147

Fulton, Arkansas, proposed terminus of Pacific railroad, 44

Garfield, James A., opposed to organization of Territory of Oklahoma, 105

Great American Desert, 262

INDEX

Greer County, jurisdiction over, disputed, 115; additional compensation to Indians, 198; assigned to Oklahoma, 203

Gregg, Josiah, on limits of Indian Territory in 1844, 15, conditions in, 28, 94

Gwin, William M., attitude toward opening of Nebraska, 41, 49; bills for Pacific railroad, 43

Guthrie, land office, 187; founded, 187; early conditions, 190, 192; population, 190, 195; capital of Oklahoma Territory, 195; favored double statehood, 246

Hall, Willard P., Nebraska bills, 38, 39; chief supporter of Richardson bill, 40; mentioned, 262

Hamilton, Edward L., bills for admission of Oklahoma and Indian Territory, 248, 254

Harlan, James, removal of Indians from Kansas supported, 84; bill to organize Indian Territory, 85, 89; secretary of the interior, 87; censure of Ross, 89, and of Five Civilized Tribes, 92

Harney, W. S., member of commission to treat with southern Indians, 88

Harrison, President, proclamation opening Oklahoma district, 185; proclamation warning cattlemen out of Cherokee outlet, 199

Harvey, David A., bill for admission of Oklahoma, 237

Hatch, Edward, estimate of amount collected by Payne from boomers, 134; breaks up colony at Rock Falls, 135, and at Stillwater, 136, 153; urges congressional action, 155

Hayes, President, proclamations warning intruders, 122, 127

Henn, Bernhart, on population of Nebraska, 39

Holman, William S., bill for formation of policy with an Indian Territory east of ninety-eighth meridian, 166, 167

Houston, Sam, opening of larger Indian Territory opposed, 41

Howard, United States vs., 142

Howard, Volney E., opening of larger Indian Territory opposed, 40

Howe, John W., on popular sovereignty, 50

Illinois, petition of legislature for opening of Oklahoma district, 146

Indian council, established, 101; Okmulgee constitution drawn up, 102; failure of plan, 103

Indian expedition 1862, 76

Indian Meridian established, 108

Indian Peace Commission, 96, 97

Indian Territory, established 1828, 12; larger Indian Territory authorized by act of May 28, 1830, 13; first use of name, 14; forms of name prior to 1854, 17; limits 1839, 1844, 1849, 14, 16; the so-called creation in 1834, 26; early bills for, 14, 25, 33; influence on movement of population, 30; confined to Oklahoma in 1854, 30, 55; abandoned by United States in 1861, 68, 74; conditions during and after the Civil War, 79, 80; plans to organize during Civil War, 83, 85; peace council at Fort Smith, 87-91; later attempts to organize, 103, 105, 267-270; first invasion, 104; entry of Sioux Indians

{ 299 }

THE FORMATION OF OKLAHOMA

and Indians of Arizona and New Mexico forbidden, 112; number of settlers in 1879, 114; lawless intruders, 126, 218; bill to remove Arizona Indians to, 151; proposals to establish court in, 102, 105, 147, 163, 218, 268, 269; Holman bill, 166, 167; court established, 175, 218; diminished by organization of Oklahoma, 194, 211; invasion by whites, 212-216, 221, 222, 226, 227; jurisdiction of court enlarged, 219, 232; new courts established, 232; conditions of non-citizens, 221, 227, 228, and attitude of Indians toward, 222, 227; bills to organize diminished Indian Territory, 223, 229, 237, 242; bill to include in Territory of Oklahoma, 240; attitude of people toward statehood, 238, 241, 245; area of reservations in 1866, and 1878, 263 (cf. 211); population in 1844, 1855, 1866, 1879, and 1907, 264-267, 277 (cf. 114, 211, 256); population 1880-1902, 213-215, 226, 233-234; admission proposed as state of Jefferson, 248, as Territory of Jefferson, 242. *See* Neosho; Oklahoma; Sequoyah

Indiana Territory, District of Louisiana attached to, 4

Indianola, Territory of, proposed, 229, 242

Iowa in 1834, part of Michigan Territory, 14; influence on, of formation of the Indian Territory, 31

Iowa Indians, in Kansas, 81; migration to Oklahoma, 114; reservation, 151; opening, 197

Jackson, President, message on con-

summation of removal of Indians, 26

Jefferson, President, on western boundary of Louisiana, 3; on the removal of Indians to the West, 5

Jefferson, State of, proposed, 248; Territory of, proposed, 243

Johnson, Robert W., Neosho bill, 55, 58, 61

Joint statehood, defined, 228. *See* single statehood

Kansas, Territory of, first proposed, 52, established, 53; petition of state legislature in 1862 for removal of Indians, 81; in 1872 for extension of southern boundary, 105; later attitude toward removal of Indians to Indian Territory, 112; memorial of legislature for opening of Indian Territory, 178; bill to authorize annexation of No Man's Land, 173, 174

Kansas City, convention in 1888, 176

Kansas-Nebraska act. *See* Nebraska

Kaws, reservation in Kansas, 23, 81; acquire land in Oklahoma, 110; absorbed in Oklahoma, 210, 255; area of reservation in 1878, 263; number in Oklahoma in 1879 and 1907, 265, 267

Kickapoo party, 190, 191

Kickapoos, reservation in Kansas, 23, 81; settlement in Oklahoma, 114; reservation, 151; opening, 203-208; number in Oklahoma in 1879 and 1907, 265, 266

Kingfisher, land office, 187; settlement of, 187, 191; population, 1890, 195; statehood convention, 238

Kiowas (Kiowa Apaches), acquisition of hunting rights in Okla-

INDEX

homa, 22; treaty with Confederates, 72; allotment proposed in 1867, 101; reservation, 108; allotment authorized, 170; opening, 207; area of reservation in 1878, 263; number in Oklahoma in 1879 and 1907, 265, 267

Knox, William S., bill to admit Oklahoma, 242

Lamar, L. Q. C., policy for Indian Territory, 161; annexation of No Man's Land to New Mexico proposed, 173

Lane, James H., bill for removal of Indians from Kansas, 83; remarks on intruders in Indian country, 274, 275

Lanniwa, Territory of, proposed, 82, 83

Lawton, drawing, 209; population in 1901, 209

Leased district, origin, 64; seized by Confederates, 72; acquired by the United States, 98; additional compensation for, 198

Leases, cattle, 115, 122; power of Indians to make doubtful, 144; objections to, 144, 152, 165; declared voidable, 160; ended, 199; mentioned, 219

Lehigh, permission secured to establish provisional municipal government, 217; population in 1890, 217, in 1900, 234

Lincoln, Territory of, proposed, 103, 267, 268

Little Rock, railroad convention, 42

Long, S. H., selection of site for Fort Smith, 261; report on the Great American Desert, 262

Louisiana Purchase, 3; district, 3; territory, 4; state, 4, 14, 15; names applied to, 16, 17

McAlester, coal discovered, 216; population in 1890, 217, in 1900, 234; court town, 220

McCulloch, Ben, dealings with Ross and the Cherokees, 70, 71

McDougall, James A., report on Pacific railroad, 43, 44, amended, 53

McGuire, Bird S., bills to admit Oklahoma, 248, 254; remarks, 249

McKee, George C., opposition to bill for organization of Territory of Oklahoma, 104, 105

McRae, Thomas C., opposition to piecemeal absorption of Indian Territory, 243

Marble, E. M., recommends legislation against intruders on Indian land, 140

Medill, W., report on opening of Nebraska in 1848, 34

Memphis, proposed terminus of Pacific railroad, 43

Merritt, Wesley, on the term boomer, 135; on activities of boomers early in 1889, 178, 186; estimate of numbers in first rush, 188; commendation of settlers, 192

Mexican cession, influence on relative position of larger Indian Territory, 35

Miami, founded, 233; population in 1896, 233, in 1900, 234

Miami Indians, reservation in Kansas, 24; removal to Oklahoma, and location with Peorias, 106; allotment authorized, 232; separation from Peorias, 232; number in Oklahoma in 1879 and 1907, 265, 267

{ 301 }

Michigan, Territory of, extended west to the Mississippi, 14

Miles, Nelson A., recommends abolition of Indian Territory, 161

Miller, John G., bill for organization of Nebraska, 45

Mills, Roger Q., provision secured forbidding removal of Sioux to Indian Territory, 112

Minnesota, in Michigan Territory, 14; terminus of proposed road to Pacific, 44; removal of Indians to Indian Territory mentioned, 82, 87

Missouri, Territory of, established, 4, name still applied to old Missouri Territory, 14, 16, 26, 47; state admitted, 5, 14; interest in Pacific Railroad, 37, 38, 41, 52; petition of legislature for opening of larger Indian Territory, 38; petition of legislature for better organization of Indian Territory, 124

Missouri Compromise, repeal of: important in history of Oklahoma, 30, 56, 57, amendments effecting, 52, 53, effect on Southern attitude toward opening of Indian Territory, 55, 56, 57, attitude of South toward, 46-48, 51, North toward, 51; cause of southern opposition to opening of larger Indian Territory, 41, 47, 48; repeal, 52, 53

Missouri Indians. *See* Otoes and Missouris

Missouri, Kansas and Texas Railroad, constructed across Indian Territory, 100, 115, 215; interest of, in opening of Indian Territory, 117, 120, 129

Modocs, reservation in Indian Territory, 112; allotment authorized, 170, completed, 232, 233; area of reservation in 1878, 263; number in Oklahoma in 1879 and 1907, 265, 266

Moon, John A., bills for separation of Indian Territory from Oklahoma, 242, 243, 248

Monroe, President, authorized to arrange land and government for Indians, 13

Munsee, reservation in Kansas, 23

Muscogee (variant of Creek), Territory of, proposed, 58

Muskogee, seat of court, 175, 218, 220; population in 1890, 217, in 1900, 234; sentiment as to form of statehood, 247

National Commercial Convention, at Saint Louis, 105

Nebraska, opening proposed, 33; Hall's bills, 38, 39; population in 1862, 39; Richardson's bills, 39, 53; sectional opposition to organization, 40, 41, 47, 48; Dodge bill, 45, reported with amendments, 52, passed by Senate, 53; establishment of Territory, 53

Neosho, Johnson bill for territory and state, 55, 57-61; plan for a mixed state, 62, probable acceptance of by Five Civilized Tribes, 63; reintroduction of Johnson bill asked, 65

Neutral land. *See* Cherokee neutral land

New Mexico, removal of Indians to Indian Territory forbidden, 112; annexation proposed of Oklahoma Panhandle, 173; admission of Oklahoma complicated by inclusion in statehood bill with, 242, 243, 248, 249, 254, 255

INDEX

New Orleans, proposed terminus of Pacific railroad, 43
New York Indians, treaty of 1838, 15; reservation in Kansas, 24, 28
Nez Perces, transported to Indian Territory, 113; removed, 160; numbers in Oklahoma in 1879, 265
No Man's Land. *See* Oklahoma Panhandle. *See also* Cimarron Territory
Norman, population in 1890, 195; seat of university, 196
North Carolina, petition of legislature for Indian state, 35
North Dakota, in Michigan Territory, 14
North Fork village, treaties of 1861, 72
Northwest Territory, name applied to part of Louisiana Purchase, 16, mentioned, 35; not part of Indian Territory, 45

Oklahoma, part of Louisiana Purchase, 3; early political history, 3, 4; Indian migration, 5; first white settlers, 4, 5, 31; name first applied to Indian Territory, 102, 103, temporarily limited to Oklahoma district, 116; applied to districts west of area of Five Civilized Tribes, 175; bills to establish Territory of, 103, 105, 115, 148, 163, 171, 175, 175, 176, 193, 267-270; bill to establish Province of Oklahoma, 116; Payne's colony, 132; opening of, petitions for, 146, 164, 171, 176, 177, 270-272; beginnings of, 184; organization of territory, 193, 194; development of, 1890: 1902, 195-210; admission of, 236, 237, 238, 241-248, 253, 254; joined with Indian Territory, 255, finally admitted, 257; population, in 1890, 195, in 1907, 256; bill to extend territory to include diminished Indian Territory, 240; attitude of people toward form of statehood, 238, 240, 245-247, 249; constitutional convention, 255-257; the Indian state, 258. *See* Boomers. *See also* Greer County; Indian Territory, etc.

Oklahoma City, founded, 188; early history, 188-192; population in 1889, 191, in 1890, 195; statehood conventions, 237, 247; attitude toward form of statehood, 246

Oklahoma district, ceded by Creeks and Seminoles in 1866 with restrictions, 98, 276, restrictions removed, 179-182, 185, 275, 276; first application of name, 116; status fixed by judicial decision, 130; negotiations authorized for purchase, 137, 156; cattle in, 145; opening, 184-192; population in 1889, 190, in 1890, 195; area in 1878, 217, in 1889, 186

Oklahoma Panhandle (No Man's Land), not part of Louisiana Purchase, 3; acquired by United States, 60; inclusion in Chelokee Territory proposed, 60, in Oklahoma, 164; history, 1884-1889, 171-175; area and population in 1890 and 1900, 173; included in Territory of Oklahoma, 194. *See* Cimarron Territory

Okmulgee constitution, adopted by Indian council, 102; ratification bills, 105, 269

Old Settlers. *See* Cherokees, Western

Opothleyoholo, leader of Union

Creeks, 75; retreat to Kansas, 75, 76; death, 89; praise of, 89

Oregon Territory, northwest part of Louisiana purchase included under, 16

Oregon trail, influence upon opening of larger Indian Territory, 31, 40

Orleans, Territory of, established, 4; becomes state of Louisiana, 4

Osages, treaties of 1818 and 1825 ceding land in Oklahoma, 8; reservation in Kansas, 9; population in 1844, 27; treaty with Confederates, 72; during Civil War, 72, 73; not wanted in Kansas, 81; removed to Oklahoma, 110; reservation in 1901, 210, in 1906, 255, area of in 1878, 263; number in Oklahoma in 1879 and 1907, 265, 267

Ottawas, reservation in Kansas, 23, 81; land acquired in Oklahoma, 106; allotment authorized, 170, completed, 233; area of reservation in 1878, 263; number in Oklahoma in 1879 and 1907, 265, 266

Otoes and Missouris, reservation in Nebraska, 23, in Oklahoma, 113; absorbed in Oklahoma, 210, 255; number in Oklahoma in 1883 and 1907, 266, 267

Oury, Granville H., bill to remove Arizona Indians to Indian Territory, 151

Owen, Robert L., estimates of population of Indian Territory, 1885-1888, 213, 214

Pacific coast, the five proposed routes for railroad to, 32; influence upon opening of larger Indian Territory, 30-34, 40, 55. *See* Railroads

Panhandle. *See* Oklahoma Panhandle

Park Hill, village in 1844, 28; treaties of 1861, 72

Parker, E. S., member of council at Fort Smith, 88; report on Indian affairs, 96

Parkville, Missouri, petition for opening of larger Indian Territory, 38

Patterson, report, 100, 115, 116, 120, 212, 217

Pawnees, reservation in Nebraska, 24; population in 1844, 27, 28; reservation in Oklahoma, 113, opening, 200, area of in 1878, 263; number in Oklahoma in 1881 and 1907, 265, 267

Payne, David L., early history, 127; in Washington, 128, 129; leader of boomers, 1880-1884, 127-135; relations with the courts, 130, 131, 132, 139-142

Payne, United States vs., 130, 139, 149

Pea Ridge, effect of battle in Indian Territory, 76

Peel, Samuel W., secures provision for opening of part of Oklahoma district, 181; bill for admission of Indian Territory, 223

Pennsylvania, legislature petitions for removal of Indians from larger Indian Territory, 35

Peorias, and others, reservation in Kansas, 23, reservation in Oklahoma, 107; allotment authorized, 232; area of reservation in 1878, 263; number in Oklahoma in 1879 and 1907, 263, 267

Perkins, Bishop, of New York, on northern route to Pacific, 44

Perkins, Bishop W., of Kansas,

INDEX

bills for opening of unoccupied Indian country, 156, for better organization of Indian Territory, 162, 163, 193, for admission of Oklahoma and Indian Territory, 224

Piecemeal absorption, 239, 242, 243

Pike, Albert, treaties with southern Indians, 71-74; defense, 93

Plumb, Preston B., bill to open unoccupied Indian land to settlement, 153, 163; resolution of inquiry, 153, 154, 155; bill to authorize annexation of the public land strip (No Man's Land) to Kansas, 174, 175

Pomeroy, Samuel C., bill for removal of Indians from Kansas, 82, 83, for Territory of Lanniwa, 82, 83

Plains Tribes, rights acquired in western Oklahoma, 22; war against, 127. *See* Comanches; Kiowas; Wichitas

Platte, Orville H., bill for organization of Territory of Oklahoma, 193

Poncas, removal to Oklahoma, 113; absorbed in Oklahoma, 210, 255; number in 1879 and 1907, 265, 267

Popular sovereignty, 49, 50, 51

Pope John, reports and recommendations, 116, 123, 125, 126, 131; sued by Payne, 131

Porter, Pleasant, leader of Creeks in sale of Oklahoma district, 179

Pottawatomies, reservation in Kansas, 23, 81; land acquired in Oklahoma, 108; allotment authorized, 170; reservation opened, 197; area of reservation shared with Shawnees in 1878, 263; number in 1879 and 1907, 265, 266

Price, H., plan of settling freedmen in Oklahoma district, 150

Price, William C., quoted, 47

Prohibition, 256, 257

Province of Oklahoma, proposed, 116

Public land strip. *See* Oklahoma Panhandle

Purcell, starting point for settlers from the south in the first opening of Oklahoma district, 188; population in 1890, 217, in 1900, 234; statehood convention, 238; sentiment as to form of statehood, 246-247

Quapaws, cession of Oklahoma to United States in 1818, 7; reservation in Oklahoma, 18; treaty with Confederates, 72; attitude during Civil War, 72; reservation diminished, 106; invaded, 123, 126; allotment authorized, 170, completed, 232, 233; area of reservation in 1866 and 1878, 263; number in 1844, 1855, 1866, 1879, and 1907, 264, 265, 266

Quay, Matthew S., favors Knox bill, 244; bills for statehood, 248

Railroads, development about 1850, 37, later, 205-207; not profitable in Indian Territory, 40, 100; effect of passage of Kansas-Nebraska act on proposed location of Pacific railroad, 53; provisions for, in treaty of 1855 with Chickasaws and Choctaws, 66, in Indian treaties of 1866, 100, 104; protests of Indians against, 101, 115; influence on boomer agitation, 117, 120, 146; on progress in Oklahoma Territory, 205-207, in the Indian Territory, 215; opposed by Cherokees, 216. *See* Atlantic and Pacific; Choctaw Coal and Railway Company; Choctaw, Oklahoma and Gulf; Missouri, Kansas and Texas; Pacific Coast; Rock Island; Saint Louis and San Francisco; Santa Fe; Southern Kansas Railroad Co.

Recording districts, established, 250; ignored by constitutional convention, 257

Rector, Elias, reintroduction of Neosho bill recommended, 65

Renfrow, William C., on form of statehood, 238

Republicans, attitude in Congress toward form of statehood, 238, 244; attitude in Oklahoma, 240, 245, 249

Richardson, William A., Nebraska bills, 39, 53

Ridges, Major and John, killed, 62

Rock Falls colony, 135

Rock Island railroad, aid given settlers in Oklahoma district, 197; lines constructed in Oklahoma, 205, 206

Rogers, United States vs., 140

Rollins, Edward H., bill for organization of Territory of Oklahoma, 148

Roosevelt, Theodore, recommends single statehood, 253; proclaims Oklahoma a state, 257

Ross, John, leader of Cherokees, 62; wishes to remain neutral in the Civil War, 70; refuses to treat with Pike, 72; decides to treat, 73; writes to Opothleyoholo, 75; with his party goes over to Union side, 77, 78; in Philadelphia, 78; attacked by Harlan and Cooley, 78, 89, 90; in council at Fort Smith, 90

Rusk, Thomas J., opposition to opening of larger Indian Territory, 41

Ryan, Thomas, bill to open unoccupied land in Indian Territory to settlement, 153, 156; amendment to Indian appropriation bill authorizing negotiations for unoccupied Indian land, 154, 156; opposition to Holman bill, 166; bill to open Panhandle, 172; amendment establishing land offices in Oklahoma, 181, 182

Sacs and Foxes, reservation in Kansas, 24, 81, in Oklahoma, 107, opening, 197, area of, in 1878, 263; number in Oklahoma in 1879 and 1907, 265, 266

Saint Joseph convention, 50

Saint Louis, proposed terminus of Pacific road, 3, 43; convention, 165

Saint Louis and San Francisco Railroad constructed in Indian Territory, 215, 216. *See also* Atlantic and Pacific

Salomon, Frederick, mutiny at Fort Gibson, 77; in command of brigade, 78

Santa Fe railroad, in Oklahoma district, 186; aid to settlers, 197; construction of lines in Oklahoma, 206, 216; in Indian Territory, 216; opposition of Cherokee Nation, 216

Santa Fe Trail, influence upon opening of larger Indian Territory, 31, 40, 54

Schurz, Carl, desire to keep Indian Territory intact, 148; allotment favored, 167

Sears, T. C., attorney for Missouri Kansas, and Texas, 117, 120

Seay, Abraham J., on statehood for Oklahoma, 237

INDEX

Sebastian, William K., fixes the northern boundary of Oklahoma, 54

Sells, Elijah, on "jayhawkers," 80; member of council at Fort Smith, 88; on loyalty of southern Indians, 91

Seminole party, 190, 191

Seminoles, removal to Oklahoma and union with Creeks, 18, 19; separate reservation secured, 63, 65; treaty with Confederates, 72; attitude during Civil War, 74; sufferings of Union faction, 76; in council at Fort Smith, 89; old reservation ceded and new one acquired in 1866, 97, 275; reservation enlarged, 97, 98; agree to the removal of restrictions on the Oklahoma district, 180, 182, 185, 276; agreements with Dawes Commission, 231, 234; declared citizens, 234; area of reservation in 1866 and 1878, 263; in 1882, 98; number in Oklahoma in 1844, 1855, 1866, 1879, 1907, 264-267, 277. *See* Dawes Commission; Five Civilized Tribes; Indian Territory; Neosho

Seneca-Shawnee band, reservation established, 18; treaty with Confederates, 72; attitude during Civil War, 72; band dissolved, 106; area of reservation in 1866, 263; number in 1844, 1855, and 1866, 264, 265. *See* Eastern Shawnees; Senecas

Senecas, reservation in Oklahoma established, 17; treaty with Confederates, 72; attitude during Civil War, 72; reservation diminished, 106, 109; allotment authorized, 170; completed, 233; area of reservation in 1866 and 1878, 263; number in, 1844, 1855, 1866, 1879 and 1907, 264, 267

Sequoyah, arguments for proposed state, 250, 251; call for constitutional convention, 252; constitution submitted, 252; bill for, 253

Separate statehood, defined, 237. *See* Double statehood

Shawnee, attitude toward form of statehood, 246

Shawnee, reservation in Kansas, 23, 81; among Cherokees, 99. *See* Absentee Shawnees; Eastern Shawnees; Seneca-Shawnee band

Sheridan, Philip H., report on border conditions, 126; recommendations regarding disposition of Indian Territory, 161

Sherman, James S., attitude on reform in Indian Territory, 230

Sherman, John, favors annulling treaties with Five Civilized Tribes, in 1862, 83

Sherman, W. T., opinion as to cause of the boomer agitation, 121

Single statehood, defined, 238; favored in Oklahoma, 238, 239, 240, 241, 242, 252, by Republicans in Congress, 238, 243, 248, 253; accepted by Republicans of Oklahoma, 249; recommended by President Roosevelt, 253; adopted, 255

Sioux, removal to Indian Territory proposed, 84, 112, forbidden, 112

Slavery, effect on opening of larger Indian Territory, 47-50; among the southern Indians, 93, 94

Smith, Caleb B., on results of abandonment of Indian Territory, 74; favors removal of Indians from Kansas, 83

THE FORMATION OF OKLAHOMA

Smith, Thomas A., Fort Smith, Arkansas, named for, 261
Sooners, defined, 187, 188 (cf. 180, 181, 185)
Soule, United States vs., 149
South Dakota, in Michigan Territory, 14; encroachments on Black Hills reservation, 121
Southern Kansas Railroad Company, Cherokee Nation, vs., 216
Sparks, William A. J., report on Oklahoma Panhandle, 172
Springer, William M., supports organization of Territory of Oklahoma, 174; bill for, 176, 179; amendment to Indian appropriation act authorizing Cherokee commission, 183; bill for state of Columbia, 236
Stand Watie, leader of faction of Cherokees, 62, 73; elected principal chief by Confederates, 73
Statehood. *See* Double statehood; Joint statehood; Separate statehood; Single statehood
Steele, George W., first governor of Territory of Oklahoma, 195-197
Stillwater, colony, 136, 153, 270; town, population in 1890, 195; seat of agricultural and mechanical college, 196
Stocking, United States vs., 142
Sweetster, Charles, favors allotment, citizenship, and abolition of Indian treaties in 1853, 62

Tahlequah, proposed capital of Chelokee Territory, 58; mentioned, 70, 73-74, 77, 79; population 1890, 217; in 1900, 234
Tecumseh, government town site, 198
Teller, Henry M., favors removal of negroes to Indian Territory, 150; favors purchase of Indian claims to Oklahoma district, 155; report, 226, 227, 228
Texas, influence of formation of Indian Territory on, 30; opposition of Texan congressmen to opening of larger Indian Territory, 40, 41; proposal to include part in Indian Territory, 83; later attitude toward Indian Territory, 112
Texas, United States vs., 203
Thompson, Jacob, plan for allotment in severalty within tribal reservation, 66, 101
Tishomingo, council, 81
Tonkawas, reservation established, 160; opened 200; number of in Indian Territory, 267
Town sites, in Oklahoma, 189, 190, 191, 192, 195, 198, 201, 205, 209, in Indian Territory, 216, 227, 231, 250
Treaty of 1819 with Spain, 3, 4
Treaty of 1853 with Mexico, 45
Treaties, with Indians, discontinued, 111. *See* Comanches; Kiowas; Osages; Wichitas; Wyandottes; etc. *See also* Railroads
Tufts, John Q., on intruders in Indian Territory, 212, 213; on need for judicial reform in, 217

United States Board of Indian Commissioners, established, 115; changes in the Indian Territory favored, 101, 116, 167; attacked by tribal organization, 115, 116

Vest, George G., resolution of inquiry in 1879, 124; demand for reorganization of Indian Terri-

INDEX

tory, 124, 125; bill for, 147; resolution authorizing negotiations for unoccupied land, 153, 154; secures insertion of plan in Indian appropriation act of 1885, 156; bill for judicial organization of Indian Territory, 219; resolution for commission to Five Civilized Tribes, 224

Vicksburg, proposed terminus of Pacific railroad, 43, 44

Vilas, William F., treats with Creek delegates for release of restrictions on use of Oklahoma district, 179, 190; refuses to treat with Seminoles, 181

Waddill, James R., bill to open unoccupied land in Indian Territory, 124

Wallace, Robert M., bill to authorize annexation of Chickasaws and Choctaw districts by Arkansas, 254

Walker, Robert J., on opening of southern Indian Territory, 66

Weaver, James B., favors opening of Oklahoma, 166, 174

Weer, William, deposed by mutiny, 77; in command of brigade, 78

Western Cherokees. *See* Cherokees, Western

Western movement, influence on, of formation of larger Indian Territory, 30

Western Territory, name applied to country west of Missouri and Arkansas, 16, 25

Whitney, Asa, work in arousing public interest in Pacific railroad, 36, 262

Wheeler, Joseph, bill to admit Oklahoma, 238

Wichitas, acquire right in Oklahoma, 22, in leased district, 64, 69; treaty with Confederates, 72; reservation in Oklahoma, 110; allotment authorized, 170; County I, 202; opening of reservation, 207, area of in 1878, 263; population in 1866, 1879, and 1907, 264-266

Wichita Mountains, attract boomers, 123, 131

Wilkins, William, recommends organization of Nebraska in 1844, 32, 33

Wilson's Creek, effect of battle in Indian Territory, 70, 71, 73

Wisdom, Dew M., estimates of population, 226

Wister, Thomas, member of council at Fort Smith, 88

Wyandottes, reservation in Kansas, 24; petition for organization of a territory, 39; acquire reservation in Oklahoma, 106; allotment authorized, 170, completed, 232, area of in 1878, 263; number in Oklahoma in 1879 and 1907, 265, 267

THE FORMATION OF THE STATE OF OKLAHOMA

BY ROY GITTINGER

HAS BEEN COMPOSED ON THE MONOTYPE IN 12 POINT

BASKERVILLE, WITH TWO POINTS LEADING

UNIVERSITY OF OKLAHOMA PRESS

NORMAN, OKLAHOMA

www.ingramcontent.com/pod-product-compliance
Lightning Source LLC
Chambersburg PA
CBHW020737160426
43192CB00006B/223